The World's Best Poetry

Volume VI

Fancy and Sentiment

Poetry Anthology Press

The World's Best Poetry

Survey of American Poetry

The World's Best Poetry

Volume VI

Fancy and Sentiment

Edited by Bliss Carman

Prepared by
The Editorial Board, Granger Book Co., Inc.

 Poetry Anthology Press
Great Neck, New York

Library of Congress Catalog Card Number 80-84498
International Standard Book Number 0-89609-207-0
International Standard Book Number for
Foundation Volumes I-X, 0-89609-300-X

Manufactured in the U.S.A.

Poetry Anthology Press is a
division of Granger Book Co., Inc.

Granger Book Co. has no affiliation
with Columbia University Press or its
publication "Granger's Index to Poetry."

TABLE OF CONTENTS.

Preface

The publications of **Poetry Anthology Press** constitute a
comprehensive conspectus of international verse in English
designed to form the core of a library's poetry collection.
Covering the entire range of poetic literature, these
anthologies encompass all topics and national literatures.

Each collection, published in a multivolume continuing
series format, is devoted to a major area of the whole
undertaking and contains complete author, title, and first
line indexes. Biographical data is also provided.

The World's Best Poetry, with coverage through the 19th
century, is topically classified and arranged by subject
matter. Supplements keep the 10 volume foundation
collection current and complete.

Survey of American Poetry is an anthology of American
verse arranged chronologically in 10 volumes. Each volume
presents a significant period of American poetic history,
from 1607 to date.

THE PLACE OF POETRY IN LIFE.

BY CHARLES FRANCIS RICHARDSON.

BEAUTY, sooner or later, comes to its own; but no man perceives it all at once. Even the undying poetry of the world around us must be brought to the notice of growing minds. It is no wonder, then, that a taste for poetry in literature is often undeveloped.

Some people read a great deal of poetry, with constant zest and unfailing advantage; others, though they may be "great readers" of other classes of literature, find little pleasure or profit in poetry. Is it a duty to read poetry? Should those who seem to have no natural taste for it endeavor to cultivate a taste; or should they rest content with the conclusion that certain minds appreciate, and profit by, poetical compositions, while other minds have no capacity for their enjoyment?

It may not be a downright duty to like poetry, or to try to like it; but certainly it is a misfortune that so large and lovely a division of the world's literature should be lost to any reader. The absence of a poetic taste is a sad indication of a lack of the imaginative faculty; and without imagination what is life?

If a reader finds that the ideal has little or no place in his intellectual existence or in his daily

processes of thought and feeling, then he should
consider, with all soberness, the fact that a God-
given power is slipping away from him—a power
without which his best faculties must become atro-
phied; without which he loses the greater part of
the enjoyment of life, day by day; without which,
in very truth, he cannot see all the glory of the
open door of the Kingdom of Heaven. Children are
poets; they find fairy-land in a poor broken set of
toy crockery or in a ragged company of broken-
nosed dolls. Their powers of imagination ought
never to be lost in the humdrum affairs of a work-
a-day world; their habit of discovering the ideal in
the real is one which cannot be laid aside without
great detriment to the individual life and character.
There may, then, be persons who " have no capacity
for poetry," and who cannot cultivate a taste for it;
but this inability, if real, is to be mourned as a
mental blindness and deafness, shutting out the
greater part of the universe from sight and hearing;
for " the most real things in the world are those that
neither men nor children can see."

There is, of course, a great deal of nobly imaginative literature which is not poetry, in the tech-
nical sense; but if one can read Hawthorne or the
Waverley Novels with pleasure, he is quite sure to
find no stumbling-block in " Ulalume " or " The
Lady of the Lake." It is the poetic spirit that we
should recognize and take to our hearts, whatever
may be the outward form in which it may be en-
shrined. Poetry, said Poe, is " the rhythmical
creation of beauty ";—that is, it is one of many
ways of expressing in permanently beautiful form

man's ideas of what he has seen or imagined. No other division of creative art possesses such universality, such intelligibility, as does this art of song.

The beginning of the love of poetry lies in the individual mind; for its development one must seek his material from the treasures around him, and must work out his methods of utilizing that material with the same care that he applies to other departments of intellectual exercise. Let him, if he finds his taste in need of cultivation, begin with such poems as he likes; read them more than once; learn their teachings; apprehend their inner spirit and purpose. Whatever the beginning, it is sure to lead to something better, if the reader will but resolutely determine to know what the writer meant to say; to see the picture that he portrayed; and to share his enthusiasm and warmth of feeling.

This cultivation of the intelligence is essential to the highest success even in daily drudgery, in politics, and in the commercial business of the world. No one is too dull, or too prosaic, or too much absorbed in the routine of "practical life," to be absolved from the care of his imaginative powers; and no one is likely to find that this care will not repay him even in a practical sense. It is the old alternative of "eyes and no eyes." He who thinks wisely, he who perceives quickly that which others do not see at all, is better equipped for any work than one whose mind works slowly and feebly, and whose apprehensions have grown rusty from disuse.

Poetry is not for the few, but for the many, for all. The world's greatest poems, with few exceptions, have been poems whose meaning has been

perfectly clear and whose language has been simple,
—poems which have addressed themselves to the
direct intelligence of men. Homer, and Chaucer,
and Shakespeare need no mystical commentary to
explain their meaning; like Mark Antony, they
" only speak right on." If a poem is obscure, after
a reasonably intelligent reading, you may know by
that mark alone that it is not worth your while to
vex your brain over it. If a poet has not made
himself clear, it is his fault and not yours, if you are a
person of intellectual capacity. Sunlight, air, water,
these are not for the few; nor is poetry to be cooped
and confined any more than these.

True poetry has a far nobler mission than to
puzzle, or to amuse, or even to excite; it is the voice
of all that is best in humanity, speaking from man
to man. Not all of us can thus speak, but we can
hear, and incorporate the poetic spirit in our best
and fullest life, day by day.

What is that spirit? Many have been the at-
tempts to define it; but, after all, we can only say,
in the words of Shelley, " All feel, yet see thee
never." Or again, is not poetry to be described, as
nearly as we can describe it, in two more lines from
the same fine song of the " Voice in the Air "?

> " Lamp of Earth, where'er thou movest
> Its dim shapes are clad with brightness."

Matter is ruled by mind, and the best power of
mind is sentiment. The Kingdom of God, said the
founder of the Christian religion, is within you. It
is the mission of poetry, by means of noble words in
fit metrical forms, to show to man the supernal

beauty of the world of things and thought and action, and to lead him therewith to broaden his own life and other lives in the eternal upward march.

Let us turn, for an illustration of the place of sentiment in the intellectual life, to the heart of that great quickening movement in the world's history which we call the Renaissance, or New Birth.

Of all the cities in the world, none is so rich as Florence in memorials of mind. As one stands beneath the magisterial pinnacle of the Palazzo Vecchio, beholds the unrivalled proportions of Brunelleschi's dome, marks the serious yet cheerful unity of Giotto's tower, studies the stories on the bronze gates of the Baptistery, reads the mortuary inscriptions in the somewhat monotonous nave of the church of Santa Croce, bares his head in the cell of Savonarola, springs heavenward with the thought and the vision of Fra Angelico's angels, is touched with the humanity of Andrea del Sarto's tenderly sweet Madonna on the frescoed wall, or roams through the incomparable riches of the Uffizi and the Pitti, the glory of the City of Flowers seems an epitome of all that man has ever done or dreamed. On the steps of Santa Maria Novella, Boccaccio's gay refugees, in all the lust of life, stood preparing their flight from the plague-smitten town; through Florentine streets walked Petrarch with the soul of Laura imprisoned in his heart; and in the shade of the cathedral is still shown that Sasso di Dante where sat the greatest poet of mediæval Europe as he gazed with sad eyes on the men and women and children passing by. And all these towers and domes, these narrow streets and unspacious squares, these rich treasures of church and convent and gallery, make up the Florence of power—power displayed in the loves and hates a half-a-thousand years agone.

Indeed, if all these treasures of the Florentine past were to perish save one alone—

> "Though the many lights dwindle to one light,
> There is help if the heaven has one,"—

if only a single picture in a single art gallery remained, it would still tell us (if that picture were the "Primavera" of Botticelli) what it was that informed this strange city of the past, and made poem, palace, dome, tower, gate, cell, fagot, angel, Madonna, and Tribuna the things they were and are. On a westward wall of the Academy of Fine Arts, one of the lesser galleries of prodigal Florence, hangs what the guide-books call an "allegorical representation of Spring; on the left Mercury and the Graces, Venus in the middle, and on the right Flora, with a personification of Fertility and a god of wind." Possibly so; perhaps, as others think, an allegory of the four seasons; but surely the first great picture in which there was the unmistakable and perennial glory of pure imagination, amid the conventional mythology or hagiology of the time. With this picture before him one exclaims with Dante: *Incipit vita nova;* here indeed is an epitome of the Renaissance, as Florence is an epitome of the mediæval world. Life, after all, these lovely figures seem to say, is a poor and cruel thing without beauty of doing and of being; nor can beauty really be, without the heart that makes—the sentiment that shapes and consecrates. And the poet or the painter in our age, as in Botticelli's, is he who puts these lessons of the beautiful before the ears and eyes of man.

" We usually," says Ruskin, " fall into much error by considering the intellectual powers as having dignity in themselves, and separable from the heart; whereas the truth is, that the intellect becomes noble and ignoble according to the food we give it, and the kind of subjects with which it is conversant." So we relearn an old lesson from an old text.

The opening years of the twentieth century are in some ways strikingly similar to the beginning of the eighteenth. The reigns of the Georges, in our motherland, were a period of rationalism; the first years of Edward's rule are a time of materialism, in which the ancient truths of art and righteousness must be restated for an " engineering age." Feeling can never die while man lives, nor can art cease to strive to portray what man has seen or dreamed; but in the history of the world a period of imagination is ever followed by a time of criticism and comment or perhaps dull negation. After Shakespeare and Spenser and Milton came Pope and Johnson and the echoes of Voltaire; after Scott and Tennyson Spencer and Huxley. Just a hundred years ago appeared the lyrical ballads of Wordsworth and Coleridge, that " new world " of romantic poetry; and thus genius is ever reincarnated from time to time. The new man must ever and anon be summoned forth by the new prophet; the poet must cry out in the arid waste of a mere life that is not true living. A time of national expansion is the very time for us to exclaim anew that we are children of ideas, and that ideas are born of sentiment.

When a scientist declares that literature is a " frill " which ought not to have any place in a modern college curriculum, so crowded with scientific and really useful studies, there is need to go back to Botticelli for a fresh start and a little elementary instruction; for to-day, as in his picture, the cold north wind is cruelly blowing upon the gaysome-hearted spirit of creative beauty, and clutching her with his freezing fingers. He who despises, or deems superfluous in a practical age, the " frills " of Dante or Tennyson, should read for his reproof and instruction in righteousness such wise words as those lately spoken by an American who stood alike for letters and for right living:

" Commonly, a man is said to be practical who looks out keenly for his own interests, and succeeds in getting possession of much property. He may do this by industry and thrift, or he may do it by taking advantage of the weakness of his fellows. In either case success entitles him to the reputation of being practical. Or a man may be entitled to this epithet if he concerns himself only with material things, and if the product of his effort is strictly utilitarian. In short, a man is practical if he gets what he wants, and keeps it. This is a low view of life, and wholly leaves out of consideration the most important part of it. The true and broad meaning of ' practical ' is a wise adaptation of means to the end in view, and the end in view is an essential part of the practicality. A man who succeeds in making a good sonnet is as practical as a man who manu-

factures a good wheelbarrow. A perfect sonnet is
rare. All the ages have produced only a few—some
say not a hundred altogether. Yet a little group
of Shakespeare's is of more value, has been of more
use to mankind, than the millions of wheelbarrows.
Yet the world could get on without sonnets, and
it could not dispense with wheelbarrows? Yes:
but that depends upon your idea of the world. To
me a world constructed wholly on the wheelbarrow
plan would be intolerable. It is bad enough with
the sonnets mixed in."

In the progress of the world, whether in republic
or in monarchy, the few lead and the many are led,
often very slowly and imperfectly. The old lessons
must be taught anew to every generation. It is not
enough to say that " progress is in the air "; we
must define progress with accuracy and promote it
with patience as well as zeal. Patriotism, liberty,
religion, duty, art—these may be in the air indeed;
it is our business to put them into men's souls and
lives. Philosophy is the guide of life; but philosophy is more than wisdom, it is the love of wisdom, and love is sentiment. It was sentiment that
dominated the work of Jesus and Paul in founding
Christian ethics upon the basis of love. The " min-
istry " to-day is service, and service of every sort
must be consecrated by feeling for the served. The
man of medicine, from Sir Thomas Browne and his
" Christian Morals " to John Brown and his " Rab
and his Friends," may become, and sometimes has
become, even more than his fellow-worker from the
divinity school, a messenger of intimate good to the
individual and the home. American politics and

civics would have been poor indeed without the
sentiment that shaped the constructive order of our
constitutions and laws.   Jefferson, with all his
varied practicalities, was an idealist; and even in
the cool papers composing *The Federalist* there
runs, as through the ages, " one increasing purpose "
that is often a passion.   Jefferson, in his first in-
augural, spoke of " that harmony and affection without which liberty and life itself are but dreary
things " ; and Hamilton, in the opening lines of the
first of *The Federalist* papers, made haste to claim
that the settlement of the Union would " add the
inducements of philanthropy to those of patriotism."
Thus the leader, in any field, is he who, as in the
Greek torch-race, holds in his hand a burning fire
and transmits it to others.

In order to perceive to the full, the intellect must
apprehend the wish as well as the fact.   Still more
is such perception demanded of him who would
portray.   Said Dryden of Shakespeare :   " When
he describes anything, you more than see it, you feel
it too."   That is why Dumas declared that the
greatest of the Elizabethans " has gone to the bottom of everything, divined everything, said everything."   There can be no divination without sympathy between the seer—and the poet is a seer in a
double sense—and the seen.   Hard and narrow is
Dryden's famous

> " Three poets, in three distant ages born,
>   Greece, Italy, and England did adorn ;
>   The first in loftiness of thought surpassed ;
>   The next, in majesty ; in both, the last.
>   The force of nature could no further go ;
>   To make a third, she joined the former two."

Dryden did not see, or did not say, that a certain
lack of sympathy, of sentiment, in a way sets Milton below Chaucer or Shakespeare.

So much of art depends upon portrayal in painting, sculpture, music, words, that too much empha-
sis can hardly be put upon this truth. It is the
business of intellectual leadership, especially in
every form of art, to unfold or to interpret what
men have missed or but half understood, in life or
in its background of the natural world. " Art,"
averred Coleridge, " cannot exist without, or apart
from, nature ; and what has man of his own to give
to his fellow-men but his own thoughts and feelings, and his observations, so far as they are modi-
fied by his own thoughts or feelings ? " So Ruskin :
" The grandest aim of imaginative art [is] to give
men noble grounds for noble emotion." We move
in a circle, or rather we receive and give ; sympathy
and sentiment perceive, art interprets, and the re-
ceiver of the artist's gift transmits that gift to
others. If there is

> " A motion and a spirit which impels
> All thinking things, all objects of all thought,
> And rolls through all things,"

that spirit is assuredly something more than hard
intellectuality. Intellect, after all, is human and
mortal ; soul is divine and eternal. Never in my
life did this sense of the verities of the universe and
the triumph of life over death come nearer to my
mind than when once I stood on that hillock in
Concord's Sleepy Hollow cemetery where rest, almost side by side, Hawthorne and Emerson, with

the Alcotts and Thoreau not far away.   From their
graves the spirits of our first writer and of our chief
philosopher of optimism rise to tell us that we
too have our Westminster Abbeys and St. Pauls,
though overhanging branches replace upspringing
arches of stone, and the dome of the blue vault is
substituted for that which Christopher Wren upreared.   When such dust was laid in mother earth
men said not,

> "Death . . . adds
> Him to his land, a lump of mold the more —"

but, instead, " Now our soil is consecrated, and made
part of the universe of mind as well as of matter."

> " The restless sea resounds along the shore,
>   The light land-breeze flows outward with a sigh,
> And each to each seems chanting evermore
>   A mournful memory of days gone by.

> " Here, where they lived, all holy thoughts revive,
>   Of patient striving and of faith held fast ;
> Here, where they died, their buried records live,
>   Silent they speak from out the shadowy past."

Shelley, I suppose, represented more than any poet
of his time a sort of ethereal mentality in the nature
of his imaginative genius.   Yet it was he who said,
in his "Defense of Poetry " : "The great instrument of moral good is imagination. . . . What were
virtue, love, patriotism, friendship—what were the
scenery of this beautiful universe which we in-
habit, what were our consolations on this side of the
grave, and what were our aspirations beyond it, if
poetry did not ascend to bring light and fire from
those eternal regions where the owl-winged faculty

of calculation dare not ever soar?" Andrew Lang
had the same thought in mind when he declared
that "Coleridge is, or may be reckoned, a great poet,
because every now and again he captures in verse
that indefinable emotion which is less articulately
expressed in music, and in some unutterable way he
transports us into the world of dream and desire.
This is a very vague fashion of saying what hardly
permits itself to be said. We might put it that
Coleridge has, on occasion, the power to move us, as
we are moved by the most rarely beautiful cosmic
effects of magic lights and shadows; by the silver
on lakes for a chosen moment in the dawn or twilight; by the fragrant deeps of dewy forests; by
sudden infrequent passions of heart and memory,
and by unexpected potencies of imagination." Piti-
fully did Shelley and Coleridge—not less than Milton
himself—fall short of Milton's declaration that "he
who would not be frustrate of his hope to write
well hereafter in laudable things ought himself to
be a true poem." Literary men are as human as
other folks, and a little more so. But sometimes the
stream appears to rise higher than its source, because we do not really know what the artist's highest level is. "An artist's creations are the best . . .
test of his nature. When we do not know all the
facts of a man's life—and how seldom we know even
half of them—it is dangerous to make what facts we
do know overbear the evidence of his works." An
author's book or a painter's picture, we may say,
represents both the *is* and the *would-be ;* and can
there be an ideal without aspiration? Benvenuto
Cellini was, as he has lately been characterized, a

" scoundrel," but his Perseus did not come from the scoundrelly part of him. Many of the great artists of the world have been moral weaklings, while some of its noblest souls have lacked not only the creative power, but any apparent sense of appreciation of beautiful things made. But art consecrated by ethics is that which produces a Divina Commedia out of the experiences and ideas of what otherwise would be a mere Comédie Humaine.

The poet, or other artist, is he who scans life and nature, and presents them to us in significant and enduring forms. He stands for what all mankind half hopes to be, and he is directly successful in proportion to his representative power. Ill-regulated superficiality is fatal to the artist, and therefore to the leader;—and we ought all to be leaders of something, if only of ourselves. The ruler, the director, must correlate many things. His is the " breadth of life." If he finds that honesty is the best policy, he also perceives that " he is not an honest man who is honest for this reason." To him, at his best, belongs what Theodore Watts-Dunton calls Tennyson's—that is to say any great poet's—" instinct for confronting the universe as a whole." And in the presence of the universe, he solemnly says with the possessor of one of the greatest of American " fortunes "—how foolish to speak of money and fortune as synonymous !—that " the poorest man I know is the man who has nothing but money."

The poet beholds and interprets. In the great book of nature and life he reads, and from a thousand texts unfolds to humanity the perennial beauty and the divine lessons of the universe. He learns by insight what others miss in the slow processes of external investigation. For him nature is the mirror of God and the mentor of man. As naturally as a mountain brook, he sings because he must. He studies the whole created universe, and finds God in the bush as well as in the libraries.

American literature furnishes in the case of Longfellow, whom it is now the fashion to decry, a pleasant illustration of the way in which the poet may combine many things for the benefit of his time. He was a college teacher, but no pedant; a text-book maker, but also a singer; an adapter, but not, as Poe called him, a plagiarist; an early follower of Heine, but at last the creator of two of our most characteristically American books, in story and in form; the scholarly student and translator of Dante, but likewise the simple singer of " Excelsior " and " A Psalm of Life." In a sentimental time he knew how to use and to better the fashions of his day; and in the crude and crass period of American *isms* and *ologies* he helped us because he was both sympathetic and wise.

The time-spirit, as far as it affects the intellectual life of a people, is simply the intelligence of man, dominated by a high purpose. The countrymen of Franklin, Washington, Jefferson, and Webster do not need to be reminded that the brain is the servant of the soul, not less in politics than in art. The history of the United States is the history of the evolution of ideas. Evolution is in one sense inexorable; in another and far truer sense it is the sum-total of our own use of the powers and means at hand, which we have inherited or earned. Sentiment is worthless unless transmuted into character, and character demands action. We are ourselves results; we must likewise be causes; if the nineteenth, and eighteenth, and seventeenth centuries have been in some ways good, the twentieth ought to be best of all. The past explains the present, and the present the past. We may interpret the coming century by its predecessors, for, however great its changes may be, from our followers there surely will not depart the quickening spirit of their Aryan ancestors, especially of the Teutonic branch. Though the future be in a true sense an unknown world, with its potencies of material and spiritual development—for the child is the son of the centuries, and in truth an Emerson or a Browning can peer beyond the horizon of a Shakespeare—still the verities of human nature can never be lost.

We may be living in a literary or artistic interregnum, but the stuff of literature is ever at hand—of that silent literature which is, as it were, the background of the literature which is written. First the deed, then its eidolon. Not one of the twice four hundred men who went down with Kempenfelt could have written " Toll for the Brave " ; but a great act—and one supposes that they died with courage—is not far, in essence, from a great creation. Surely, as the century begins, one sees the heroic on every hand; men were never braver than to-day— sometimes with a bravery which is glorified by a self-sacrifice all the truer because it is not reckless.

We occasionally speak of our own days—days of

brief wars and of the better victories of peaceful education—as though they were late finalities; who knows but we ourselves are living in the earliest ages of the ancient earth? This is the first period in which social decency has been attained even in any moderate degree; the first in which men have travelled by steam; talked by electricity; multiplied cheap books; relieved the handicraftsman of much of his weary toil; brought fresh food from the ends of the earth for eaters who find it cheaper to buy than to produce. In mechanics we may well be modest so long as man cannot, unaided, fly a tenfoot distance ten inches above the surface of the earth which gave him birth; while in philosophy we have not one glimmer of real knowledge concerning the creating cause or actual character of time, space, matter, life; nor can we tell, any more than the kitten at our feet or the house fly on the ceiling, the connection between the end of a thought and the end of a nerve. "The truth is," wrote John Addington Symonds, "that in many senses we are still in mid-Renaissance. The evolution has not been completed. The life is our own and is progressive. As in the transformation-scene of some great masque, so here, the waning and the waxing shapes are mingled; the new forms, at first shadowy and filmy, gain upon the old, and now both blend; and now the old scene fades into the background; still, who shall say whether the new scene be finally set up?"

The poet, therefore, is now and must forever be the searcher for ultimate truth.

"Happier to chase a flying goal
Than to sit counting laurelled gains;
To guess the soul within the soul,
Than to be lord of what remains.

" Hide still, best good, in subtle wise,
Beyond my nature's utmost scope ;
Be ever absent from mine eyes
To be twice present in my hope ! "

The one thing which distinguishes the leader from the led is the vision behind the mist. The poet, as Plato told us long ago, has many functions: " His it is to teach and enlighten the state, to make life beautiful, and to draw the soul insensibly into harmony with reason. But among them all none, assuredly, is greater than the mission which he has received from heaven—-to keep alive the senses of a world that is out of sight, and to show how the troubled waves of human life may dimly reflect the beauty and mystery of God."

Charles F. Richardson.

The World's Best Poetry

Volume VI

Fancy and Sentiment

POEMS OF FANCY.

I.

THE IMAGINATION.

FANTASY.

FROM "THE VISION OF DELIGHT."

Break, Fantasy, from thy cave of cloud,
  And spread thy purple wings,
Now all thy figures are allowed,
  And various shapes of things ;
Create of airy forms a stream,
It must have blood, and naught of phlegm ;
And though it be a waking dream,
    Yet let it like an odor rise
      To all the senses here,
    And fall like sleep upon their eyes,
      Or music in their ear.

BEN JONSON.

HALLO, MY FANCY.

  In melancholic fancy,
    Out of myself,
  In the vulcan dancy,

3

All the world surveying,
Nowhere staying,
Just like a fairy elf;
Out o'er the tops of highest mountains skipping,
Out o'er the hills, the trees and valleys tripping,
Out o'er the ocean seas, without an oar or shipping.
Hallo, my fancy, whither wilt thou go?

Amidst the misty vapors,
Fain would I know
What doth cause the tapers;
Why the clouds benight us,
And affright us
While we travel here below.
Fain would I know what makes the roaring thunder,
And what these lightnings be that rend the clouds
asunder,
And what these comets are on which we gaze and
wonder.
Hallo, my fancy, whither wilt thou go?

Fain would I know the reason
Why the little ant,
All the summer season,
Layeth up provision,
On condition
To know no winter's want:
And how these little fishes, that swim beneath salt
water,
Do never blind their eyes; methinks it is a matter
An inch above the reach of old Erra Pater!
Hallo, my fancy, whither wilt thou go?

Fain would I be resolved
   How things are done ;
And where the bull was calved
Of bloody Phalaris,
And where the tailor is
   That works to the man i' the moon!
Fain would I know how Cupid aims so rightly ;
And how these little fairies do dance and leap so
     lightly ;
And where fair Cynthia makes her ambles nightly.
  Hallo, my fancy, whither wilt thou go?

In conceit like Phaeton,
   I 'll mount Phœbus' chair,
Having ne'er a hat on,
All my hair a-burning
In my journeying,
   Hurrying through the air.
Fain would I hear his fiery horses neighing,
And see how they on foamy bits are playing ;
All the stars and planets I will be surveying!
  Hallo, my fancy, whither wilt thou go ?

O, from what ground of nature
   Doth the pelican,
That self-devouring creature,
Prove so froward
And untoward,
   Her vitals for to strain ?
And why the subtle fox, while in death's wounds is
     lying,
Doth not lament his pangs by howling and by
     crying ;

And why the milk-white swan doth sing when
        she 's a-dying.
    Hallo, my fancy, whither wilt thou go ?

        Fain would I conclude this,
            At least make essay,
        What similitude is ;
        Why fowls of a feather
        Flock and fly together,
            And lambs know beasts of prey :
How Nature's alchymists, these small laborious
        creatures,
Acknowledge still a prince in ordering their matters,
And suffer none to live, who slothing lose their
        features.
    Hallo, my fancy, whither wilt thou go ?

        I 'm rapt with admiration,
            When I do ruminate,
        Men of an occupation,
        How each one calls him brother,
        Yet each envieth other,
            And yet still intimate !
Yea, I admire to see some natures farther sun-
        d'red,
Than antipodes to us.   Is it not to be wond'red ?
In myriads ye 'll find, of one mind scarce a hun-
        dred ?
    Hallo, my fancy, whither wilt thou go ?

        What multitude of notions
            Doth perturb my pate,
        Considering the motions,

How the heavens are preserved,
And this world served
In moisture, light, and heat!
If one spirit sits the outmost circle turning,
Or one turns another, continuing in journeying,
If rapid circles' motion be that which they call
burning!
  Hallo, my fancy, whither wilt thou go!

Fain also would I prove this,
  By considering
What that, which you call love, is:
Whether it be a folly
Or a melancholy,
  Or some heroic thing!
Fain I'd have it proved, by one whom love hath
wounded,
And fully upon one his desire hath founded,
Whom nothing else could please though the world
were rounded.
  Hallo, my fancy, whither wilt thou go?

To know this world's centre,
  Height, depth, breadth, and length,
Fain would I adventure
To search the hid attractions
Of magnetic actions,
  And adamantine strength.
Fain would I know, if in some lofty mountain,
Where the moon sojourns, if there be trees or
fountain;
If there be beasts of prey, or yet be fields to
hunt in.
  Hallo, my fancy, whither wilt thou go?

  Fain would I have it tried
   By experiment,
  By none can be denied !
  If in this bulk of nature,
  There be voids less or greater,
   Or all remains complete.
Fain would I know if beasts have any reason ;
If falcons killing eagles do commit a treason ;
If fear of winter's want make swallows fly the
   season.
  Hallo, my fancy, whither wilt thou go ?

  Hallo, my fancy, hallo !
   Stay, stay at home with me,
  I can thee no longer follow,
  For thou hast betrayed me,
  And bewrayed me ;
   It is too much for thee.
Stay, stay at home with me ; leave off thy lofty
   soaring ;
Stay thou at home with me, and on thy books be
   poring ;
For he that goes abroad lays little up in storing :
  Thou 'rt welcome home, my fancy, welcome home
   to me.
       WILLIAM CLELAND.

IDEALITY.

T<small>HE</small> vale of Tempe had in vain been fair,
Green Ida never deemed the nurse of Jove ;
Each fabled stream, beneath its covert grove,
Had idly murmured to the idle air ;
The shaggy wolf had kept his horrid lair

In Delphi's cell, and old Trophonius' cave,
And the wild wailing of the Ionian wave
Had never blended with the sweet despair
Of Sappho's death-song : if the sight inspired
Saw only what the visual organs show,
If heaven-born phantasy no more required
Than what within the sphere of sense may grow.
The beauty to perceive of earthly things,
The mounting soul must heavenward prune her
    wings.

                  HARTLEY COLERIDGE.

FANCY.

EVER let the Fancy roam,
Pleasure never is at home :
At a touch sweet Pleasure melteth,
Like to bubbles when rain pelteth ;
Then let wingèd Fancy wander
Through the thought still spread beyond her :
Open wide the mind's cage-door,
She 'll dart forth, and cloudward soar.

O sweet Fancy ! let her loose ;
Summer's joys are spoilt by use,
And the enjoying of the Spring
Fades as does its blossoming :.
Autumn's red-lipped fruitage too,
Blushing through the mist and dew,
Cloys with tasting.   What do then ?
Sit thee by the ingle, when
The sear fagot blazes bright,
Spirit of a winter's night ;

When the soundless earth is muffled,
And the cakèd snow is shuffled
From the ploughboy's heavy shoon;
When the Night doth meet the Noon
In a dark conspiracy
To banish Even from her sky.
—Sit thee there, and send abroad
With a mind self-overawed
Fancy, high-commissioned:—send her!
She has vassals to attend her;
She will bring, in spite of frost,
Beauties that the earth hath lost;
She will bring thee, all together,
All delights of summer weather;
All the buds and bells of May
From dewy sward or thorny spray;
All the heapèd Autumn's wealth,
With a still, mysterious stealth;
She will mix these pleasures up
Like three fit wines in a cup,
And thou shalt quaff it;—thou shalt hear
Distant harvest-carols clear;
Rustle of the reapèd corn;
Sweet birds antheming the morn;
And in the same moment—hark!
'T is the early April lark,
Or the rooks, with busy caw,
Foraging for sticks and straw.
Thou shalt, at one glance, behold
The daisy and the marigold;
White-plumed lilies, and the first
Hedge-grown primrose that hath burst;
Shaded hyacinth, alway
Sapphire queen of the mid-May;

And every leaf, and every flower
Pearlèd with the self-same shower.
Thou shalt see the field-mouse peep
Meagre from its cellèd sleep;
And the snake all winter-thin
Cast on sunny bank its skin;
Freckled nest-eggs thou shalt see
Hatching in the hawthorn tree,
When the hen-bird's wing doth rest
Quiet on her mossy nest;
Then the hurry and alarm
When the beehive casts its swarm;
Acorns ripe down-pattering
While the autumn breezes sing.

O sweet Fancy! let her loose;
Everything is spoilt by use:
Where 's the cheek that doth not fade,
Too much gazed at?   Where 's the maid
Whose lip mature is ever new?
Where 's the eye, however blue,
Doth not weary?   Where 's the face
One would meet in every place?
Where 's the voice, however soft,
One would hear so very oft?
At a touch sweet Pleasure melteth
Like to bubbles when rain pelteth.
Let then wingèd Fancy find
Thee a mistress to thy mind:
Dulcet-eyed as Ceres' daughter,
Ere the god of torment taught her
How to frown and how to chide;
With a waist and with a side

White as Hebe's, when her zone
Split its golden clasp, and down
Fell her kirtle to her feet
While she held the goblet sweet,
And Jove grew languid.—Break the mesh
Of the Fancy's silken leash ;
Quickly break her prison-string,
And such joys as these she 'll bring :
—Let the wingèd Fancy roam,
Pleasure never is at home.

JOHN KEATS.

IMAGINATION.

FROM "A MIDSUMMER NIGHT'S DREAM," ACT V. SC. 2.

THE lunatic, the lover, and the poet
Are of imagination all compact :
One sees more devils than vast hell can hold,
That is, the madman : the lover, all as frantic,
Sees Helen's beauty in a brow of Egypt :
The poet's eye, in a fine frenzy rolling,
Doth glance from heaven to earth, from earth to
      heaven ;
And as imagination bodies forth
The forms of things unknown, the poet's pen
Turns them to shapes, and gives to airy nothing
A local habitation and a name.

SHAKESPEARE.

II.

FAIRIES: ELVES: SPRITES.

QUEEN MAB.

FROM "ROMEO AND JULIET," ACT I. SC. 4.

O, THEN, I see, Queen Mab hath been with you.
She is the fairies' midwife; and she comes
In shape no bigger than an agate-stone
On the fore-finger of an alderman,
Drawn with a team of little atomies
Athwart men's noses as they lie asleep:
Her wagon-spokes made of long spinners' legs;
The cover, of the wings of grasshoppers;
The traces, of the smallest spider's web;
The collars, of the moonshine's watery beams;
Her whip, of cricket's bone; the lash, of film;
Her wagoner, a small gray-coated gnat,
Not half so big as a round little worm
Pricked from the lazy finger of a maid:
Her chariot is an empty hazel-nut,
Made by the joiner squirrel, or old grub,
Time out of mind the fairies' coach-makers.
And in this state she gallops night by night
Through lovers' brains, and then they dream of
    love;

13

On courtiers' knees, that dream on court'sies
    straight ;
O'er lawyers' fingers, who straight dream on fees ;
O'er ladies' lips, who straight on kisses dream,—
Which oft the angry Mab with blisters plagues,
Because their breaths with sweetmeats tainted are :
Sometime she gallops o'er a courtier's nose,
And then dreams he of smelling out a suit ;
And sometime comes she with a tithe-pig's tail,
Tickling a parson's nose as 'a lies asleep,
Then dreams he of another benefice :
Sometime she driveth o'er a soldier's neck,
And then dreams he of cutting foreign throats,
Of breaches, ambuscadoes, Spanish blades,
Of healths five fathom deep ; and then anon
Drums in his ear, at which he starts, and wakes ;
And, being thus frighted, swears a prayer or two,
And sleeps again.   This is that very Mab
That plats the manes of horses in the night ;
And bakes the elf-locks in foul sluttish hairs,
Which, once untangled, much misfortune bodes :
This is the hag, when maids lie on their backs,
That presses them, and learns them first to bear,
Making them women of good carriage.

SHAKESPEARE.

OBERON'S FEAST.

Shapcot ! to thee the Fairy State
I with discretion dedicate :
Because thou prizest things that are
Curious and unfamiliar,
Take first the feast ; these dishes gone,
We'll see the Fairy-court anon.

A little mushroom-table spread,
After short prayers, they set on bread,
A moon-parched grain of purest wheat,
With some small glitt'ring grit, to eat
His choice bits with ; then in a trice
They make a feast less great than nice.
But all this while his eye is served,
We must not think his ear was sterved ;
But that there was in place to stir
His spleen, the chirring grasshopper,
The merry cricket, puling fly,
The piping gnat for minstrelsy.
And now, we must imagine first,
The elves present, to quench his thirst,
A pure seed-pearl of infant dew,
Brought and besweetened in a blue
And pregnant violet ; which done,
His kitling eyes begin to run
Quite through the table, where he spies
The horns of papery butterflies,
Of which he eats ; and tastes a little
Of that we call the cuckoo's spittle ;
A little fuz-ball pudding stands
By, yet not blessèd by his hands,
That was too coarse ; but then forthwith
He ventures boldly on the pith
Of sugared rush, and eats the sagge
And well-bestrutted bees' sweet bag ;
Gladding his palate with some store
Of emmet's eggs ; what would he more ?
But beards of mice, a newt's stewed thigh,
A bloated earwig, and a fly ;
With the red-capt worm, that 's shut
Within the concave of a nut,

Brown as his tooth.　A little moth,
Late fattened in a piece of cloth;
With withered cherries, mandrakes' ears,
Moles' eyes: to these the slain stag's tears;
The unctuous dew-laps of a snail,
The broke-heart of a nightingale
O'ercome in music; with a wine
Ne'er ravished from the flattering vine,
But gently prest from the soft side
Of the most sweet and dainty bride,
Brought in a dainty daisy, which
He fully quaffs up, to bewitch
His blood to height; this done, commended
Grace by his priest; The feast is ended.

ROBERT HERRICK.

FAIRY'S SONG.

FROM "A MIDSUMMER NIGHT'S DREAM," ACT II. SC. 1.

Over hill, over dale,
　Thorough bush, thorough brier,
Over park, over pale,
　Thorough flood, thorough fire,
I do wander everywhere,
Swifter than the moon's sphere;
And I serve the fairy queen,
To dew her orbs upon the green;
The cowslips tall her pensioners be;
In their gold coats, spots you see;
These be rubies, fairy favors—
In those freckles live their savors.
I must go seek some dewdrops here,
And hang a pearl in every cowslip's ear.

SHAKESPEARE.

COMPLIMENT TO QUEEN ELIZABETH.

FROM " A MIDSUMMER NIGHT'S DREAM," ACT II. SC. 2.

OBERON.—My gentle Puck, come hither. Thou
    remember'st
Since once I sat upon a promontory,
And heard a mermaid, on a dolphin's back,
Uttering such dulcet and harmonious breath,
That the rude sea grew civil at her song,
And certain stars shot madly from their spheres,
To hear the sea-maid's music.
    PUCK.—   I remember.
    OBERON.—That very time I saw (but thou couldst
    not),
Flying between the cold moon and the earth,
Cupid all armed : a certain aim he took
At a fair vestal thronèd by the west,
And loosed his love-shaft smartly from his bow,
As it should pierce a hundred thousand hearts :
But I might see young Cupid's fiery shaft
Quenched in the chaste beams of the watery moon,
And the imperial votaress passed on,
In maiden meditation, fancy free.
Yet marked I where the bolt of Cupid fell :
It fell upon a little western flower
Before milk-white, now purple with love's wound,
And maidens call it Love-in-idleness.
Fetch me that flower.
                        SHAKESPEARE.

  2

THE FAIRIES' LULLABY.

FROM "A MIDSUMMER NIGHT'S DREAM," ACT II. SC. 3.

Enter TITANIA, *with her train.*

TITANIA.—Come, now a roundel, and a fairy song;
Then, for the third part of a minute, hence;—
Some, to kill cankers in the musk-rose buds;
Some war with rear-mice for their leathern wings,
To make my small elves coats; and some keep back
The clamorous owl, that nightly hoots, and wonders
At our quaint spirits.   Sing me now asleep;
Then to your offices, and let me rest.

SONG.

1 FAIRY.— *You spotted snakes, with double tongue,*
  Thorny hedgehogs, be not seen;
  Newts and blind-worms, do no wrong:
  Come not near our fairy queen.

CHORUS. *Philomel, with melody,*
  Sing in our sweet lullaby;
Lulla, lulla, lullaby; lulla, lulla, lullaby:
  Never harm,
  Nor spell nor charm,
  Come our lovely lady nigh;
  So, good-night, with lullaby.

2 FAIRY.— *Weaving spiders, come not here,*
  Hence, you long-legged spinners, hence!
  Beetles black, approach not near;
  Worm, nor snail, do no offence.

CHORUS. *Philomel, with melody,* etc.

1 Fairy.—Hence away; now all is well:
   One, aloof, stand sentinel.
      [*Exeunt Fairies.* Titania *sleeps.*
                              SHAKESPEARE.

FAIRIES' SONG.

We the fairies blithe and antic,
Of dimensions not gigantic,
Though the moonshine mostly keep us,
Oft in orchards frisk and peep us.

Stolen sweets are always sweeter;
Stolen kisses much completer;
Stolen looks are nice in chapels;
Stolen, stolen be your apples.

When to bed the world are bobbing,
Then 's the time for orchard-robbing;
Yet the fruit were scarce worth peeling
Were it not for stealing, stealing.

> From the Latin of THOMAS RANDOLPH.
> Translation of LEIGH HUNT.

THE FAIRIES.

Up the airy mountain,
   Down the rushy glen,
We daren't go a hunting
   For fear of little men;
Wee folk, good folk,
   Trooping all together;
Green jacket, red cap,
   And white owl's feather!

Down along the rocky shore
    Some make their home,—
They live on crispy pancakes
    Of yellow tide-foam;
Some in the reeds
    Of the black mountain-lake,
With frogs for their watch-dogs,
    All night awake.

High on the hill-top
    The old King sits;
He is now so old and gray
    He 's nigh lost his wits.
With a bridge of white mist
    Columbkill he crosses,
On his stately journeys
    From Slieveleague to Rosses:
Or going up with music
    On cold starry nights,
To sup with the Queen
    Of the gay Northern Lights.

They stole little Bridget
    For seven years long;
When she came down again
    Her friends were all gone.
They took her lightly back,
    Between the night and morrow;
They thought that she was fast asleep,
    But she was dead with sorrow.
They have kept her ever since
    Deep within the lakes,
On a bed of flag-leaves,
    Watching till she wakes.

By the craggy hillside,
    Through the mosses bare,
They have planted thorn-trees
    For pleasure here and there.
Is any man so daring
    To dig one up in spite,
He shall find the thornies set
    In his bed at night.

Up the airy mountain,
    Down the rushy glen,
We daren't go a hunting
    For fear of little men ;
Wee folk, good folk,
    Trooping all together ;
Green jacket, red cap,
    And white owl's feather !
WILLIAM ALLINGHAM.

KILMENY.

FROM "THE QUEEN'S WAKE."

Bᴏɴɴʏ Kɪʟᴍᴇɴʏ gaed up the glen ;
But it wasna to meet Duneira's men,
Nor the rosy monk of the isle to see,
For Kilmeny was pure as pure could be.
It was only to hear the yorlin sing,
And pu' the cress-flower round the spring,—
The scarlet hypp, and the hindberrye,
And the nut that hung frae the hazel-tree ;
For Kilmeny was pure as pure could be.
But lang may her minny look o'er the wa',
And lang may she seek i' the green-wood shaw ;

Lang the laird of Duneira blame,
And lang, lang greet or Kilmeny come hame.

When many a day had come and fled,
When grief grew calm, and hope was dead,
When mass for Kilmeny's soul had been sung,
When the bedesman had prayed, and the dead-bell
    rung ;
Late, late in a gloamin, when all was still,
When the fringe was red on the westlin hill,
The wood was sear, the moon i' the wane,
The reek o' the cot hung over the plain,—
Like a little wee cloud in the world its lane ;
When the ingle lowed with an eiry leme,
Late, late in the gloamin Kilmeny came hame !

" Kilmeny, Kilmeny, where have you been ?
Lang hae we sought baith holt and den,—
By linn, by ford, and green-wood tree ;
Yet you are halesome and fair to see.
Where got you that joup o' the lily sheen ?
That bonny snood of the birk sae green ?
And these roses, the fairest that ever was seen ?
Kilmeny, Kilmeny, where have you been ? "

Kilmeny looked up with a lovely grace,
But nae smile was seen on Kilmeny's face ;
As still was her look, and as still was her ee,
As the stillness that lay on the emerant lea,
Or the mist that sleeps on a waveless sea.
For Kilmeny had been she knew not where,
And Kilmeny had seen what she could not declare.
Kilmeny had been where the cock never crew,
Where the rain never fell, and the wind never blew ;

But it seemed as the harp of the sky had rung,
And the airs of heaven played round her tongue,
When she spake of the lovely forms she had seen,
And a land where sin had never been,—
A land of love, and a land of light,
Withouten sun or moon or night;
Where the river swa'd a living stream,
And the light a pure celestial beam:
The land of vision it would seem,
A still, an everlasting dream.

In yon green-wood there is a waik,
And in that waik there is a wene,
And in that wene there is a maike,
That neither has flesh, blood, nor bane;
And down in yon green-wood he walks his lane.

In that green wene Kilmeny lay,
Her bosom happed wi' the flowerets gay;
But the air was soft, and the silence deep,
And bonny Kilmeny fell sound asleep;
She kend nae mair, nor opened her ee,
Till waked by the hymns of a far countrye.

She 'wakened on a couch of the silk sae slim,
All striped wi' the bars of the rainbow's rim;
And lovely beings around were rife,
Who erst had travelled mortal life;
And aye they smiled, and 'gan to speer:
" What spirit has brought this mortal here?"

" Lang have I journeyed the world wide,"
A meek and reverend fere replied;
" Baith night and day I have watched the fair
Eident a thousand years and mair.

Yes, I have watched o'er ilk degree,
Wherever blooms femenitye;
But sinless virgin, free of stain,
In mind and body, fand I nane.
Never, since the banquet of time,
Found I a virgin in her prime,
Till late this bonny maiden I saw,
As spotless as the morning snaw.
Full twenty years she has lived as free
As the spirits that sojourn in this countrye.
I have brought her away frae the snares of men,
That sin or death she may never ken."

They clasped her waist and her hands sae fair;
They kissed her cheek, and they kemed her hair;
And round came many a blooming fere,
Saying, " Bonny Kilmeny, ye 're welcome here;
Women are freed of the littand scorn;
O, blest be the day Kilmeny was born!
Now shall the land of the spirits see,
Now shall it ken, what a woman may be!
Many a lang year in sorrow and pain,
Many a lang year through the world we 've gane,
Commissioned to watch fair womankind,
For it 's they who nurice the immortal mind.
We have watched their steps as the dawning shone,
And deep in the greenwood walks alone;
By lily bower and silken bed
The viewless tears have o'er them shed;
Have soothed their ardent minds to sleep,
Or left the couch of love to weep.
We have seen! we have seen! but the time must
        come,
And the angels will weep at the day of doom!

" O, would the fairest of mortal kind
Aye keep the holy truths in mind,
That kindred spirits their motions see,
Who watch their ways with anxious ee,
And grieve for the guilt of humanitye !
O, sweet to Heaven the maiden's prayer,
And the sigh that heaves a bosom sae fair !
And dear to Heaven the words of truth
And the praise of virtue frae beauty's mouth !
And dear to the viewless forms of air
The minds that kythe as the body fair !

" O bonny Kilmeny ! free frae stain,
If ever you seek the world again,—
That world of sin, of sorrow and fear,—
O, tell of the joys that are waiting here ;
And tell of the signs you shall shortly see ;
Of the times that are now, and the times that shall
        be."

They lifted Kilmeny, they led her away,
And she walked in the light of a sunless day ;
The sky was a dome of crystal bright,
The fountain of vision, and fountain of light ;
The emerald fields were of dazzling glow,
And the flowers of everlasting blow.
Then deep in the stream her body they laid,
That her youth and beauty never might fade ;
And they smiled on heaven, when they saw her lie
In the stream of life that wandered by.
And she heard a song,—she heard it sung,
She kend not where ; but sae sweetly it rung,
It fell on her ear like a dream of the morn,—
" O, blest be the day Kilmeny was born !

Now shall the land of the spirits see,
Now shall it ken, what a woman may be!
The sun that shines on the world sae bright,
A borrowed gleid frae the fountain of light;
And the moon that sleeks the sky sae dun,
Like a gouden bow, or a beamless sun,
Shall wear away, and be seen nae mair;
And the angels shall miss them, travelling the air.
But lang, lang after baith night and day,
When the sun and the world have dyed away,
When the sinner has gane to his waesome doom,
Kilmeny shall smile in eternal bloom!"

They bore her away, she wist not how,
For she felt not arm nor rest below;
But so swift they wained her through the light,
'T was like the motion of sound or sight;
They seemed to split the gales of air,
And yet nor gale nor breeze was there.
Unnumbered groves below them grew;
They came, they past, and backward flew,
Like floods of blossoms gliding on,
In moment seen, in moment gone.
O, never vales to mortal view
Appeared like those o'er which they flew,
That land to human spirits given,
The lowermost vales of the storied heaven;
From whence they can view the world below,
And heaven's blue gates with sapphires glow,—
More glory yet unmeet to know.

They bore her far to a mountain green,
To see what mortal never had seen;

And they seated her high on a purple sward,
And bade her heed what she saw and heard,
And note the changes the spirits wrought ;
For now she lived in the land of thought.—
She looked, and she saw nor sun nor skies,
But a crystal dome of a thousand dyes ;
She looked, and she saw nae land aright,
But an endless whirl of glory and light ;
And radiant beings went and came,
Far swifter than wind or the linkèd flame ;
She hid her een frae the dazzling view ;
She looked again, and the scene was new.

She saw a sun on a summer sky,
And clouds of amber sailing by ;
A lovely land beneath her lay,
And that land had glens and mountains gray ;
And that land had valleys and hoary piles,
And marlèd seas, and a thousand isles ;
Its fields were speckled, its forests green,
And its lakes were all of the dazzling sheen,
Like magic mirrors, where slumbering lay
The sun and the sky and the cloudlet gray,
Which heaved and trembled, and gently swung ;
On every shore they seemed to be hung ;
For there they were seen on their downward plain
A thousand times and a thousand again ;
In winding lake and placid firth,—
Little peaceful heavens in the bosom of earth.

Kilmeny sighed and seemed to grieve,
For she found her heart to that land did cleave ;
She saw the corn wave on the vale ;
She saw the deer run down the dale ;

She saw the plaid and the broad claymore,
And the brows that the badge of freedom bore ;
And she thought she had seen the land before.

She saw a lady sit on a throne,
The fairest that ever the sun shone on :
A lion licked her hand of milk,
And she held him in a leish of silk ;
And a leifu' maiden stood at her knee,
With a silver wand and melting ee ;
Her sovereign shield till love stole in,
And poisoned all the fount within.

Then a gruff untoward bedesman came,
And hundit the lion on his dame ;
And the guardian maid wi' the dauntless ee,
She dropped a tear, and left her knee ;
And she saw till the queen frae the lion fled,
Till the bonniest flower of the world lay dead ;
A coffin was set on a distant plain,
And she saw the red blood fall like rain :
Then bonny Kilmeny's heart grew sair,
And she turned away, and could look nae mair.

Then the gruff grim carle girnèd amain,
And they trampled him down, but he rose again ;
And he baited the lion to deeds of weir,
Till he lapped the blood to the kingdom dear ;
And weening his head was danger-preef,
When crowned with the rose and clover leaf,
He growled at the carle, and chased him away
To feed wi' the deer on the mountain gray.
He growled at the carle, and he gecked at Heaven ;
But his mark was set, and his arles given.

Kilmeny a while her een withdrew;
She looked again, and the scene was new.

She saw below her fair unfurled
One half of all the glowing world,
Where oceans rolled, and rivers ran,
To bound the aims of sinful man.
She saw a people, fierce and fell;
Burst frae their bounds like fiends of hell;
There lilies grew, and the eagle flew,
And she herked on her ravening crew,
Till the cities and towers were wrapt in a blaze,
And the thunder it roared o'er the lands and the
     seas.
The widows they wailed, and the red blood ran,
And she threatened an end to the race of man:
She never lened, nor stood in awe,
Till caught by the lion's deadly paw.
Oh! then the eagle swinked for life,
And brainzelled up a mortal strife;
But flew she north, or flew she south,
She met wi' the growl of the lion's mouth.

With a mooted wing and waefu' maen,
The eagle sought her eiry again;
But lang may she cower in her bloody nest,
And lang, lang sleek her wounded breast,
Before she sey another flight,
To play wi' the norland lion's might.

But to sing the sights Kilmeny saw,
So far surpassing nature's law,
The singer's voice wad sink away,
And the string of his harp wad cease to play.

But she saw till the sorrows of man were by,
And all was love and harmony ;—
Till the stars of heaven fell calmly away,
Like the flakes of snaw on a winter's day.

Then Kilmeny begged again to see
The friends she had left in her own countrye,
To tell the place where she had been,
And the glories that lay in the land unseen ;
To warn the living maidens fair,
The loved of heaven, the spirits' care,
That all whose minds unmeled remain
Shall bloom in beauty when time is gane.

With distant music, soft and deep,
They lulled Kilmeny sound asleep;
And when she awakened, she lay her lane,
All happed with flowers in the green-wood wene.
When seven long years had come and fled ;
When grief was calm, and hope was dead ;
When scarce was remembered Kilmeny's name,
Late, late in a gloamin, Kilmeny came hame !
And O, her beauty was fair to see,
But still and steadfast was her ee !
Such beauty bard may never declare,
For there was no pride nor passion there;
And the soft desire of maidens' een
In that mild face could never be seen.
Her seymar was the lily flower,
And her cheek the moss-rose in the shower;
And her voice like the distant melodye
That floats along the twilight sea.
But she loved to raike the lanely glen,
And keeped afar frae the haunts of men;

Her holy hymns unheard to sing,
To suck the flowers and drink the spring.
But wherever her peaceful form appeared,
The wild beasts of the hills were cheered;
The wolf played blythely round the field;
The lordly byson lowed and kneeled;
The dun deer wooed with manner bland,
And cowered aneath her lily hand.
And when at even the woodlands rung,
When hymns of other worlds she sung
In ecstasy of sweet devotion,
O, then the glen was all in motion!
The wild beasts of the forest came,
Broke from their bughts and faulds the tame,
And goved around, charmed and amazed;
Even the dull cattle crooned, and gazed,
And murmured, and looked with anxious pain
For something the mystery to explain.
The buzzard came with the throstle-cock,
The corby left her houf in the rock;
The blackbird alang wi' the eagle flew;
The hind came tripping o'er the dew;
The wolf and the kid their raike began;
And the tod, and the lamb, and the leveret ran;
The hawk and the hern attour them hung,
And the merl and the mavis forhooyed their young;
And all in a peaceful ring were hurled:
It was like an eve in a sinless world!

When a month and day had come and gane,
Kilmeny sought the green-wood wene;
There laid her down on the leaves sae green,
And Kilmeny on earth was never mair seen.

But O the words that fell from her mouth
Were words of wonder, and words of truth!
But all the land were in fear and dread,
For they kend na whether she was living or dead.
It wasna her hame, and she couldna remain;
She left this world of sorrow and pain,
And returned to the land of thought again.

JAMES HOGG.

THE FAIRY CHILD.

THE summer sun was sinking
  With a mild light, calm and mellow;
It shone on my little boy's bonnie cheeks,
  And his loose locks of yellow.

The robin was singing sweetly,
  And his song was sad and tender;
And my little boy's eyes, while he heard the song,
  Smiled with a sweet, soft splendor.

My little boy lay on my bosom
  While his soul the song was quaffing;
The joy of his soul had tinged his cheek,
  And his heart and his eye were laughing.

I sate alone in my cottage,
  The midnight needle plying;
I feared for my child, for the rush's light
  In the socket now was dying;

There came a hand to my lonely latch,
  Like the wind at midnight moaning;
I knelt to pray, but rose again,
  For I heard my little boy groaning.

I crossed my brow and I crossed my breast,
  But that night my child departed,—
They left a weakling in his stead,
  And I am broken-hearted !

O, it cannot be my own sweet boy,
  For his eyes are dim and hollow ;
My little boy is gone—is gone,
  And his mother soon will follow.

The dirge for the dead will be sung for me,
  And the mass be chanted meetly,
And I shall sleep with my little boy,
  In the moonlight churchyard sweetly.

JOHN ANSTER.

GARDEN FAIRIES.

KEEN was the air, the sky was very light,
Soft with shed snow my garden was, and white,
And, walking there, I heard upon the night
  Sudden sound of little voices,
  Just the prettiest of noises.

It was the strangest, subtlest, sweetest sound,
It seemed above me, seemed upon the ground,
Then swiftly seemed to eddy round and round,
  Till I said : " To-night the air is
  Surely full of garden fairies."

And all at once it seemed I grew aware
That little, shining presences were there,—
White shapes and red shapes danced upon the air ;
  Then a peal of silver laughter,
  And such singing followed after
3

As none of you, I think, have heard.
More soft it was than call of any bird,
Note after note, exquisitely deferred,
　　Soft as dew-drops when they settle
　　In a fair flower's open petal.

" What are these fairies ? " to myself I said ;
For answer, then, as from a garden's bed,
On the cold air a sudden scent was shed,—
　　Scent of lilies, scent of roses,
　　Scent of Summer's sweetest posies.

And said a small, sweet voice within my ear :
" We flowers, that sleep through winter, once a year
Are by our flower queen sent to visit here,
　　That this fact may duly flout us,—
　　Gardens can look fair without us.

" A very little time we have to play,
Then must we go, oh, very far away,
And sleep again for many a long, long day,
　　Till the glad birds sing above us,
　　And the warm sun comes to love us.

" Hark what the roses sing now, as we go ; "
Then very sweet and soft, and very low,—
A dream of sound across the garden snow,—
　　Came the chime of roses singing
　　To the lily-bell's faint ringing.

ROSES' SONG.

" Softly sinking through the snow,
To our winter rest we go,
Underneath the snow to house
Till the birds be in the boughs,

And the boughs with leaves be fair,
And the sun shine everywhere.

" Softly through the snow we settle,
Little snow-drops press each petal.
Oh, the snow is kind and white,—
Soft it is, and very light;
Soon we shall be where no light is,—
But where sleep is, and where night is,—
Sleep of every wind unshaken,
Till our Summer bids us waken."

Then toward some far-off goal that singing drew;
Then altogether ceased ; more steely blue
The blue stars shone; but in my spirit grew
    Hope of Summer, love of Roses,
    Certainty that Sorrow closes.
                    PHILIP BOURKE MARSTON.

THE CULPRIT FAY.

" My visual orbs are purged from film, and, lo !
    Instead of Anster's turnip-bearing vales,
I see old fairy land's miraculous show !
    Her trees of tinsel kissed by freakish gales,
Her ouphs that, cloaked in leaf-gold, skim the breeze,
    And fairies, swarming————————"
                    —TENNANT'S " ANSTER FAIR."

'T is the middle watch of a summer's night,—
The earth is dark, but the heavens are bright;
Naught is seen in the vault on high
But the moon, and the stars, and the cloudless sky,
And the flood which rolls its milky hue,
A river of light on the welkin blue.

The moon looks down on old Cro'nest;
She mellows the shades on his shaggy breast,
And seems his huge gray form to throw
In a silver cone on the wave below.
His sides are broken by spots of shade,
By the walnut bough and the cedar made;
And through their clustering branches dark
Glimmers and dies the firefly's spark,—
Like starry twinkles that momently break
Through the rifts of the gathering tempest's rack.

The stars are on the moving stream,
　And fling, as its ripples gently flow,
A burnished length of wavy beam
　In an eel-like, spiral line below;
The winds are whist, and the owl is still;
　The bat in the shelvy rock is hid;
And naught is heard on the lonely hill
But the cricket's chirp, and the answer shrill
　Of the gauze-winged katydid;
And the plaint of the wailing whippoorwill,
　Who moans unseen, and ceaseless sings
Ever a note of wail and woe,
　Till morning spreads her rosy wings,
And earth and sky in her glances glow.

'T is the hour of fairy ban and spell:
The wood-tick has kept the minutes well;
He has counted them all with click and stroke
Deep in the heart of the mountain-oak,
And he has awakened the sentry elve
　Who sleeps with him in the haunted tree,
To bid him ring the hour of twelve,
　And call the fays to their revelry;

Twelve small strokes on his tinkling bell
('T was made of the white snail's pearly shell) :
" Midnight comes, and all is well !
Hither, hither wing your way !
'T is the dawn of the fairy-day."

They come from beds of lichen green,
They creep from the mullein's velvet screen ;
   Some on the backs of beetles fly
From the silver tops of moon-touched trees,
     Where they swung in their cobweb hammocks
       high,
And rocked about in the evening breeze ;
   Some from the hum-bird's downy nest,—
They had driven him out by elfin power,
   And, pillowed on plumes of his rainbow breast,
Had slumbered there till the charmêd hour ;
   Some had lain in the scoop of the rock,
With glittering ising-stars inlaid ;
   And some had opened the four-o'clock,
And stole within its purple shade.
   And now they throng the moonlight glade,
Above, below, on every side,—
   Their little minim forms arrayed
In the tricksy pomp of fairy pride !

They come not now to print the lea,
In freak and dance around the tree,
Or at the mushroom board to sup,
And drink the dew from the buttercup ;
A scene of sorrow waits them now,
For an ouphe has broken his vestal vow ;
He has loved an earthly maid,
And left for her his woodland shade ;

He has lain upon her lip of dew,
And sunned him in her eye of blue,
Fanned her cheek with his wing of air,
Played in the ringlets of her hair,
And nestling on her snowy breast,
Forgot the lily-king's behest.
For this the shadowy tribes of air
   To the elfin court must haste away :
And now they stand expectant there,
   To hear the doom of the culprit fay.

The throne was reared upon the grass,
Of spice-wood and of sassafras ;
On pillars of mottled tortoise-shell
   Hung the burnished canopy,—
And o'er it gorgeous curtains fell
   Of the tulip's crimson drapery.
The monarch sat on his judgment-seat,
   On his brow the crown imperial shone,
The prisoner fay was at his feet,
   And his peers were ranged around the throne.
He waved his sceptre in the air,
   He looked around and calmly spoke ;
His brow was grave and his eye severe,
   But his voice in a softened accent broke :

" Fairy ! fairy ! list and mark :
   Thou hast broke thine elfin chain ;
Thy flame-wood lamp is quenched and dark,
   And thy wings are dyed with a deadly stain,—
Thou hast sullied thine elfin purity
   In the glance of a mortal maiden's eye ;
Thou hast scorned our dread decree,
   And thou shouldst pay the forfeit high.

But well I know her sinless mind
  Is pure as the angel forms above,
Gentle and meek, and chaste and kind,
  Such as a spirit well might love.
Fairy ! had she spot or taint,
Bitter had been thy punishment :
Tied to the hornet's shardy wings ;
Tossed on the pricks of nettles' stings ;
Or seven long ages doomed to dwell
With the lazy worm in the walnut-shell ;
Or every night to writhe and bleed
Beneath the tread of the centipede ;
Or bound in a cobweb-dungeon dim,
Your jailer a spider, huge and grim,
Amid the carrion bodies to lie
Of the worm, and the bug, and the murdered fly :
These it had been your lot to bear,
Had a stain been found on the earthly fair.
Now list, and mark our mild decree,—
Fairy, this your doom must be :

" Thou shalt seek the beach of sand
Where the water bounds the elfin land ;
Thou shalt watch the oozy brine
Till the sturgeon leaps in the bright moonshine,
Then dart the glistening arch below,
And catch a drop from his silver bow.
The water-sprites will wield their arms
  And dash around, with roar and rave,
And vain are the woodland spirits' charms ;
  They are the imps that rule the wave.
Yet trust thee in thy single might :
If thy heart be pure and thy spirit right,
Thou shalt win the warlock fight.

"If the spray-bead gem be won,
    The stain of thy wing is washed away ;
But another errand must be done
    Ere thy crime be lost for aye :
Thy flame-wood lamp is quenched and dark,
Thou must re-illume its spark.
Mount thy steed, and spur him high
To the heaven's blue canopy ;
And when thou seest a shooting star,
Follow it fast, and follow it far,—
The last faint spark of its burning train
Shall light the elfin lamp again.
Thou hast heard our sentence, fay ;
Hence ! to the water-side, away ! "

The goblin marked his monarch well ;
    He spake not, but he bowed him low,
Then plucked a crimson colen-bell,
    And turned him round in act to go.
The way is long, he cannot fly,
    His soilèd wing has lost its power,
And he winds adown the mountain high,
    For many a sore and weary hour.
Through dreary beds of tangled fern,
Through groves of nightshade dark and dern,
Over the grass and through the brake,
Where toils the ant and sleeps the snake ;
    Now o'er the violet's azure flush
He skips along in lightsome mood ;
    And now he thrids the bramble-bush,
Till its points are dyed in fairy blood.
He has leaped the bog, he has pierced the brier,
He has swum the brook, and waded the mire,

Till his spirits sank, and his limbs grew weak,
And the red waxed fainter in his cheek.
He had fallen to the ground outright,
  For rugged and dim was his onward track,
But there came a spotted toad in sight,
  And he laughed as he jumped upon her back;
He bridled her mouth with a silkweed twist,
  He lashed her sides with an osier thong;
And now, through evening's dewy mist,
  With leap and spring they bound along,
Till the mountain's magic verge is past,
And the beach of sand is reached at last.

Soft and pale is the moony beam,
Moveless still the glassy stream;
The wave is clear, the beach is bright
  With snowy shells and sparkling stones;
The shore-surge comes in ripples light,
  In murmurings faint and distant moans;
And ever afar in the silence deep
Is heard the splash of the sturgeon's leap,
And the bend of his graceful bow is seen,—
A glittering arch of silver sheen,
Spanning the wave of burnished blue,
And dripping with gems of the river-dew.

The elfin cast a glance around,
  As he lighted down from his courser toad,
Then round his breast his wings he wound,
  And close to the river's brink he strode;
He sprang on a rock, he breathed a prayer,
  Above his head his arms he threw,
Then tossed a tiny curve in air,
  And headlong plunged in the waters blue.

Up sprung the spirits of the waves
From the sea-silk beds in their coral caves;
With snail-plate armor, snatched in haste,
They speed their way through the liquid waste;
Some are rapidly borne along
On the mailèd shrimp or the prickly prong;
Some on the blood-red leeches glide,
Some on the stony star-fish ride,
Some on the back of the lancing squab,
Some on the sideling soldier-crab;
And some on the jellied quarl, that flings
At once a thousand streamy stings;
They cut the wave with the living oar,
And hurry on to the moonlight shore,
To guard their realms and chase away
The footsteps of the invading fay.

Fearlessly he skims along,
His hope his high, and his limbs are strong;
He spreads his arms like the swallow's wing,
And throws his feet with a frog-like fling;
His locks of gold on the waters shine,
   At his breast the tiny foam-bees rise,
His back gleams bright above the brine,
   And the wake-line foam behind him lies.
But the water-sprites are gathering near
   To check his course along the tide;
Their warriors come in swift career
   And hem him round on every side;
On his thigh the leech has fixed his hold,
The quarl's long arms are round him rolled,
The prickly prong has pierced his skin,
And the squab has thrown his javelin;

The gritty star has rubbed him raw,
And the crab has struck with his giant claw ;
He howls with rage, and he shrieks with pain ;
He strikes around, but his blows are vain ;
Hopeless is the unequal fight,
Fairy ! naught is left but flight.

He turned him round, and fled amain,
With hurry and dash, to the beach again ;
He twisted over from side to side,
And laid his cheek to the cleaving tide ;
The strokes of his plunging arms are fleet,
And with all his might he flings his feet,
But the water-sprites are round him still,
To cross his path and work him ill.
They bade the wave before him rise ;
They flung the sea-fire in his eyes ;
And they stunned his ears with the scallop-stroke,
With the porpoise heave and the drum-fish croak.
O, but a weary wight was he
When he reached the foot of the dogwood-tree.
Gashed and wounded, and stiff and sore,
He laid him down on the sandy shore ;
He blessed the force of the charmèd line,
    And he banned the water-goblins' spite,
For he saw around in the sweet moonshine
Their little wee faces above the brine,
    Giggling and laughing with all their might
    At the piteous hap of the fairy wight.

Soon he gathered the balsam dew
    From the sorrel-leaf and the henbane bud ;
Over each wound the balm he drew,
    And with cobweb lint he stanched the blood.

The mild west-wind was soft and low,
It cooled the heat of his burning brow;
And he felt new life in his sinews shoot,
As he drank the juice of the calamus-root;
And now he treads the fatal shore
As fresh and vigorous as before.

Wrapped in musing stands the sprite;
'T is the middle wane of night;
  His task is hard, his way is far,
But he must do his errand right
  Ere dawning mounts her beamy car,
And rolls her chariot wheels of light;
And vain are the spells of fairy-land,—
He must work with a human hand.

He cast a saddened look around;
  But he felt new joy his bosom swell,
When, glittering on the shadowed ground,
  He saw a purple muscle-shell;
Thither he ran, and he bent him low,
He heaved at the stern and he heaved at the bow,
And he pushed her over the yielding sand
Till he came to the verge of the haunted land.
She was as lovely a pleasure-boat
  As ever fairy had paddled in,
For she glowed with purple paint without,
  And shone with silvery pearl within;
A sculler's notch in the stern he made,
An oar he shaped of the bootle-blade;
Then sprung to his seat with a lightsome leap,
And launched afar on the calm, blue deep.

The imps of the river yell and rave.
They had no power above the wave;

But they heaved the billow before the prow,
  And they dashed the surge against her side,
And they struck her keel with jerk and blow,
  Till the gunwale bent to the rocking tide.
She wimpled about to the pale moonbeam,
Like a feather that floats on a wind-tossed stream ;
And momently athwart her track
The quarl upreared his island back,
And the fluttering scallop behind would float,
And patter the water about the boat ;
But he bailed her out with his colen-bell,
  And he kept her trimmed with a wary tread,
While on every side, like lightning, fell
  The heavy strokes of his bootle-blade.

Onward still he held his way,
Till he came where the column of moonshine lay,
And saw beneath the surface dim
The brown-backed sturgeon slowly swim ;
Around him were the goblin train,—
But he sculled with all his might and main,
And followed wherever the sturgeon led,
Till he saw him upward point his head ;
Then he dropped his paddle-blade,
And held his colen-goblet up
To catch the drop in its crimson cup.

With sweeping tail and quivering fin
  Through the wave the sturgeon flew,
And, like the heaven-shot javelin,
  He sprung above the waters blue.
Instant as the star-fall light
  He plunged him in the deep again.

But he left an arch of silver bright,
  The rainbow of the moony main.
It was a strange and lovely sight
  To see the puny goblin there ;
He seemed an angel form of light,
  With azure wing and sunny hair,
  Throned on a cloud of purple fair,
Circled with blue and edged with white,
And sitting, at the fall of even,
Beneath the bow of summer heaven.

A moment, and its lustre fell ;
  But ere it met the billow blue
He caught within his crimson bell
  A droplet of its sparkling dew !—
Joy to thee, fay ! thy task is done,
Thy wings are pure, for the gem is won,—
Cheerly ply thy dripping oar,
And haste away to the elfin shore.

He turns, and lo ! on either side
The ripples on his path divide ;
And the track o'er which his boat must pass
Is smooth as a sheet of polished glass.
Around, their limbs the sea-nymphs lave,
  With snowy arms half swelling out,
While on the glossed and gleamy wave
  Their sea-green ringlets loosely float.
They swim around with smile and song ;
  They press the bark with pearly hand,
And gently urge her course along
  Toward the beach of speckled sand,
And, as he lightly leaped to land,

They bade adieu with nod and bow ;
  Then gayly kissed each little hand,
And dropped in the crystal deep below.

A moment stayed the fairy there ;
He kissed the beach and breathed a prayer ;
Then spread his wings of gilded blue,
And on to the elfin court he flew.
As ever ye saw a bubble rise,
And shine with a thousand changing dyes,
Till, lessening far, through ether driven,
It mingles with the hues of heaven ;
As, at the glimpse of morning pale,
The lance-fly spreads his silken sail,
And gleams with blendings soft and bright
Till lost in the shades of fading night,—
So rose from earth the lovely fay ;
So vanished, far in heaven away !

    *   *   *   *

Up, fairy ! quit thy chickweed bower,
The cricket has called the second hour ;
Twice again, and the lark will rise
To kiss the streaking of the skies,—
Up ! thy charmèd armor don,
Thou 'lt need it ere the night be gone.

He put his acorn helmet on ;
It was plumed of the silk of the thistle-down ;
The corselet plate that guarded his breast
Was once the wild bee's golden vest ;
His cloak, of a thousand mingled dyes,
Was formed of the wings of butterflies ;
His shield was the shell of a lady-bug queen,
Studs of gold on a ground of green ;

And the quivering lance which he brandished bright
Was the sting of a wasp he had slain in fight.
Swift he bestrode his firefly steed ;
   He bared his blade of the bent-grass blue ;
He drove his spurs of the cockle-seed,
   And away like a glance of thought he flew
To skim the heavens, and follow far
The fiery trail of the rocket-star.

The moth-fly, as he shot in air,
Crept under the leaf, and hid her there ;
The katydid forgot its lay,
The prowling gnat fled fast away,
The fell mosquito checked his drone
And folded his wings till the fay was gone,
And the wily beetle dropped his head,
And fell on the ground as if he were dead ;
They crouched them close in the darksome shade,
   They quaked all o'er with awe and fear,
For they had felt the blue-bent blade,
   And writhed at the prick of the elfin spear.
Many a time, on a summer's night,
When the sky was clear, and the moon was bright,
They had been roused from the haunted ground
By the yelp and bay of the fairy hound ;
   They had heard the tiny bugle-horn,
They had heard the twang of the maize-silk string,
When the vine-twig bows were tightly drawn,
   And the needle-shaft through air was borne,
Feathered with down of the hum-bird's wing.
And now they deemed the courier ouphe
   Some hunter-sprite of the elfin ground,
And they watched till they saw him mount the roof
   That canopies the world around ;

Then glad they left their covert lair,
And freaked about in the midnight air.

Up to the vaulted firmament
His path the firefly courser bent,
And at every gallop on the wind
He flung a glittering spark behind;
He flies like a feather in the blast
Till the first light cloud in heaven is past.
 But the shapes of air have begun their work,
And a drizzly mist is round him cast:
 He cannot see through the mantle murk;
He shivers with cold, but he urges fast;
 Through storm and darkness, sleet and shade,
He lashes his steed, and spurs amain,—
For shadowy hands have twitched the rein,
 And flame-shot tongues around him played,
And near him many a fiendish eye
Glared with a fell malignity,
And yells of rage, and shrieks of fear,
Came screaming on his startled ear.

His wings are wet around his breast,
The plume hangs dripping from his crest,
His eyes are blurred with the lightning's glare,
And his ears are stunned with the thunder's blare.
But he gave a shout and his blade he drew,
 He thrust before and he struck behind,
Till he pierced their cloudy bodies through,
 And gashed their shadowy limbs of wind:
Howling the misty spectres flew,
 They rend the air with frightful cries;
For he has gained the welkin blue,
 And the land of clouds beneath him lies.

 4

Up to the cope careering swift,
   In breathless motion fast,
Fleet as the swallow cuts the drift,
   Or the sea-roc rides the blast,
The sapphire sheet of eve is shot,
   The spherèd moon is past,
The earth but seems a tiny blot
   On a sheet of azure cast.
O, it was sweet, in the clear moonlight,
   To tread the starry plain of even !
To meet the thousand eyes of night,
   And feel the cooling breath of heaven !
But the elfin made no stop or stay
Till he came to the bank of the Milky Way ;
Then he checked his courser's foot,
And watched for the glimpse of the planet-shoot.

Sudden along the snowy tide
   That swelled to meet their footsteps' fall,
The sylphs of heaven were seen to glide,
   Attired in sunset's crimson pall ;
Around the fay they weave the dance,
   They skip before him on the plain,
And one has taken his wasp-sting lance,
   And one upholds his bridle-rein ;
With warblings wild they lead him on
   To where, through clouds of amber seen,
Studded with stars, resplendent shone
   The palace of the sylphid queen.
Its spiral columns, gleaming bright,
Were streamers of the northern light ;
Its curtain's light and lovely flush
Was of the morning's rosy blush ;

And the ceiling fair that rose aboon,
The white and feathery fleece of noon.

But, O, how fair the shape that lay
    Beneath a rainbow bending bright!
She seemed to the entrancèd fay
    The loveliest of the forms of light;
Her mantle was the purple rolled
    At twilight in the west afar;
'T was tied with threads of dawning gold,
    And buttoned with a sparkling star.
Her face was like the lily roon
    That veils the vestal planet's hue;
Her eyes, two beamlets from the moon,
    Set floating in the welkin blue.
Her hair is like the sunny beam,
And the diamond gems which round it gleam
Are the pure drops of dewy even
That ne'er have left their native heaven.

She raised her eyes to the wondering sprite,
    And they leaped with smiles; for well I ween
Never before in the bowers of light
    Had the form of an earthly fay been seen.
Long she looked in his tiny face;
    Long with his butterfly cloak she played;
She smoothed his wings of azure lace,
    And handled the tassel of his blade;
And as he told, in accents low,
The story of his love and woe,
She felt new pains in her bosom rise,
And the tear-drop started in her eyes.
And "O, sweet spirit of earth," she cried,
    "Return no more to your woodland height,

But ever here with me abide
  In the land of everlasting light !
Within the fleecy drift we 'll lie,
  We 'll hang upon the rainbow's rim ;
And all the jewels of the sky
  Around thy brow shall brightly beam !
And thou shalt bathe thee in the stream
  That rolls its whitening foam aboon,
And ride upon the lightning's gleam,
  And dance upon the orbèd moon !
We 'll sit within the Pleiad ring,
  We 'll rest on Orion's starry belt,
And I will bid my sylphs to sing
  The song that makes the dew-mist melt ;
Their harps are of the umber shade
  That hides the blush of waking day,
And every gleamy string is made
  Of silvery moonshine's lengthened ray ;
And thou shalt pillow on my breast,
  While heavenly breathings float around,
And, with the sylphs of ether blest,
  Forget the joys of fairy ground."

She was lovely and fair to see,
And the elfin's heart beat fitfully ;
But lovelier far, and still more fair,
The earthly form imprinted there ;
Naught he saw in the heavens above
Was half so dear as his mortal love,
For he thought upon her looks so meek,
And he thought of the light flush on her cheek.
Never again might he bask and lie
On that sweet cheek and moonlight eye ;

But in his dreams her form to see,
To clasp her in his revery,
To think upon his virgin bride,
Was worth all heaven, and earth beside.

" Lady," he cried, " I have sworn to-night,
On the word of a fairy knight,
To do my sentence-task aright;
My honor scarce is free from stain,—
I may not soil its snows again;
Betide me weal, betide me woe,
Its mandate must be answered now."
Her bosom heaved with many a sigh,
The tear was in her drooping eye;
But she led him to the palace gate,
  And called the sylphs who hovered there,
And bade them fly and bring him straight,
  Of clouds condensed, a sable car.
With charm and spell she blessed it there,
From all the fiends of upper air;
Then round him cast the shadowy shroud,
And tied his steed behind the cloud;
And pressed his hand as she bade him fly
Far to the verge of the northern sky,
For by its wane and wavering light
There was a star would fall to-night.

Borne afar on the wings of the blast,
Northward away he speeds him fast,
And his courser follows the cloudy wain
Till the hoof-strokes fall like pattering rain.
The clouds roll backward as he flies,
Each flickering star behind him lies,

And he has reached the northern plain,
And backed his firefly steed again,
Ready to follow in its flight
The streaming of the rocket-light.

The star is yet in the vault of heaven,
  But it rocks in the summer gale;
And now 't is fitful and uneven,
  And now 't is deadly pale;
And now 't is wrapped in sulphur-smoke,
  And quenched is its rayless beam;
And now with a rattling thunder-stroke
  It bursts in flash and flame.
As swift as the glance of the arrowy lance
  That the storm-spirit flings from high,
The star-shot flew o'er the welkin blue,
  As it fell from the sheeted sky.
As swift as the wind in its train behind
  The elfin gallops along:
The fiends of the clouds are bellowing loud,
  But the sylphid charm is strong;
He gallops unhurt in the shower of fire,
  While the cloud-fiends fly from the blaze;
He watches each flake till its sparks expire,
  And rides in the light of its rays.
But he drove his steed to the lightning's speed,
  And caught a glimmering spark;
Then wheeled around to the fairy ground,
  And sped through the midnight dark.
        *   *   *   *
Ouphe and goblin! imp and sprite!
  Elf of eve! and starry fay!
Ye that love the moon's soft light,
  Hither,—hither wend your way;

Twine ye in a jocund ring,
  Sing and trip it merrily,
Hand to hand, and wing to wing,
  Round the wild witch-hazel tree.

Hail the wanderer again
  With dance and song, and lute and lyre;
Pure his wing and strong his chain,
  And doubly bright his fairy fire.
Twine ye in an airy round,
  Brush the dew and print the lea;
Skip and gambol, hop and bound,
  Round the wild witch-hazel tree.

The beetle guards our holy ground,
  He flies about the haunted place,
And if mortal there be found,
  He hums in his ears and flaps his face;
The leaf-harp sounds our roundelay,
  The owlet's eyes our lanterns be;
Thus we sing and dance and play
  Round the wild witch-hazel tree.

But hark! from tower to tree-top high,
  The sentry-elf his call has made;
A streak is in the eastern sky,
  Shapes of moonlight! flit and fade!
The hill-tops gleam in morning's spring,
The skylark shakes his dappled wing,
The day-glimpse glimmers on the lawn,
The cock has crowed, and the fays are gone.

JOSEPH RODMAN DRAKE.

OH! WHERE DO FAIRIES HIDE THEIR HEADS?

Oh! where do fairies hide their heads,
    When snow lies on the hills,
When frost has spoiled their mossy beds,
    And crystallized their rills?
Beneath the moon they cannot trip
    In circles o'er the plain;
And draughts of dew they cannot sip,
    Till green leaves come again.

Perhaps, in small, blue diving-bells
    They plunge beneath the waves,
Inhabiting the wreathed shells
    That lie in coral caves.
Perhaps, in red Vesuvius
    Carousals they maintain;
And cheer their little spirits thus,
    Till green leaves come again.

When they return, there will be mirth
    And music in the air,
And fairy wings upon the earth,
    And mischief everywhere.
The maids, to keep the elves aloof,
    Will bar the doors in vain;
No key-hole will be fairy-proof,
    When green leaves come again.

THOMAS HAYNES BAYLY.

SONGS OF ARIEL.

FROM "THE TEMPEST," ACT I. SC. 2.

I.

COME unto these yellow sands,
    And then take hands ;
Court'sied when you have, and kissed.
    (The wild waves whist!)
Foot it featly here and there ;
And, sweet sprites, the burthen bear.
    Hark, hark !
    Burthen [*dispersedly*]—Bow-wow.
    The watch-dogs bark—
    Burthen [*dispersedly*]—Bow-wow.
Hark, hark ! I hear
The strain of strutting chanticleer
Cry Cock-a diddle-dow.

II.

Full fathom five thy father lies ;
    Of his bones are coral made ;
Those are pearls that were his eyes ;
    Nothing of him that doth fade
But doth suffer a sea-change
Into something rich and strange.
Sea-nymphs hourly ring his knell :
    Burthen.—Ding-dong !
Hark ! now I hear them—ding, dong, bell !

III.

ACT V. SC. 1.

Where the bee sucks, there suck I :
In a cowslip's bell I lie ;

There I couch when owls do cry;
On the bat's back I do fly
After summer merrily.
Merrily, merrily, shall I live now,
Under the blossom that hangs on the bough.

SHAKESPEARE.

AIRY NOTHINGS.

FROM "THE TEMPEST," ACT IV. SC. 1.

OUR revels now are ended.   These our actors,
As I foretold you, were all spirits, and
Are melted into air, into thin air;
And, like the baseless fabric of this vision,
The cloud-capped towers, the gorgeous palaces,
The solemn temples, the great globe itself,
Yea, all which it inherit, shall dissolve,
And, like this insubstantial pageant faded,
Leave not a rack behind.   We are such stuff
As dreams are made on; and our little life
Is rounded with a sleep.

SHAKESPEARE.

THE ERL–KING

WHO rides so late through the midnight blast?
'T is a father spurs on with his child full fast;
He gathers the boy well into his arm,
He clasps him close and he keeps him warm.

"My son, why thus to my arm dost cling?"—
"Father, dost thou not see the elfin-king?
The elfin-king with his crown and train!"
"My son, 't is a streak of the misty rain!"

" *Come hither, thou darling, come, go with me!*
Fine games I know that I'll play with thee;
Flowers many and bright do my kingdoms hold,
My mother has many a robe of gold."

" O father, dear father, and dost thou not hear
What the elfin-king whispers so low in mine
  ear? "—
" Calm, calm thee, my boy, it is only the breeze,
As it rustles the withered leaves under the trees."

" *Wilt thou go, bonny boy, wilt thou go with me?*
My daughters shall wait on thee daintily;
My daughters around thee in dance shall sweep,
And rock thee and kiss thee and sing thee to sleep."

" O father, dear father, and dost thou not mark
The elf-king's daughters move by in the dark? "—
" I see it, my child; but it is not they,
'T is the old willow nodding its head so gray."

" *I love thee! thy beauty it charms me so;*
And I'll take thee by force, if thou wilt not go! "
" O father, dear father, he 's grasping me,—
My heart is as cold as cold can be! "

The father rides swiftly,—with terror he gasps,—
The sobbing child in his arms he clasps;
He reaches the castle with spurring and dread;
But alack! in his arms the child lay dead!

From the German of GOETHE.
Translation of MARTIN and AYTOUN.

THE DJINNS.

Town, tower,
Shore, deep,
Where lower
Cliffs steep;
Waves gray,
Where play
Winds gay,—
All sleep.

Hark ! a sound,
Far and slight,
Breathes around
On the night:
High and higher,
Nigh and nigher,
Like a fire
Roaring bright.

Now on 't is sweeping
With rattling beat,
Like dwarf imp leaping
In gallop fleet:
He flies, he prances,
In frolic fancies,
On wave-crest dances
With pattering feet.

Hark, the rising swell,
With each nearer burst
Like the toll of bell
Of a convent cursed;

Like the billowy roar
On a storm-lashed shore,—
Now hushed, now once more
Maddening to its worst.

O God! the deadly sound
Of the Djinns' fearful cry!
Quick, 'neath the spiral round
Of the deep staircase fly!
See, see our lamplight fade!
And of the balustrade
Mounts, mounts the circling shade
Up to the ceiling high!

'T is the Djinns' wild streaming swarm
Whistling in their tempest-flight;
Snap the tall yews 'neath the storm,
Like a pine-flame crackling bright.
Swift and heavy, lo, their crowd
Through the heavens rushing loud,
Like a livid thunder-cloud
With its bolt of fiery night!

Ha! they are on us, close without!
Shut tight the shelter where we lie!
With hideous din the monster rout,
Dragon and vampire, fill the sky!
The loosened rafter overhead
Trembles and bends like quivering reed;
Shakes the old door with shuddering dread,
As from its rusty hinge 't would fly!

Wild cries of hell! voices that howl and shriek!
The horrid swarm before the tempest tossed—
O Heaven!—descends my lowly roof to seek:
Bends the strong wall beneath the furious host.

Totters the house, as though, like dry leaf shorn
From autumn bough and on the mad blast borne,
Up from its deep foundations it were torn
To join the stormy whirl.   Ah! all is lost!

O Prophet! if thy hand but now
Save from these foul and hellish things,
A pilgrim at thy shrine I 'll bow,
Laden with pious offerings.
Bid their hot breath its fiery rain
Stream on my faithful door in vain,
Vainly upon my blackened pane
Grate the fierce claws of their dark wings!

They have passed!—and their wild legion
Cease to thunder at my door;
Fleeting through night's rayless region,
Hither they return no more.
Clanking chains and sounds of woe
Fill the forests as they go;
And the tall oaks cower low,
Bent their flaming flight before.

On! on! the storm of wings
Bears far the fiery fear,
Till scarce the breeze now brings
Dim murmurings to the ear;
Like locusts' humming hail,
Or thrash of tiny flail
Plied by the pattering hail
On some old roof-tree near.

Fainter now are borne
Fitful mutterings still;
As, when Arab horn
Swells its magic peal,

Shoreward o'er the deep
Fairy voices sweep,
And the infant's sleep
Golden visions fill.

Each deadly Djinn,
Dark child of fright,
Of death and sin,
Speeds the wild flight.
Hark, the dull moan,
Like the deep tone
Of ocean's groan,
Afar, by night!

More and more
Fades it now,
As on shore
Ripple's flow,—
As the plaint
Far and faint
Of a saint
Murmured low.

Hark! hist!
Around,
I list!
The bounds
Of space
All trace
Efface
Of sound.

From the French of **VICTOR MARIE HUGO.**

THE LADY LOST IN THE WOOD.

THE LADY.—This way the noise was, if mine ear be
    true,
My best guide now ; methought it was the sound
Of riot and ill-managed merriment,
Such as the jocund flute or gamesome pipe
Stirs up amongst the loose, unlettered hinds,
When for their teeming flocks and granges full
In wanton dance they praise the bounteous Pan,
And thank the gods amiss.   I should be loath
To meet the rudeness and swilled insolence
Of such late wassailers ; yet O, where else
Shall I inform my unacquainted feet
In the blind mazes of this tangled wood ?
My brothers, when they saw me wearied out
With this long way, resolving here to lodge
Under the spreading favor of these pines,
Stepped, as they said, to the next thicket side
To bring me berries, or such cooling fruit
As the kind, hospitable woods provide.
They left me then, when the gray-hooded even,
Like a sad votarist in palmer's weed,
Rose from the hindmost wheels of Phœbus' wain.
But where they are, and why they came not back,
Is now the labor of my thoughts : 't is likeliest
They had engaged their wandering steps too far,
And envious darkness, ere they could return,
Had stole them from me ; else, O thievish night,
Why shouldst thou, but for some felonious end,
In thy dark lantern thus close up the stars,

That nature hung in heaven, and filled their lamps
With everlasting oil, to give due light
To the misled and lonely traveller ?
This is the place, as well as I may guess,
Whence even now the tumult of loud mirth
Was rife, and perfect in my listening ear,
Yet naught but single darkness do I find.
What might this be ?   A thousand fantasies
Begin to throng into my memory,
Of calling shapes, and beckoning shadows dire,
And airy tongues, that syllable men's names
On sands and shores and desert wildernesses.
These thoughts may startle well, but not astound
The virtuous mind, that ever walks attended
By a strong-siding champion, Conscience.
O welcome, pure-eyed Faith, white-handed Hope,
Thou hovering angel girt with golden wings,
And thou unblemished form of Chastity ;
I see you visibly, and now believe
That he, the Supreme Good, to whom all things ill
Are but as slavish officers of vengeance,
Would send a glistering guardian, if need were,
To keep my life and honor unassailed.
Was I deceived, or did a sable cloud
Turn forth her silver lining on the night ?
I did not err, there does a sable cloud
Turn forth her silver lining on the night,
And casts a gleam over this tufted grove.
I cannot halloo to my brothers ; but
Such noise as I can make, to be heard farthest,
I 'll venture, for my new-enlivened spirits
Prompt me ; and they perhaps are not far off.

MILTON.

5

THE NYMPH OF THE SEVERN.

FROM " COMUS."

SPIRIT.—There is a gentle nymph not far from hence
That with moist curb sways the smooth Severn
    stream.
Sabrina is her name, a virgin pure ;
Whilom she was the daughter of Locrine,
That had the sceptre from his father Brute.
She, guiltless damsel, flying the mad pursuit
Of her enragèd stepdame Guendolen,
Commended her fair innocence to the flood
That stayed her flight with his cross-flowing course.
The water-nymphs that in the bottom played
Held up their pearlèd wrists, and took her in,
Bearing her straight to aged Nereus' hall,
Who, piteous of her woes, reared her lank head,
And gave her to his daughters to imbathe
In nectared lavers strewed with asphodel,
And through the porch and inlet of each sense
Dropped in ambrosial oils, till she revived,
And underwent a quick immortal change,
Made Goddess of the river : still she retains
Her maiden gentleness, and oft at eve
Visits the herds along the twilight meadows,
Helping all urchin blasts, and ill-luck signs
That the shrewd meddling elf delights to make,
Which she with precious vialed liquors heals ;
For which the shepherds at their festivals
Carol her goodness loud in rustic lays,
And throw sweet garland wreaths into her stream

Of pansies, pinks, and gaudy daffodils.
And, as the old swain said, she can unlock
The clasping charm, and thaw the mumming spell,
If she be right invoked in warbled song;
For maidenhood she loves, and will be swift
To aid a virgin, such as was herself,
In hard besetting need; this will I try,
And add the power of some adjuring verse.

SONG.

Sabrina fair,
 Listen where thou art sitting
Under the glassy, cool, translucent wave,
 In twisted braids of lilies knitting
The loose train of thy amber-dropping hair;
 Listen, for dear honor's sake,
 Goddess of the silver lake,
  Listen and save!
Listen, and appear to us
In name of great Oceanus;
By th' earth-shaking Neptune's mace.
And Tethy's grave majestic pace;
By hoary Nereus' wrinkled look,
And the Carpathian wizard's hook;
By scaly Triton's winding shell,
And old sooth-saying Glaucus' spell;
By Leucothea's lovely hands,
And her son that rules the strands;
By Thetis' tinsel-slippered feet,
And the songs of sirens sweet;
By dead Parthenope's dear tomb,
And fair Ligea's golden comb,
Wherewith she sits on diamond rocks,
Sleeking her soft alluring locks;

By all the nymphs that nightly dance
Upon thy streams with wily glance—
Rise, rise, and heave thy rosy head
From thy coral-paven bed,
And bridle in thy headlong wave,
Till thou our summons answered have.
　　　　Listen and save !

SABRINA *rises, attended by water-nymphs, and sings.*

　　SABRINA.—By the rushy-fringèd bank,
Where grows the willow and the osier dank
　　　My sliding chariot stays,
Thick set with agate, and the azure sheen
　　Of turkois blue, and emerald green,
　　　　That in the channel strays ;
　　Whilst from off the waters fleet
　　Thus I set my printless feet
　　O'er the cowslip's velvet head,
　　　　That bends not as I tread ;
　　Gentle swain, at thy request
　　　I am here.
　　SPIRIT.—Goddess, dear,
We implore thy powerful hand
To undo the charmèd band
Of true virgin here distressed,
Through the force and through the wile
Of unblest enchanter vile.
　　SABRINA.—Shepherd, 't is my office best
To help ensnarèd chastity :
Brightest lady, look on me !
Thus I sprinkle on thy breast
Drops that from my fountain pure
I have kept of precious cure,

Thrice upon thy finger's tip,
Thrice upon thy rubied lip ;
Next this marble venomed seat,
Smeared with gums of glutinous heat,
I touch with chaste palms moist and cold :
Now the spell hath lost his hold ;
And I must haste ere morning hour
To wait in Amphitritè's bower.

SABRINA *descends, and the* LADY *rises out of her seat.*

SPIRIT.—Virgin, daughter of Locrine,
Sprung from old Anchises' line,
  May thy brimmèd waves for this
  Their full tribute never miss
From a thousand petty rills,
That tumble down the snowy hills ;
Summer drought, or singèd air,
Never scorch thy tresses fair,
Nor wet October's torrent flood
Thy molten crystal fill with mud ;
May thy billows roll ashore
The beryl, and the golden ore ;
May thy lofty head be crowned
With many a tower and terrace round,
And here and there thy banks upon
With groves of myrrh and cinnamon.
  Come, lady ! while heaven lends us grace,
Let us fly this cursèd place,
Lest the sorcerer us entice
With some other new device.
Not a waste or needless sound,
Till we come to holier ground ;

I shall be your faithful guide
Through this gloomy covert wide ;
And not many furlongs thence
Is your father's residence,
Where this night are met in state
Many a friend to gratulate
His wished presence, and beside
All the swains that near abide,
With jigs and rural dance resort ;
We shall catch them at their sport,
And our sudden coming there
Will double all their mirth and cheer ;
Come, let us haste, the stars grow high,
But night sits monarch yet in the mid sky.

MILTON.

TAM O' SHANTER.

A TALE.

"Of Brownyis and of Bogilis full is this Buke."
—GAWIN DOUGLAS.

WHEN chapman billies leave the street,
And drouthy neebors neebors meet,
As market-days are wearing late,
An' folk begin to tak the gate ;
While we sit bousing at the nappy,
An' getting fou and unco happy,
We think na on the lang Scots miles,
The mosses, waters, slaps, and styles,
That lie between us and our hame,
Whare sits our sulky, sullen dame,
Gathering her brows like gathering storm,
Nursing her wrath to keep it warm.

This truth fand honest Tam O' Shanter,
As he frae Ayr ae night did canter
(Auld Ayr, wham ne'er a town surpasses,
For honest men and bonnie lasses).
 O Tam! hadst thou been but sae wise
As taen thy ain wife Kate's advice!
She tauld thee weel thou was a skellum,
A blethering, blustering, drunken blellum:
That frae November till October,
Ae market-day thou was na sober;
That ilka melder, wi' the miller,
Thou sat as lang as thou had siller;
That every naig was ca'd a shoe on,
The smith and thee gat roaring fou on;
That at the L—d's house, ev'n on Sunday,
Thou drank wi' Kirton Jean till Monday.
She prophesied that, late or soon,
Thou would be found deep drowned in Doon;
Or catched wi' warlocks in the mirk,
By Alloway's auld haunted kirk.
 Ah, gentle dames! it gars me greet
To think how monie counsels sweet,
How monie lengthened sage advices,
The husband frae the wife despises!
 But to our tale: Ae market night
Tam had got planted unco right,
Fast by an ingle, bleezing finely,
Wi' reaming swats, that drank divinely;
And at his elbow souter Johnny,
His ancient, trusty, drouthy crony.
Tam lo'ed him like a vera brither;
They had been fou for weeks thegither.
The night drave on wi' sangs and clatter,
And aye the ale was growing better;

The landlady and Tam grew gracious,
Wi' favors secret, sweet, and precious;
The souter tauld his queerest stories;
The landlord's laugh was ready chorus;
The storm without might rair and rustle,
Tam did na mind the storm a whistle.

Care, mad to see a man sae happy,
E'en drowned himself amang the nappy;
As bees flee hame wi' lades o' treasure,
The minutes winged their way wi' pleasure;
Kings may be blest, but Tam was glorious,
O'er a' the ills o' life victorious.

But pleasures are like poppies spread;
You seize the flower, its bloom is shed;
Or like the snow-fall in the river,
A moment white,—then melts forever;
Or like the borealis race,
That flit ere you can point their place;
Or like the rainbow's lovely form
Evanishing amid the storm.
Nae man can tether time or tide;
The hour approaches Tam maun ride;
That hour o' night's black arch the keystane,
That dreary hour he mounts his beast in;
And sic a night he takes the road in
As ne'er poor sinner was abroad in.

The wind blew as 't wad blawn its last;
The rattling showers rose on the blast;
The speedy gleams the darkness swallowed;
Loud, deep, and lang the thunder bellowed;
That night a child might understand
The Deil had business on his hand.

Weel mounted on his gray mare, Meg,
(A better never lifted leg,)

Tam skelpit on thro' dub and mire,
Despising wind and rain and fire,—
Whyles holding fast his guid blue bonnet,
Whyles crooning o'er some auld Scots sonnet,
Whyles glowering round wi' prudent cares,
Lest bogles catch him unawares;
Kirk-Alloway was drawing nigh,
Whare ghaists and houlets nightly cry.
  By this time he was cross the ford,
Whare in the snaw the chapman smoored;
And past the birks and meikle stane,
Whare drunken Charlie brak 's neck-bane;
And through the whins, and by the cairn,
Whare hunters fand the murdered bairn;
And near the thorn, aboon the well,
Whare Mungo's mither hanged hersel'.
Before him Doon pours all his floods;
The doubling storm roars through the woods;
The lightnings flash from pole to pole;
Near and more near the thunders roll;
When, glimmering through the groaning trees,
Kirk-Alloway seemed in a bleeze!
Through ilka bore the beams were glancing,
And loud resounded mirth and dancing.
  Inspiring bold John Barleycorn!
What dangers thou canst make us scorn!
Wi' tippenny we fear nae evil;
Wi' usquebae we 'll face the Devil!—
The swats sae reamed in Tammie's noddle,
Fair play, he cared na Deils a bodle.
But Maggie stood right sair astonished,
Till, by the heel and hand admonished,
She ventured forward on the light;
And, wow! Tam saw an unco sight!

Warlocks and witches in a dance :
Nae cotillon brent new frae France,
But hornpipes, jigs, strathspeys, and reels
Put life and mettle in their heels.
A winnock-bunker in the east,
There sat auld Nick, in shape o' beast,—
A towzie tyke, black, grim, and large,—
To gie them music was his charge ;
He screwed the pipes and gart them skirl
Till roof an' rafters a' did dirl.
Coffins stood round like open presses,
That shawed the dead in their last dresses ;
And by some devilish cantrip sleight,
Each in its cauld hand held a light,
By which heroic Tam was able
To note, upon the haly table,
A murderer's banes, in gibbet airns ;
Twa span-lang, wee, unchristened bairns ;
A thief, new cutted frae a rape,
Wi' his last gasp his gab did gape ;
Five tomahawks, wi' bluid red rusted ;
Five scymitars, wi' murder crusted ;
A garter, which a babe had strangled ;
A knife, a father's throat had mangled,
Whom his ain son o' life bereft,—
The gray hairs yet stack to the heft ;
Three lawyers' tongues turned inside out,
Wi' lies seamed like a beggar's clout ;
And priests' hearts, rotten, black as muck,
Lay stinking, vile, in every neuk :
Wi' mair o' horrible and awfu'
Which even to name wad be unlawfu'.
  ms Tammie glowered, amazed and curious,
The mirth and fun grew fast and furious ;

The piper loud and louder blew;
The dancers quick and quicker flew;
They reeled, they set, they crossed, they cleekit,
Till ilka carlin swat and reekit,
And coost her duddies to the wark,
And linket at it in her sark!
　　Now Tam, O Tam! had they been queans,
A' plump and strapping in their teens:
Their sarks, instead of creeshie flannen,
Been snaw-white seventeen-hunder linen;
Thir breeks o' mine, my only pair,
That ance were plush, o' guid blue hair,
I wad hae gi'en them off my hurdies
For ae blink o' the bonnie burdies!
　　But withered beldams, auld and droll,
Rigwoodie hags wad spean a foal,
Lowping an' flinging on a crummock,—
I wonder didna turn thy stomach.
　　But Tam kenn'd what was what fu' brawlie.
There was ae winsome wench and walie,
That night inlisted in the core
(Lang after kenned on Carrick shore;
For monie a beast to dead she shot,
And perished monie a bonnie boat,
And shook baith meikle corn and bear,
And kept the country-side in fear).
Her cutty-sark o' Paisley harn,
That while a lassie she had worn,
In longitude though sorely scanty,
It was her best, and she was vaunty.—
Ah! little kenned thy reverend grannie
That sark she coft for her wee **Nannie**
Wi' twa pund Scots ('t was a' her riches)
Wad ever graced a dance o' witches!

But here my Muse her wing maun cower,
Sic flights are far beyond her power ;
To sing how Nannie lap and flang
(A souple jade she was and strang),
And how Tam stood like ane bewitched,
And thought his very een enriched.
Ev'n Satan glowered, and fidged fu' fain,
And hotched and blew wi' might and main ;
Till first ae caper, syne anither,—
Tam tint his reason a' thegither,
And roars out, " Weel done, Cutty-sark ! "
And in an instant a' was dark ;
And scarcely had he Maggie rallied,
When out the hellish legion sallied.

As bees bizz out wi' angry fyke,
When plundering herds assail their byke ;
As open pussie's mortal foes,
When, pop ! she starts before their nose ;
As eager runs the market-crowd,
When *Catch the thief !* resounds aloud ;
So Maggie runs,—the witches follow,
Wi' monie an eldritch skreech and hollow.

Ah, Tam ! ah, Tam ! thou 'll get thy fairin' !
In hell they 'll roast thee like a herrin !
In vain thy Kate awaits thy comin'—
Kate soon will be a woefu' woman !
Now, do thy speedy utmost, Meg,
And win the key-stane of the brig ;
There at them thou thy tail may toss,—
A running stream they dare na cross.
But ere the key-stane she could make,
The fient a tail she had to shake ;
For Nannie, far before the rest,
Hard upon noble Maggie prest,

And flew at Tam wi' furious ettle :
But little wist she Maggie's mettle,—
Ae spring brought aff her master hale,
But left behind her ain gray tail :
The carlin claught her by the rump,
And left poor Maggie scarce a stump.

Now, wha this tale o' truth shall read,
Ilk man and mother's son take heed ;
Whene'er to drink you are inclined,
Or cutty-sarks run in your mind,
Think, ye may buy the joys o'er dear,
Remember Tam O' Shanter's mare.

ROBERT BURNS.

THE LORE–LEI.

I KNOW not whence it rises,
  This thought so full of woe ;—
But a tale of times departed
  Haunts me—and will not go.

The air is cool, and it darkens,
  And calmly flows the Rhine ;
The mountain peaks are sparkling
  In the sunny evening-shine.

And yonder sits a maiden,
  The fairest of the fair ;
With gold is her garment glittering,
  And she combs her golden hair.

With a golden comb she combs it,
  And a wild song singeth she,

That melts the heart with a wondrous
And powerful melody.

The boatman feels his bosom
  With a nameless longing move ;
He sees not the gulfs before him,
  His gaze is fixed above,

Till over boat and boatman
  The Rhine's deep waters run ;
And this with her magic singing
  The Lore-Lei hath done !

From the German of HEINRICH HEINE.

* * *

THE FISHER.

The waters purled, the waters swelled,—
  A fisher sat near by,
And earnestly his line beheld
  With tranquil heart and eye ;
And while he sits and watches there,
  He sees the waves divide,
And, lo! a maid, with glistening hair,
  Springs from the troubled tide.

She sang to him, she spake to him,—
  " Why lur'st thou from below,
In cruel mood, my tender brood,
  To die in day's fierce glow ?
Ah ! didst thou know how sweetly there
  The little fishes dwell,
Thou wouldst come down their lot to share,
  And be forever well.

" Bathes not the smiling sun at night—
    The moon too—in the waves ?
Comes he not forth more fresh and bright
    From ocean's cooling caves ?
Canst thou unmoved that deep world see,
    That heaven of tranquil blue,
Where thine own face is beckoning thee
    Down to the eternal dew ? "

The waters purled, the waters swelled,—
    They kissed his naked feet ;
His heart a nameless transport held,
    As if his love did greet.
She spake to him, she sang to him ;
    Then all with him was o'er,—
Half drew she him, half sank he in,—
    He sank to rise no more.

From the German of GOETHE
Translation of CHARLES TIMOTHY BROOKS.

THE SIRENS' SONG.

FROM THE " INNER TEMPLE MASQUE."

STEER hither, steer your winged pines,
    All beaten mariners :
Here lie undiscovered mines,
    A prey to passengers ;
Perfumes far sweeter than the best
That make the phœnix urn and nest :
    Fear not your ships,
Nor any to oppose you save our lips ;
    But come on shore,
Where no joy dies till love has gotten more.

For swelling waves our panting breasts,
   Where never storms arise,
Exchange ; and be awhile our guests :
   For stars, gaze on our eyes.
The compass, love shall hourly sing ;
And, as he goes about the ring,
   We will not miss
To tell each point he nameth with a kiss.

WILLIAM BROWNE.

THE FORSAKEN MERMAN.

Come, dear children, let us away ;
   Down and away below.
Now my brothers call from the bay ;
Now the great winds shorewards blow ;
Now the salt tides seaward flow ;
Now the wild white horses play,
Champ and chafe and toss in the spray.
   Children dear, let us away.
     This way, this way.

Call her once before you go.
   Call once yet,
In a voice that she will know :
   " Margaret ! Margaret ! "
Children's voices should be dear
(Call once more) to a mother's ear
Children's voices wild with pain,
   Surely she will come again.
Call her once, and come away,
   This way, this way.
" Mother dear, we cannot stay !

The wild white horses foam and fret,
Margaret! Margaret!"

Come, dear children, come away down.
Call no more.
One last look at the white-walled town,
And the little gray church on the windy shore,
Then come down.
She will not come, though you call all day.
Come away, come away.

Children dear, was it yesterday
We heard the sweet bells over the bay?
In the caverns where we lay,
Through the surf and through the swell,
The far-off sound of a silver bell?

Sand-strewn caverns cool and deep,
Where the winds are all asleep;
Where the spent lights quiver and gleam;
Where the salt weed sways in the stream;
Where the sea-beasts, ranged all round,
Feed in the ooze of their pasture-ground;
Where the sea-snakes coil and twine,
Dry their mail and bask in the brine;
Where great whales come sailing by,
Sail and sail, with unshut eye,
Round the world forever and aye?
When did music come this way?
Children dear, was it yesterday?

Children dear, was it yesterday
(Call yet once) that she went away?

6

Once she sat with you and me,
  On a red gold throne in the heart of the sea.
And the youngest sat on her knee.
She combed its bright hair, and she tended it well,
When down swung the sound of the far-off bell,
She sighed, she looked up through the clear green
    sea,
She said, "I must go, for my kinsfolk pray
In the little gray church on the shore to-day.
'T will be Easter-time in the world,—ah me!
And I lose my poor soul, Merman, here with thee."
I said : "Go up, dear heart, through the waves :
Say thy prayer, and come back to the kind sea-caves."
She smiled, she went up through the surf in the
    bay,
  Children dear, was it yesterday?

  Children dear, were we long alone?
" The sea grows stormy, the little ones moan ;
Long prayers," I said, "in the world they say."
" Come," I said, and we rose through the surf in the
    bay.
We went up the beach in the sandy down
Where the sea-stocks bloom, to the white-walled
    town,
Through the narrow paved streets, where all was
    still,
To the little gray church on the windy hill.
From the church came a murmur of folk at their
    prayers,
But we stood without in the cold blowing airs.
We climbed on the graves, on the stones worn with
    rains,
And we gazed up the aisle through the small leaded
    panes,

She sat by the pillar; we saw her clear;
" Margaret, hist! come quick, we are here.
Dear heart," I said, " we are here alone.
The sea grows stormy, the little ones moan."
But, ah, she gave me never a look,
For her eyes were sealed to the holy book.
    " Loud prays the priest; shut stands the door."
    Come away, children, call no more,
    Come away, come down, call no more.

    Down, down, down,
    Down to the depths of the sea.
She sits at her wheel in the humming town,
    Singing most joyfully.
Hark what she sings: " O joy, O joy,
From the humming street, and the child with its toy,
From the priest and the bell, and the holy well,
    From the wheel where I spun,
    And the blessed light of the sun."
    And so she sings her fill,
    Singing most joyfully
    Till the shuttle falls from her hand,
    And the whizzing wheel stands still.
She steals to the window, and looks at the sand,
    And over the sand at the sea;
    And her eyes are set in a stare;
    And anon there breaks a sigh,
    And anon there drops a tear,
    From a sorrow-clouded eye,
    And a heart sorrow-laden,
      A long, long sigh,
For the cold strange eyes of a little Mermaiden,
And the gleam of her golden hair.

Come away, away, children,
Come, children, come down.
The hoarse wind blows colder,
Lights shine in the town.
She will start from her slumber
When gusts shake the door ;
She will hear the winds howling,
Will hear the waves roar.
We shall see, while above us
The waves roar and whirl,
A ceiling of amber,
A pavement of pearl,—
Singing, " Here came a mortal,
But faithless was she,
And alone dwell forever
The kings of the sea."

But, children, at midnight,
When soft the winds blow,
When clear falls the moonlight,
When spring-tides are low ;
When sweet airs come seaward
From heaths starred with broom ;
And high rocks throw mildly
On the blanched sands a gloom :
Up the still, glistening beaches,
Up the creeks we will hie ;
Over banks of bright seaweed
The ebb-tide leaves dry.
We will gaze from the sand-hills,
At the white sleeping town ;
At the church on the hillside—
And then come back, down.

Singing, " There dwells a loved one,
    But cruel is she :
    She left lonely forever
    The kings of the sea."

MATTHEW ARNOLD.

THE FLITTING OF THE FAIRIES.

FROM " THE END OF ELFINTOWN."

.   .   .   .   .

For this holds true—too true, alas !
The sky that eve was clear as glass,
Yet no man saw the Faeries pass
    Where azure pathways glisten ;
And true it is—too true, ay me—
That nevermore on lawn or lea
Shall mortal man a Faery see,
    Though long he look and listen.

Only the twilit woods among
A wild-winged breeze hath sometimes flung
Dim echoes borne from strains soft sung
    Beyond sky-reaches hollow ;
Still further, fainter up the height,
Receding past the deep-zoned night—
Far chant of Fays who lead that flight,
    Faint call of Fays who follow.

JANE BARLOW.

III.

MYTHICAL : MYSTICAL : LEGENDARY.

A MUSICAL INSTRUMENT.

WHAT was he doing, the great god Pan,
  Down in the reeds by the river?
Spreading ruin and scattering ban,
Splashing and paddling with hoofs of a goat,
And breaking the golden lilies afloat
  With the dragon-fly on the river?

He tore out a reed, the great god Pan,
  From the deep, cool bed of the river,
The limpid water turbidly ran,
And the broken lilies a-dying lay,
And the dragon-fly had fled away,
  Ere he brought it out of the river.

High on the shore sat the great god Pan,
  While turbidly flowed the river,
And hacked and hewed as a great god can
With his hard, bleak steel at the patient reed,
Till there was not a sign of a leaf indeed
  To prove it fresh from the river.

He cut it short, did the great god Pan,
  (How tall it stood in the river!)
Then drew the pith like the heart of a man,

Steadily from the outside ring,
Then notched the poor dry empty thing
  In holes, as he sate by the river.

" This is the way," laughed the great god Pan,
  (Laughed while he sate by the river!)
" The only way since gods began
To make sweet music, they could succeed."
Then dropping his mouth to a hole in the reed,
  He blew in power by the river.

Sweet, sweet, sweet, O Pan,
  Piercing sweet by the river!
Blinding sweet, O great god Pan!
The sun on the hill forgot to die,
And the lilies revived, and the dragon-fly
  Came back to dream on the river.

Yet half a beast is the great god Pan,
  To laugh, as he sits by the river,
Making a poet out of a man.
The true gods sigh for the cost and the pain,—
For the reed that grows nevermore again
  As a reed with the reeds of the river.

ELIZABETH BARRETT BROWNING.

A TRANSFORMATION.

FROM " THE METAMORPHOSES."

WEARY and travel-worn,—her lips unwet
With water,—at a straw-thatched cottage door
The wanderer knocked. An ancient crone came
    forth
And saw her need, and hospitable brought

Her bowl of barley-broth, and bade her drink.
Thankful she raised it; but a graceless boy
And impudent stood by, and, ere the half
Was drained, "Ha! ha! see how the glutton
    swills!"
With insolent jeer he cried.   The goddess's ire
Was roused; and as he spoke, what liquor yet
The bowl retained, full in his face she dashed.
His cheeks broke out in blotches; what were arms
Turned legs, and from the shortened trunk a tail
Tapered behind.   Small mischief evermore
Might that small body work: the lizard's self
Was larger now than he.   With terror shrieked
The crone, and weeping, stooped her altered child
To raise; the little monster fled her grasp
And wriggled into hiding.   Still his name
His nature tells, and, from the star-light spots
That mark him, known as Stellio, crawls the Newt.

From the Latin of OVID.
Translation of HENRY KING.

THE COMET.

OCTOBER, 1858.

ERRATIC Soul of some great Purpose, doomed
To track the wild illimitable space,
Till sure propitiation has been made
For the divine commission unperformed!
What was thy crime?   Ahasuerus' curse
Were not more stern on earth than thine in heaven!

Art thou the Spirit of some Angel World,
For grave rebellion banished from thy peers,
Compelled to watch the calm, immortal stars

Circling in rapture the celestial void,
While the avenger follows in thy train
To spur thee on to wretchedness eterne?

Or one of Nature's wildest fantasies,
From which she flies in terror so profound,
And with such whirl of torment in her breast,
That mighty earthquakes yawn where'er she treads ;
While War makes red its terrible right hand,
And Famine stalks abroad all lean and wan?

To us thou art as exquisitely fair
As the ideal visions of the seer,
Or gentlest fancy that e'er floated down
Imagination's bright, unruffled stream,
Wedding the thought that was too deep for words
To the low breathings of inspirèd song.

When the stars sang together o'er the birth
Of the poor Babe at Bethlehem, that lay
In the coarse manger at the crowded Inn,
Didst thou, perhaps a bright exalted star,
Refuse to swell the grand, harmonious lay,
Jealous as Herod of the birth divine?

Or when the crown of thorns on Calvary
Pierced the Redeemer's brow, didst thou disdain
To weep, when all the planetary worlds
Were blinded by the fulness of their tears?
E'en to the flaming sun, that hid his face
At the loud cry, " Lama Sabachthani ! "

No rest ! No rest ! the very damned have that
In the dark councils of remotest Hell,
Where the dread scheme was perfected that sealed

Thy disobedience and accruing doom.
Like Adam's sons, hast thou, too, forfeited
The blest repose that never pillowed Sin?

No! none can tell thy fate, thou wandering
  Sphinx!
Pale Science, searching by the midnight lamp
Through the vexed mazes of the human brain,
Still fails to read the secret of its soul
As the superb enigma flashes by,
A loosed Prometheus burning with disdain.

CHARLES SANGSTER.

THE BALLAD OF JUDAS ISCARIOT.

'T was the body of Judas Iscariot
  Lay in the Field of Blood;
'T was the soul of Judas Iscariot
  Beside the body stood.

Black was the earth by night,
  And black was the sky;
Black, black were the broken clouds,
  Tho' the red Moon went by.

'T was the body of Judas Iscariot
  Strangled and dead lay there;
'T was the soul of Judas Iscariot
  Looked on it in despair.

The breath of the World came and went
  Like a sick man's in rest;
Drop by drop on the World's eyes
  The dews fell cool and blest.

Then the soul of Judas Iscariot
  Did make a gentle moan—
" I will bury underneath the ground
  My flesh and blood and bone.

" I will bury deep beneath the soil,
  Lest mortals look thereon,
And when the wolf and raven come
  The body will be gone !

" The stones of the field are sharp as steel,
  And hard and bold, God wot ;
And I must bear my body hence
  Until I find a spot ! "

'T was the soul of Judas Iscariot
  So grim, and gaunt, and gray,
Raised the body of Judas Iscariot,
  And carried it away.

And as he bare it from the field
  Its touch was cold as ice,
And the ivory teeth within the jaw
  Rattled aloud, like dice.

As the soul of Judas Iscariot
  Carried its load with pain,
The Eye of Heaven, like a lanthorn's eye,
  Opened and shut again.

Half he walked, and half he seemed
  Lifted on the cold wind ;
He did not turn, for chilly hands
  Were pushing from behind.

The first place that he came unto
   It was the open wold,
And underneath were prickly whins,
   And a wind that blew so cold.

The next place that he came unto
   It was a stagnant pool,
And when he threw the body in
   It floated light as wool.

He drew the body on his back,
   And it was dripping chill,
And the next place that he came unto
   Was a Cross upon a hill.

A Cross upon the windy hill,
   And a Cross on either side,
Three skeletons that swing thereon,
   Who had been crucified.

And on the middle cross-bar sat
   A white Dove slumbering ;
Dim it sat in the dim light,
   With its head beneath its wing.

And underneath the middle Cross
   A grave yawned wide and vast,
But the soul of Judas Iscariot
   Shivered, and glided past.

The fourth place that he came unto
   It was the Brig of Dread,
And the great torrents rushing down
   Were deep, and swift, and red.

He dared not fling the body in
   For fear of faces dim,
And arms were waved in the wild water
   To thrust it back to him.

'T was the soul of Judas Iscariot
   Turned from the Brig of Dread,
And the dreadful foam of the wild water
   Had splashed the body red.

For days and nights he wandered on
   Upon an open plain,
And the days went by like blinding mist,
   And the nights like rushing rain.

For days and nights he wandered on,
   All thro' the Wood of Woe;
And the nights went by like moaning wind,
   And the days like drifting snow.

'T was the soul of Judas Iscariot
   Came with a weary face—
Alone, alone, and all alone,
   Alone in a lonely place !

He wandered east, he wandered west
   And heard no human sound ;
For months and years, in grief and tears,
   He wandered round and round.

For months and years, in grief and tears,
   He walked the silent night ;
Then the soul of Judas Iscariot
   Perceived a far-off light.

A far-off light across the waste,
  As dim as dim might be,
That came and went like a lighthouse gleam
  On a black night at sea.

'T was the soul of Judas Iscariot
  Crawled to the distant gleam;
And the rain came down, and the rain was blown
  Against him with a scream.

For days and nights he wandered on,
  Pushed on by hands behind;
And the days went by like black, black rain,
  And the nights like rushing wind.

'T was the soul of Judas Iscariot,
  Strange, and sad, and tall,
Stood all alone at dead of night
  Before a lighted hall.

And the wold was white with snow,
  And his foot-marks black and damp,
And the ghost of the silver Moon arose,
  Holding her yellow lamp.

And the icicles were on the eaves,
  And the walls were deep with white,
And the shadows of the guests within
  Passed on the window light.

The shadows of the wedding guests
  Did strangely come and go,
And the body of Judas Iscariot
  Lay stretched along the snow.

The body of Judas Iscariot
  Lay stretched along the snow;
'T was the soul of Judas Iscariot
  Ran swiftly to and fro.

To and fro, and up and down,
  He ran so swiftly there,
As round and round the frozen Pole
  Glideth the lean white bear.

'T was the Bridegroom sat at the table-head,
  And the lights burned bright and clear—
" Oh, who is that," the Bridegroom said,
  " Whose weary feet I hear ? "

'T was one looked from the lighted hall,
  And answered soft and slow,
" It is a wolf runs up and down
  With a black track in the snow."

The Bridegroom in his robe of white
  Sat at the table-head—
" Oh, who is that who moans without ? "
  The blessèd Bridegroom said.

'T was one looked from the lighted hall,
  And answered fierce and low,
" 'T is the soul of Judas Iscariot
  Gliding to and fro."

'T was the soul of Judas Iscariot
  Did hush itself and stand,
And saw the Bridegroom at the door
  With a light in his hand.

The Bridegroom stood in the open door,
And he was clad in white,
And far within the Lord's Supper
Was spread so long and bright.

The Bridegroom shaded his eyes and looked,
And his face was bright to see—
"What dost thou here at the Lord's Supper
With thy body's sins?" said he.

'Twas the soul of Judas Iscariot
Stood black, and sad, and bare—
"I have wandered many nights and days ;
There is no light elsewhere."

'T was the wedding guests cried out within,
And their eyes were fierce and bright—
"Scourge the soul of Judas Iscariot
Away into the night!"

The Bridegroom stood in the open door,
And he waved hands still and slow,
And the third time that he waved his hands
The air was thick with snow.

And of every flake of falling snow,
Before it touched the ground,
There came a dove, and a thousand doves
Made sweet sound.

'T was the body of Judas Iscariot
Floated away full fleet,
And the wings of the doves that bare it off
Were like its winding-sheet.

'T was the Bridegroom stood at the open door,
  And beckoned, smiling sweet;
'T was the soul of Judas Iscariot
  Stole in, and fell at his feet.

" The Holy Supper is spread within,
  And the many candles shine,
And I have waited long for thee
  Before I poured the wine ! "

The supper wine is poured at last,
  The lights burn bright and fair,
Iscariot washes the Bridegroom's feet,
  And dries them with his hair.

BOBERT BUCHANAN.

THE BLESSÈD DAMOZEL.*

THE blessèd damozel leaned out
  From the gold bar of Heaven ;
Her eyes were deeper than the depth
  Of waters stilled at even,
She had three lilies in her hand,
  And the stars in her hair were seven.

Her robe, ungirt from clasp to hem,
  No wrought flowers did adorn,
But a white rose of Mary's gift,
  For service meetly worn;
Her hair that lay along her back
  Was yellow like ripe corn.

Her seemed she scarce had been a day
  One of God's choristers ;

* Written in the author's nineteenth year.

7

The wonder was not yet quite gone
  From that still look of hers ;
Albeit, to them she left, her day
  Had counted as ten years.

(To one, it is ten years of years.
  . . . Yet now, and in this place,
Surely she leaned o'er me—her hair
  Fell all about my face. . . .
Nothing : the autumn-fall of leaves.
  The whole year sets apace.)

It was the rampart of God's house
  That she was standing on :
By God built over the sheer depth
  The which is Space begun ;
So high, that looking downward thence
  She scarce could see the sun.

It lies in Heaven, across the flood
  Of ether, as a bridge.
Beneath, the tides of day and night
  With flame and darkness ridge
The void, as low as where this earth
  Spins like a fretful midge.

Around her, lovers, newly met
  'Mid deathless love's acclaims,
Spoke evermore among themselves
  Their heart-remembered names ;
And the souls mounting up to God
  Went by her like thin flames.

And still she bowed herself and stooped
  Out of the circling charm ;

Until her bosom must have made
  The bar she leaned on warm,
And the lilies lay as if asleep
  Along her bended arm.

From the fixed place of Heaven she saw
  Time like a pulse shake fierce
Through all the worlds. Her gaze still strove
  Within the gulf to pierce
Its path ; and now she spoke as when
  The stars sang in their spheres.

The sun was gone now, the curled moon
  Was like a little feather
Fluttering far down the gulf ; and now
  She spoke through the still weather.
Her voice was like the voice the stars
  Had when they sang together.

(Ah sweet ! Even now, in that bird's song,
  Strove not her accents there,
Fain to be hearkened ? When those bells
  Possessed the mid-day air,
Strove not her steps to reach my side
  Down all the echoing stair ?)

" I wish that he were come to me,
  For he will come," she said.
" Have I not prayed in Heaven ?—on earth,
  Lord, Lord, has he not prayed ?
Are not two prayers a perfect strength ?
  And shall I feel afraid ?

" When round his head the aureole clings,
  And he is clothed in white,

I'll take his hand and go with him
To the deep wells of light;
As unto a stream we will step down,
And bathe there in God's sight.

" We two will stand beside that shrine,
Occult, withheld, untrod,
Whose lamps are stirred continually
With prayer sent up to God;
And see our old prayers, granted, melt
Each like a little cloud.

" We two will lie i' the shadow of
That living mystic tree
Within whose secret growth the Dove
Is sometimes felt to be,
While every leaf that His plumes touch
Saith His Name audibly.

" And I myself will teach to him,
I myself, lying so,
The songs I sing here; which his voice
Shall pause in, hushed and slow,
And find some knowledge at each pause,
Or some new thing to know."

(Alas! we two, we two, thou say'st!
Yea, one wast thou with me
That once of old. But shall God lift
To endless unity
The soul whose likeness with thy soul
Was but its love for thee?)

" We two," she said, " will seek the groves
Where the lady Mary is,

With her five handmaidens, whose names
  Are five sweet symphonies,
Cecily, Gertrude, Magdalen,
  Margaret and Rosalys.

" Circlewise sit they, with bound locks
  And foreheads garlanded ;
Into the fine cloth white like flame
  Weaving the golden thread,
To fashion the birth-robes for them
  Who are just born, being dead.

" He shall fear, haply, and be dumb :
  Then will I lay my cheek
To his, and tell about our love,
  Not once abashed or weak :
And the dear Mother will approve
  My pride, and let me speak.

" Herself shall bring us, hand in hand,
  To Him round whom all souls
Kneel, the clear-ranged unnumbered heads
  Bowed with their aureoles :
And angels meeting us shall sing
  To their citherns and citoles.

" There will I ask of Christ the Lord
  Thus much for him and me :—
Only to live as once on earth
  With Love,—only to be,
As then awhile, forever now
  Together, I and he."

She gazed and listened and then said,
  Less sad of speech than mild,—
" All this is when he comes." She ceased.
  The light thrilled towards her, filled

With angels in strong level flight.
  Her eyes prayed, and she smiled.

(I saw her smile.)   But soon their path
  Was vague in distant spheres :
And then she cast her arms along
  The golden barriers,
And laid her face between her hands,
  And wept.   (I heard her tears.)

DANTE GABRIEL ROSSETTI.

THE KING'S HIGHWAY.

OCTOBER 6, 1892.*

I 'll wake and watch this autumn night,
  Till the slow dawn is gray ;
Lest I should miss a noble sight
  Upon the King's highway.

For now the far-enthronèd King
  To whom all flesh shall come,
A glorious message sends, to bring
  His exiled minstrel home ;

And I may see the guards in white
  Troop round him, crowned with bay,
And many a starry torch alight,
  Along the King's highway ;—

May see against the ebon skies,
  The banners backward blow,
And hear the *io pæan* rise
  About them, as they go.

What vigil would it not requite,
  That glorious array,

* The day of Tennyson's death.

That sure and stately march, forthright
  Along the King's highway?

   .   .   .   .

I heard the bells of midnight sound
  From many an unseen tower,
But for the minstrel homeward bound
  I could not watch one hour.

And now, how strange the growing light,
  How blank the morning gray!
What stillness, after yesternight,
  Broods on the King's highway!

HARRIET WATERS PRESTON.

RHŒCUS.

God sends his teachers unto every age,
To every clime, and every race of men,
With revelations fitted to their growth
And shape of mind, nor gives the realm of truth,
Into the selfish rule of one sole race.
Therefore each form of worship that hath swayed
The life of man, and given it to grasp
The master-key of knowledge, reverence,
Enfolds some germs of goodness and of right;
Else never had the eager soul, which loathes
The slothful down of pampered ignorance,
Found in it even a moment's fitful rest.

   .   .   .   .   .

Hear now this fairy legend of old Greece,
As full of freedom, youth, and beauty still
As the immortal freshness of that grace
Carved for all ages on some Attic frieze.

A youth named Rhœcus, wandering in the wood,
Saw an old oak just trembling to its fall;
And, feeling pity of so fair a tree,
He propped its gray trunk with admiring care,
And with a thoughtless footstep loitered on.
But, as he turned, he heard a voice behind
That murmured "Rhœcus!"—'T was as if the leaves,
Stirred by a passing breath, had murmured it;
And, while he paused bewildered, yet again
It murmured " Rhœcus ! " softer than a breeze.
He started and beheld with dizzy eyes
What seemed the substance of a happy dream
Stand there before him, spreading a warm glow
Within the green glooms of the shadowy oak.
It seemed a woman's shape, yet all too fair
To be a woman, and with eyes too meek
For any that were wont to mate with gods.
All naked like a goddess stood she there,
And like a goddess all too beautiful
To feel the guilt-born earthliness of shame.
" Rhœcus, I am the dryad of this tree—"
Thus she began, dropping her low-toned words,
Serene, and full, and clear, as drops of dew—
" And with it I am doomed to live and die ;
The rain and sunshine are my caterers,
Nor have I other bliss than simple life ;
Now ask me what thou wilt, that I can give,
And with a thankful heart it shall be thine."

Then Rhœcus, with a flutter at the heart,
Yet, by the prompting of such beauty, bold,
Answered : " What is there that can satisfy
The endless craving of the soul but love ?
Give me thy love, or but the hope of that

Which must be evermore my spirit's goal."
After a little pause she said again,
But with a glimpse of sadness in her tone,
" I give it, Rhœcus, though a perilous gift;
An hour before the sunset meet me here."
And straightway there was nothing he could see
But the green glooms beneath the shadowy oak ;
And not a sound came to his straining ears
But the low trickling rustle of the leaves,
And, far away upon an emerald slope,
The falter of an idle shepherd's pipe.

Now, in those days of simpleness and faith,
Men did not think that happy things were dreams
Because they overstepped the narrow bourne
Of likelihood, but reverently deemed
Nothing too wondrous or too beautiful
To be the guerdon of a daring heart.
So Rhœcus made no doubt that he was blest;
And all along unto the city's gate
Earth seemed to spring beneath him as he walked;
The clear, broad sky looked bluer than its wont,
And he could scarce believe he had not wings—
Such sunshine seemed to glitter through his veins
Instead of blood, so light he felt and strange.

Young Rhœcus had a faithful heart enough,
But one that in the present dwelt too much,
And, taking with blithe welcome whatsoe'er
Chance gave of joy, was wholly bound in that,
Like the contented peasant of a vale,
Deemed it the world, and never looked beyond.
So, haply meeting in the afternoon

Some comrades who were playing at the dice,
He joined them and forgot all else beside.

The dice was rattling at the merriest,
And Rhœcus, who had met but sorry luck,
Just laughed in triumph at a happy throw,
When through the room there hummed a yellow bee
That buzzed about his ear with down-dropped legs,
As if to light.   And Rhœcus laughed and said,
Feeling how red and flushed he was with loss,
" By Venus ! does he take me for a rose ? "
And brushed him off with rough, impatient hand.
But still the bee came back, and thrice again
Rhœcus did beat him off with growing wrath.
Then through the window flew the wounded bee ;
And Rhœcus, tracking him with angry eyes,
Saw a sharp mountain-peak of Thessaly
Against the red disc of the setting sun,
And instantly the blood sank from his heart,
As if its very walls had caved away.
Without a word he turned, and rushing forth,
Ran madly through the city and the gate,
And o'er the plain, which now the wood's long shade,
By the low sun thrown forward broad and dim,
Darkened well-nigh unto the city's wall.

Quite spent and out of breath, he reached the tree ;
And, listening fearfully, he heard once more
The low voice murmur " Rhœcus ! " close at hand ;
Whereat he looked around him, but could see
Nought but the deepening glooms beneath the oak.
Then sighed the voice : " O Rhœcus ! nevermore
Shalt thou behold me, or by day or night—
Me, who would fain have blest thee with a love

More ripe and bounteous than ever yet
Filled up with nectar any mortal heart;
But thou didst scorn my humble messenger,
And sent'st him back to me with bruisèd wings.
We spirits only show to gentle eyes—
We ever ask an undivided love;
And he who scorns the least of nature's works
Is thenceforth exiled and shut out from all.
Farewell! for thou canst never see me more."

Then Rhœcus beat his breast, and groaned aloud,
And cried, " Be pitiful! forgive me yet
This once, and I shall never need it more!"
" Alas!" the voice returned, "'t is thou art blind,
Not I unmerciful; I can forgive,
But have no skill to heal thy spirit's eyes;
Only the soul hath power o'er itself."
With that again there murmured "Nevermore!"
And Rhœcus after heard no other sound,
Except the rattling of the oak's crisp leaves,
Like the long surf upon a distant shore,
Raking the sea-worn pebbles up and down.
The night had gathered round him; o'er the plain
The city sparkled with its thousand lights,
And sounds of revel fell upon his ear
Harshly and like a curse; above, the sky,
With all its bright sublimity of stars,
Deepened, and on his forehead smote the breeze;
Beauty was all around him, and delight;
But from that eve he was alone on earth,

JAMES RUSSELL LOWELL.

UNA AND THE RED CROSSE KNIGHT.

FROM "THE FAËRIE QUEENE," BOOK I. CANTO I.

A GENTLE Knight was pricking on the plaine,
Ycladd in mightie armes and silver shielde,
Wherein old dints of deepe woundes did remaine,
The cruell markes of many a bloody fielde ;
Yet armes till that time did he never wield :
His angry steede did chide his foming bitt,
As much disdayning to the curbe to yield ;
Full iolly knight he seemed, and faire did sitt,
As one for knightly giusts and fierce encounters
fitt.

And on his brest a bloodie crosse he bore,
The deare remembrance of his dying Lord,
For whose sweete sake that glorious badge he
wore,
And dead, as living ever, him adored :
Upon his shield the like was also scored,
For soveraine hope, which in his helpe he had,
Right, faithfull, true he was in deede and word ;
But of his cheere,* did seeme too solemne sad ;
Yet nothing did he dread, but ever was ydrad.†

Upon a great adventure he was bond,
That greatest Gloriana to him gave,
That greatest glorious queene of Faëry lond,
To winne him worshippe, and her grace to have,
Which of all earthly thinges he most did crave :
And ever, as he rode, his hart did earne
To prove his puissance in battell brave

* countenance.   † dreaded.

Upon his foe, and his new force to learne ;
Upon his foe, a Dragon horrible and stearne.

A lovely Ladie rode him faire beside,
Upon a lowly asse more white then snow ;
Yet she much whiter; but the same did hide
Under a vele, that wimpled was full low ;
And over all a blacke stole shee did throw :
As one that inly mournd, so was she sad,
And heavie sate upon her palfrey slow ;
Seemèd in heart some hidden care she had ;
And by her in a line a milke-white lambe she lad.

So pure and innocent as that same lambe
She was in life and every vertuous lore ;
And by descent from royall lynage came
Of ancient kinges and queenes, that had of yore
Their scepters stretcht from east to westerne
      shore,
And all the world in their subiection held ;
Till that infernall feend with foule uprore
Forwasted all their land, and then expeld ;
Whom to avenge, she had this Knight from far
      compeld.

Behind her farre away a Dwarfe did lag,
That lasie seemd, in being ever last,
Or wearièd with bearing of her bag
Of needments at his backe. Thus as they past,
The day with cloudes was suddeine overcast,
And angry Iove an hideous storme of raine
Did poure into his lemans lap so fast,
That everie wight to shrowd it did constrain ;
And this faire couple eke to shrowd themselves were
      fain.

Enforst to seeke some covert nigh at hand,
A shadie grove not farr away they spide,
That promist ayde the tempest to withstand ;
Whose loftie trees, yclad with sommers pride,
Did spred so broad, that heavens light did hide,
Not perceable with power of any starr ;
And all within were pathes and alleies wide,
With footing worne, and leading inward farr :
Faire harbour that them seemes ; so in they entred
    ar.

EDMUND SPENSER.

UNA AND THE LION.

FROM THE "FAËRIE QUEENE," BOOK I. CANTO III.

ONE day, nigh wearie of the yrkesome way,
From her unhastie beast she did alight ;
And on the grasse her dainty limbs did lay
In secrete shadow, far from all mens sight ;
From her fayre head her fillet she undight,
And layd her stole aside. Her angels face,
As the great eye of heaven, shyned bright,
And made a sunshine in the shady place ;
Did never mortall eye behold such heavenly grace.

It fortunèd, out of the thickest wood
A ramping lyon rushèd suddeinly,
Hunting full greedy after salvage blood :
Soone as the royall virgin he did spy,
With gaping mouth at her ran greedily,
To have attonce devoured her tender corse ;
But to the pray whenas he drew more ny,
His bloody rage aswagèd with remorse
And, with the sight amazd, forgat his furious forse.

Instead thereof, he kist her wearie feet,
And lickt her lilly hands with fawning tong
As he her wrongèd innocence did weet.*
O how can beautie maister the most strong,
And simple truth subdue avenging wrong!
Whose yielded pryde and proud submission,
Still dreading death, when she had markèd long,
Her hart gan melt in great compassion ;
And drizling teares did shed for pure affection.

" The lyon, lord of everie beast in field,"
Quoth she, " his princely puissance doth abate,
And mightie proud to humble weake does yield,
Forgetfull of the hungry rage, which late
Him prickt, in pittie of my sad estate :—
But he, my lyon, and my noble lord,
How does he find in cruell hart to hate
Her, that him lovd, and ever most adord
As the god of my life ? why hath he me abhord ? "

Redounding tears did choke th' end of her plaint,
Which softly ecchoed from the neighbour wood ;
And, sad to see her sorrowfull constraint,
The kingly beast upon her gazing stood ;
With pittie calmd, downe fell his angry mood.
At last, in close hart shutting up her payne,
Arose the virgin borne of heavenly brood,
And to her snowy palfrey got agayne,
To seek her strayèd champion if she might attayne.

The lyon would not leave her desolate,
But with her went along, as a strong gard

* understand.

Of her chast person, and a faythfull mate
Of her sad troubles and misfortunes hard :
Still, when she slept, he kept both watch and
    ward ;
And, when she wakt, he wayted diligent,
With humble service to her will prepard ;
From her fayre eyes he took commandment,
And ever by her lookes conceivèd her intent.

EDMUND SPENSER.

THE BOWER OF BLISS.

FROM THE "FAËRIE QUEENE," BOOK II. CANTO XII.

THERE the most daintie paradise on ground
Itselfe doth offer to his sober eye,
In which all pleasures plenteously abownd,
And none does others happinesse envye ;
The painted flowres ; the trees upshooting hye ;
The dales for shade ; the hilles for breathing
    space ;
The trembling groves ; the christall running by ;
And, that which all faire workes doth most ag-
    grace,
The art, which all that wrought, appearèd in no
    place.

One would have thought (so cunningly the rude
And scornèd partes were mingled with the fine)
That Nature had for wantonesse ensude *
Art, and that Art at Nature did repine ;
So striving each th' other to undermine,
Each did the others worke more beautify ;

* followed, imitated.

So diff'ring both in willes agreed in fine:
So all agreed, through sweete diversity,
This gardin to adorne with all variety.

And in the midst of all a fountaine stood,
Of richest substance that on earth might bee,
So pure and shiny that the silver flood
Through every channell running one might see;
Most goodly it with curious ymageree
Was over wrought, and shapes of naked boyes,
Of which some seemed with lively iollitee
To fly about, playing their wanton toyes,
Whylest others did themselves embay in liquid
    ioyes.

And over all, of purest gold, was spred
A trayle of yvie in his native hew;
For the rich metall was so colourèd,
That wight, who did not well avised † it vew,
Would surely deeme it to bee yvie trew:
Low his lascivious armes adown did creepe,
That, themselves dipping in the silver dew,
Their fleecy flowres they fearefully did steepe,
Which drops of christall seemed for wantones to
    weep.

Infinit streames continually did well
Out of this fountaine, sweet and faire to see,
The which into an ample laver fell,
And shortly grew to so great quantitie,
That like a little lake it seemed to bee;
Whose depth exceeded not three cubits hight,

† with attention.

8

That through the waves one might the bottom
    see,
All paved beneath with iaspar shining bright,
That seemd the fountaine in that sea did sayle up-
    right.

.   .   .   .   .   .

Eftsoons they heard a most melodious sound,
Of all that mote delight a daintie eare,
Such as attonce might not on living ground,
Save in this paradise, be heard elsewhere.
Right hard it was for wight which did it heare,
To read what manner musicke that mote bee;
For all that pleasing is to living eare
Was there consorted in one harmonee ;
Birdes, voices, instruments, windes, waters, all
    agree :

The ioyous birdes, shrouded in cheerfull shade,
Their notes unto the voice attempred sweet;
Th' angelicall soft trembling voyces made
To th' instruments divine respondence meet ;
The silver-sounding instruments did meet
With the base murmure of the waters fall ;
The waters fall, with difference discreet,
Now soft, now loud, unto the wind did call;
The gentle warbling wind low answerèd to all.

                          EDMUND SPENSER.

THE CAVE OF SLEEP.

FROM THE "FAËRIE QUEENE," BOOK I. CANTO I.

HE, making speedy way through spersèd ayre,
And through the world of waters wide and deepe,

To Morpheus house doth hastily repaire,
Amid the bowels of the earth full steepe,
And low, where dawning day doth never peepe,
His dwelling is; there Tethys his wet bed
Doth ever wash, and Cynthia still doth steepe
In silver deaw his ever-drouping hed,
Whiles sad Night over him her mantle black doth
    spred.

   .   .   .   .   .   .

And, more to lulle him in his slumber soft,
A trickling streame from high rock tumbling
    downe,
And ever-drizling raine upon the loft,
Mixt with a murmuring winde, much like the
    sowne
Of swarming bees, did cast him in a swowne.
No other noyse, nor peoples troublous cryes,
As still are wont t' annoy the wallèd towne,
Might there be heard; but carelesse Quiet lyes
Wrapt in eternall silence, farre from enimyes.

EDMUND SPENSER.

THE CASTLE OF INDOLENCE.

FROM CANTO I.

> The castle hight of Indolence,
>   And its false luxury ;
> Where for a little time, alas!
>   We lived right jollily.

O MORTAL man, who livest here by toil,
Do not complain of this thy hard estate ;
That like an emmet thou must ever moil,
Is a sad sentence of an ancient date ;

And, certes, there is for it reason great;
For, though sometimes it makes thee weep and
    wail,
And curse thy star, and early drudge and late;
Withouten that would come a heavier bale,
Loose life, unruly passions, and diseases pale.

In lowly dale, fast by a river's side,
With woody hill o'er hill encompassed round,
A most enchanting wizard did abide,
Than whom a fiend more fell is nowhere found.
It was, I ween, a lovely spot of ground;
And there a season atween June and May,
Half prankt with spring, with summer half
    embrowned,
A listless climate made, where, sooth to say,
No living wight could work, ne cared even for
    play.

Was naught around but images of rest:
Sleep-soothing groves, and quiet lawns between;
And flowery beds that slumbrous influence kest,
From poppies breathed; and beds of pleasant
    green,
Where never yet was creeping creature seen.
Meantime, unnumbered glittering streamlets
    played,
And hurlèd everywhere their waters sheen;
That, as they bickered through the sunny glade,
Though restless still themselves, a lulling murmur
    made.

Joined to the prattle of the purling rills
Were heard the lowing herds along the vale,

And flocks loud bleating from the distant hills,
And vacant shepherds piping in the dale :
And, now and then, sweet Philomel would wail,
Or stockdoves plain amid the forest deep,
That drowsy rustled to the sighing gale ;
And still a coil the grasshopper did keep ;
Yet all these sounds yblent inclinèd all to sleep.

Full in the passage of the vale, above,
A sable, silent, solemn forest stood ;
Where naught but shadowy forms was seen to
　　move,
As Idless fancied in her dreaming mood :
And up the hills, on either side, a wood
Of blackening pines, aye waving to and fro,
Sent forth a sleepy horror through the blood ;
And where this valley winded out, below,
The murmuring main was heard, and scarcely
　　heard, to flow.

A pleasing land of drowsyhed it was,
Of dreams that wave before the half-shut eye ;
And of gay castles in the clouds that pass,
Forever flushing round a summer sky :
There eke the soft delights, that witchingly
Instil a wanton sweetness through the breast,
And the calm pleasures always hovered nigh ;
But whate'er smacked of noyance or unrest
Was far, far off expelled from this delicious nest.

The landscape such, inspiring perfect ease,
Where Indolence (for so the wizard hight)
Close-hid his castle mid embowering trees,
That half shut out the beams of Phœbus bright,
And made a kind of checkered day and night ;

Meanwhile, unceasing at the massy gate,
Beneath a spacious palm, the wicked wight
Was placed ; and to his lute, of cruel fate
And labor harsh, complained, lamenting man's
    estate.

Thither continual pilgrims crowded still,
From all the roads of earth that pass there by :
For, as they chanced to breathe on neighboring hill,
The freshness of this valley smote their eye,
And drew them ever and anon more nigh ;
Till clustering round the enchanter false they
    hung,
Ymolten with his siren melody ;
While o'er the enfeebling lute his hand he flung,
And to the trembling chords these tempting verses
    sung :

" Behold ! ye pilgrims of this earth, behold !
See all, but man, with unearned pleasure gay :
See her bright robes the butterfly unfold,
Broke from her wintry tomb in prime of May !
What youthful bride can equal her array ?
Who can with her for easy pleasure vie ?
From mead to mead with gentle wing to stray,
From flower to flower on balmy gales to fly,
Is all she has to do beneath the radiant sky.

" Behold the merry minstrels of the morn,
The swarming songster of the careless grove,
Ten thousands throats ! that, from the flowering-
    thorn,
Hymn their good God, and carol sweet of love,
Such grateful kindly raptures them emove :

They neither plough nor sow; ne, fit for flail,
E'er to the barn the nodden sheaves they drove :
Yet theirs each harvest dancing in the gale,
Whatever crowns the hill, or smiles along the vale.

"Outcast of nature, man! the wretched thrall
Of bitter dropping sweat, of sweltry pain,
Of cares that eat away the heart with gall,
And of the vices, an inhuman train,
That all proceed from savage thirst of gain :
For when hard-hearted interest first began
To poison earth, Astræa left the plain;
Guile, violence, and murder seized on man,
And, for soft milky streams, with blood the rivers ran.

"Come, ye who still the cumbrous load of life
Push hard up hill; but as the furthest steep
You trust to gain, and put an end to strife,
Down thunders back the stone with mighty
    sweep,
And hurls your labors to the valley deep,
Forever vain : come, and withouten fee,
I in oblivion will your sorrows steep,
Your cares, your toils; will steep you in a sea
Of full delight: O, come, ye weary wights, to me!

"With me, you need not rise at early dawn,
To pass the joyless day in various stounds;
Or, louting low, on upstart fortune fawn,
And sell fair honor for some paltry pounds;
Or through the city take your dirty rounds,
To cheat, and dun, and lie, and visit pay,
Now flattering base, now giving secret wounds;
Or prowl in courts of law for human prey,
In venal senate thieve, or rob on broad highway.

" No cocks, with me, to rustic labor call,
From village on to village sounding clear:
To tardy swain no shrill-voiced matrons squall;
No dogs, no babes, no wives, to stun your ear;
No hammers thump; no horrid blacksmith sear,
Ne noisy tradesman your sweet slumbers start,
With sounds that are a misery to hear:
But all is calm, as would delight the heart
Of Sybarite of old, all nature, and all art.

" Here naught but candor reigns, indulgent ease,
Good-natured lounging, sauntering up and down:
They who are pleased themselves must always
    please;
On others' ways they never squint a frown,
Nor heed what haps in hamlet or in town:
Thus, from the source of tender Indolence,
With milky blood the heart is overflown,
Is soothed and sweetened by the social sense;
For interest, envy, pride, and strife are banished
    hence.

" What, what is virtue, but repose of mind,
A pure ethereal calm, that knows no storm;
Above the reach of wild ambition's wind,
Above those passions that this world deform,
And torture man, a proud malignant worm?
But here, instead, soft gales of passion play,
And gently stir the heart, thereby to form
A quicker sense of joy; as breezes stray
Across the enlivened skies, and make them still
    more gay.

" The best of men have ever loved repose:
They hate to mingle in the filthy fray;

Where the soul sours, and gradual rancor grows,
Imbittered more from peevish day to day.
E'en those whom fame has lent her fairest ray,
The most renowned of worthy wights of yore,
From a base world at last have stolen away :
So Scipio, to the soft Cumæan shore
Retiring, tasted joy he never knew before.

" But if a little exercise you choose,
Some zest for ease, 't is not forbidden here :
Amid the groves you may indulge the Muse,
Or tend the blooms, and deck the vernal year ;
Or softly stealing, with your watery gear,
Along the brooks, the crimson-spotted fry
You may delude : the whilst, amused, you hear
Now the hoarse stream, and now the zephyr's
    sigh,
Attunèd to the birds, and woodland melody.

" O grievous folly ! to heap up estate,
Losing the days you see beneath the sun ;
When, sudden, comes blind unrelenting fate,
And gives the untasted portion you have won
With ruthless toil, and many a wretch undone,
To those who mock you, gone to Pluto's reign,
There with sad ghosts to pine, and shadows dun ;
But sure it is of vanities most vain,
To toil for what you here untoiling may obtain."

He ceased.   But still their trembling ears retained
The deep vibrations of his witching song ;
That, by a kind of magic power, constrained
To enter in, pell-mell, the listening throng.
Heaps poured on heaps, and yet they slipt along,
In silent ease ; as when beneath the beam

Of summer moons, the distant woods among,
Or by some flood all silvered with the gleam,
The soft-embodied fays through airy portal stream :

By the smooth demon so it ordered was,
And here his baneful bounty first began :
Though some there were who would not further
pass,
And his alluring baits suspected han.
The wise distrust the too fair-spoken man.
Yet through the gate they cast a wisful eye :
Not to move on, perdie, is all they can :
For do their very best they cannot fly,
But often each way look, and often sorely sigh.

. . . . . .

The rooms with costly tapestry were hung,
Where was inwoven many a gentle tale ;
Such as of old the rural poets sung,
Or of Arcadian or Sicilian vale :
Reclining lovers, in the lonely dale,
Poured forth at large the sweetly tortured heart ;
Or, sighing tender passion, swelled the gale,
And taught charmed echo to resound their smart ;
While flocks, woods, streams around, repose and
peace impart.

. . . . .

Each sound too here to languishment inclined,
Lulled the weak bosom, and inducèd ease ;
Aerial music in the warbling wind,
At distance rising oft, by small degrees,
Nearer and nearer came, till o'er the trees
It hung, and breathed such soul-dissolving airs,
As did, alas ! with soft perdition please :

Entangled deep in its enchanting snares,
The listening heart forgot all duties and all cares.

A certain music, never known before,
Here lulled the pensive, melancholy mind;
Full easily obtained. Behooves no more,
But sidelong, to the gently waving wind,
To lay the well-tuned instrument reclined;
From which, with airy flying fingers light,
Beyond each mortal touch the most refined,
The god of winds drew sounds of deep delight:
Whence, with just cause, the harp of Æolus it
 hight.

Ah me! what hand can touch the string so fine?
Who up the lofty diapason roll
Such sweet, such sad, such solemn airs divine,
Then let them down again into the soul?
Now rising love they fanned; now pleasing dole
They breathed, in tender musings, through the
 heart;
And now a graver sacred strain they stole,
As when seraphic hands a hymn impart:
Wild warbling nature all, above the reach of art!

JAMES THOMSON.

OUTWARD BOUND.

I LEAVE behind me the elm-shadowed square
And carven portals of the silent street,
And wander on with listless, vagrant feet
Through seaward-leading alleys, till the air
Smells of the sea, and straightway then the care

Slips from my heart, and life once more is sweet.
At the lane's ending lie the white-winged fleet.
O restless Fancy, whither wouldst thou fare?
Here are brave pinions that shall take thee far—
Gaunt hulks of Norway; ships of red Ceylon;
Slim-masted lovers of the blue Azores!
'T is but an instant hence to Zanzibar,
Or to the regions of the Midnight Sun.
Ionian isles are thine, and all the fairy shores!

THOMAS BAILEY ALDRICH.

THE LADY OF SHALOTT.

PART I.

On either side the river lie
Long fields of barley and of rye,
That clothe the wold and meet the sky,
And through the field the roads run by
        To many-towered Camelot;
And up and down the people go,
Gazing where the lilies blow
Round an island there below—
        The island of Shalott.

Willows whiten; aspens quiver;
Little breezes dusk and shiver
Through the wave that runs for ever
By the island in the river,
        Flowing down to Camelot.
Four gray walls, and four gray towers,
Overlook a space of flowers;
And the silent isle imbowers
        The lady of Shalott.

By the margin, willow-veiled,
Slide the heavy barges, trailed
By slow horses; and, unhailed,
The shallop flitteth, silken-sailed,
      Skimming down to Camelot;
But who hath seen her wave her hand?
Or at the casement seen her stand?
Or is she known in all the land—
      The lady of Shalott?

Only reapers, reaping early
In among the bearded barley,
Hear a song that echoes cheerly
From the river, winding clearly
      Down to towered Camelot;
And by the moon the reaper weary,
Piling sheaves in uplands airy,
Listening, whispers, " 'T is the fairy
      Lady of Shalott."

PART II.

There she weaves by night and day
A magic web with colors gay.
She has heard a whisper say
A curse is on her if she stay
      To look down to Camelot.
She knows not what the curse may be;
And so she weaveth steadily,
And little other care hath she—
      The lady of Shalott.

And moving through a mirror clear
That hangs before her all the year,

Shadows of the world appear.
There she sees the highway near,
      Winding down to Camelot;
There the river eddy whirls;
And there the surly village-churls,
And the red cloaks of market-girls,
      Pass onward from Shalott.

Sometimes a troop of damsels glad,
An abbot on an ambling pad—
Sometimes a curly shepherd-lad,
Or long-haired page, in crimson clad,
      Goes by to towered Camelot:
And sometimes through the mirror blue
The knights come riding, two and two:
She hath no loyal knight and true—
      The lady of Shalott.

But in her web she still delights
To weave the mirror's magic sights;
For often, through the silent nights,
A funeral, with plumes and lights
      And music, went to Camelot;
Or, when the moon was overhead,
Came two young lovers lately wed;
"I am half sick of shadows," said
      The lady of Shalott.

PART III.

A bow-shot from her bower-eaves
He rode between the barley-sheaves;
The sun came dazzling through the leaves,
And flamed upon the brazen greaves
      Of bold Sir Lancelot.

A red-cross knight for ever kneeled
To a lady in his shield,
That sparkled on the yellow field,
    Beside remote Shalott.

The gemmy bridle glittered free,
Like to some branch of stars we see
Hung in the golden galaxy.
The bridle-bells rang merrily,
    As he rode down to Camelot;
And, from his blazoned baldric slung,
A mighty silver bugle hung;
And as he rode his armor rung,
    Beside remote Shalott.

All in the blue unclouded weather
Thick-jewelled shone the saddle-leather;
The helmet and the helmet-feather
Burned like one burning flame together,
    As he rode down to Camelot:
As often, through the purple night,
Below the starry clusters bright,
Some bearded meteor, trailing light,
    Moves over still Shalott.

His broad clear brow in sunlight glowed;
On burnished hooves his war-horse trode:
From underneath his helmet flowed
His coal-black curls as on he rode,
    As he rode down to Camelot.
From the bank and from the river
He flashed into the crystal mirror:
"Tirra lirra," by the river,
    Sang Sir Lancelot.

She left the web, she left the loom ;
She made three paces through the room ;
She saw the water-lily bloom ;
She saw the helmet and the plume ;
      She looked down to Camelot;
Out flew the web, and floated wide ;
The mirror cracked from side to side ;
" The curse is come upon me !" cried
      The lady of Shalott.

PART IV.

In the stormy east-wind straining,
The pale yellow woods were waning—
The broad stream in the banks complaining,
Heavily the low sky raining
      Over towered Camelot;
Down she came and found a boat,
Beneath a willow left afloat ;
And round about the prow she wrote,
      The lady of Shalott.

And down the river's dim expanse—
Like some bold seer in a trance,
Seeing all his own mischance—
With a glassy countenance
      Did she look to Camelot.
And at the closing of the day
She loosed the chain, and down she lay ;
The broad stream bore her far away—
      The lady of Shalott.

Lying robed in snowy white,
That loosely flew to left and right—

The leaves upon her falling light—
Through the noises of the night
     She floated down to Camelot;
And as the boat-head wound along,
The willowy hills and fields among,
They heard her singing her last song—
     The lady of Shalott—

Heard a carol, mournful, holy,
Chanted loudly, chanted lowly—
Till her blood was frozen slowly,
And her eyes were darkened wholly,
     Turned to towered Camelot;
For ere she reached, upon the tide,
The first house by the water-side,
Singing, in her song she died—
     The lady of Shalott.

Under tower and balcony,
By garden-wall and gallery,
A gleaming shape, she floated by—
A corse between the houses high—
     Silent, into Camelot.
Out upon the wharfs they came,
Knight and burgher, lord and dame;
And round the prow they read her name—
     The lady of Shalott.

Who is this? and what is here?
And in the royal palace near
Died the sound of royal cheer;
And they crossed themselves for fear—
     All the knights at Camelot;

But Lancelot mused a little space :
He said, " She has a lovely face ;
God in his mercy lend her grace—
　　The lady of Shalott ! "
ALFRED, LORD TENNYSON.

RIME OF THE ANCIENT MARINER.

PART I.

An Ancient Mariner meeteth three gallants bidden to a wedding feast, and detaineth one.

It is an Ancient Mariner,
And he stoppeth one of three,
" By thy long gray beard and glittering
　　eye,
Now wherefore stopp'st thou me ?
The Bridegroom's doors are opened
　　wide,
And I am next of kin ;
The guests are met, the feast is set,—
Mayst hear the merry din."

He holds him with his skinny hand :
" There was a ship," quoth he,
"Hold　off ! unhand　me,　graybeard
　　loon ! "—
Eftsoons his hand dropt he.

The Wedding-Guest is spell bound by the eye of the old seafaring man, and constrained to hear his tale.

He holds him with his glittering eye,—
The Wedding-Guest stood still ;
He listens like a three years' child ;
The Mariner hath his will.

The Wedding-Guest sat on a stone,—
He cannot choose but hear ;
And thus spake on that ancient man,
The bright-eyed Mariner :

"The ship was cheered, the harbor
    cleared;
Merrily did we drop
Below the kirk, below the hill,
Below the light-house top.

The sun came up upon the left,
Out of the sea came he;
And he shone bright, and on the right
Went down into the sea;

The Mariner tells how the ship sailed southward, with a good wind and fair weather, till it reached the line.

Higher and higher every day,
Till over the mast at noon—"
The Wedding-Guest here beat his breast,
For he heard the loud bassoon.

The Bride hath paced into the hall—
Red as a rose is she;
Nodding their heads before her goes
The merry minstrelsy.

The Wedding-Guest heareth the bridal music; but the Mariner continueth his tale.

The Wedding-Guest he beat his breast,
Yet he cannot choose but hear;
And thus spake on that ancient man,
The bright-eyed Mariner:

"And now the Storm-blast came, and he
Was tyrannous and strong;
He struck with his o'ertaking wings,
And chased us south along.

The ship drawn by a storm toward the south pole.

With sloping masts and dipping prow—
As who pursued with yell and blow
Still treads the shadow of his foe,
And forward bends his head—

The ship drove fast; loud roared the
　　blast,
And southward aye we fled.

And now there came both mist and
　　snow,
And it grew wondrous cold;
And ice, mast-high, came floating by,
As green as emerald.

The land of ice
and of fearful
sounds.
where no living
thing was to be
seen.

And through the drifts the snowy cliffs
Did send a dismal sheen:
Nor shapes of men nor beasts we ken—
The ice was all between.

The ice was here, the ice was there,
The ice was all around;
It cracked and growled, and roared and
　　howled,
Like noises in a swound!

Till a great sea-
bird, called the
Albatross, came
through the
snow-fog, and
was received with
great joy and
hospitality.

At length did cross an Albatross—
Thorough the fog it came;
As if it had been a Christian soul,
We hailed it in God's name.

It ate the food it ne'er had eat,
And round and round it flew.
The ice did split with a thunder-fit;
The helmsman steered us through!

And lo! the Al-
batross proveth a
bird of good
omen, and fol
loweth the ship
as it returned
northward
through fog
and floating ice.

And a good south wind sprung up be-
　　hind;
The Albatross did follow,
And every day, for food or play,
Came to the mariners' hollo!

In mist or cloud, on mast or shroud,
It perched for vespers nine ;
Whiles all the night, through fog-smoke
    white,
Glimmered the white moonshine."

" God save thee, Ancient Mariner !
From the fiends, that plague thee thus !—
Why look'st thou so ? "—" With my
    cross-bow
I shot the Albatross.

The Ancient Mariner inhospitably killeth the pious bird of good omen.

PART II.

" THE Sun now rose upon the right :
Out of the sea came he,
Still hid in mist, and on the left
Went down into the sea.

And the good south wind still blew be-
    hind,
But no sweet bird did follow,
Nor any day, for food or play,
Came to the mariners' hollo !

And I had done an hellish thing,
And it would work 'em woe :
For all averred, I had killed the bird
That made the breeze to blow.
Ah wretch ! said they, the bird to slay,
That made the breeze to blow !

His shipmates cry out against the Ancient Mariner, for killing the bird of good luck.

Nor dim nor red, like God's own head
The glorious Sun uprist :
Then all averred, I had killed the bird
That brought the fog and mist.
'T was right, said they, such birds to slay,
That bring the fog and mist.

But when the fog cleared off, they justify the same, and thus make themselves accomplices in the crime.

The fair breeze
continues the
ship enters the
Pacific Ocean,
and sails north-
ward, even till it
reaches the line. The fair breeze blew, the white foam flew,
The furrow followed free;
We were the first that ever burst
Into that silent sea.

The ship hath
been suddenly be-
calmed; Down dropt the breeze, the sails dropt
    down,—
'T was sad as sad could be;
And we did speak only to break
The silence of the sea.

All in a hot and copper sky
The bloody Sun, at noon,
Right up above the mast did stand,
No bigger than the Moon.

Day after day, day after day,
We stuck,—nor breath nor motion;
As idle as a painted ship
Upon a painted ocean.

and the Albatross
begins to be
avenged. Water, water everywhere,
And all the boards did shrink;
Water, water everywhere,
Nor any drop to drink.

The very deep did rot: O Christ!
That ever this should be!
Yea, slimy things did crawl with legs
Upon the slimy sea!

About, about, in reel and rout,
The death-fires danced at night;
The water, like a witch's oils,
Burnt green, and blue, and white.

And some in dreams assurèd were
Of the Spirit that plagued us so ;
Nine fathom deep he had followed us
From the land of mist and snow.

A Spirit had followed them ; one of the invisible inhabitants of this planet, neither departed souls nor angels : concerning whom the learned Jew Josephus, and the Platonic Constantinopolitan, Michael Psellus, may be consulted. They are very numerous, and there is no climate or element without one or more.

And every tongue, through utter drought,
Was withered at the root ;
We could not speak, no more than if
We had been choked with soot.

Ah ! well-a-day ! what evil looks
Had I from old and young !
Instead of the cross the Albatross
About my neck was hung.

The shipmates, in their sore distress, would fain throw the whole guilt on the Ancient Mariner : in sign whereof they hang the dead sea-bird round his neck.

PART III.

"There passed a weary time. Each
    throat
Was parched, and glazed each eye—
A weary time ! a weary time !
How glazed each weary eye !—
When, looking westward, I beheld
A something in the sky.

The Ancient Mariner beholdeth a sign in the element atar off.

At first it seemed a little speck,
And then it seemed a mist ;
It moved and moved, and took at last
A certain shape, I wist !

A speck, a mist, a shape, I wist !
And still it neared and neared ;
As if it dodged a water-sprite,
It plunged and tacked and veered.

At its nearer approach it seemeth him to be a ship; and at a dear ransom he freeth his speech from the bonds of thirst.

With throats unslaked, with black lips
    baked,
We could nor laugh nor wail;
Through utter drought all dumb we
    stood!
I bit my arm, I sucked the blood,
And cried, ' A sail! a sail!'

With throats unslaked, with black lips
    baked,
Agape they heard me call;
Gramercy! they for joy did grin,

A flash of joy. And all at once their breath drew in,
As they were drinking all.

And horror follows. For can it be a ship that comes onward without wind or tide! ' See! see!' I cried, 'she tacks no more!
Hither to work us weal—
Without a breeze, without a tide,
She steadies with upright keel!'

The western wave was all a-flame;
The day was well nigh done;
Almost upon the western wave
Rested the broad bright Sun,
When that strange shape drove suddenly
Betwixt us and the Sun.

It seemeth him but the skeleton of a ship. And straight the Sun was flecked with
    bars,
(Heaven's mother send us grace!)
As if through a dungeon-grate he peered
With broad and burning face.

Alas! thought I—and my heart beat
    loud—
How fast she nears and near

Are those her sails that glance in the sun,
Like restless gossameres?

Are those her ribs through which the Sun And its ribs are seen as bars on the face of the setting sun. The spectre-woman and her death-mate, and no other on board the skeleton ship.
Did peer, as through a grate?
And is that woman all her crew?
Is that a death? and are there two?
Is Death that woman's mate?

Her lips were red, her looks were free,
Her locks were yellow as gold; Like vessel, like crew!
Her skin was as white as leprosy:
The night-mare, Life-in-Death, was she,
Who thicks man's blood with cold.

The naked hulk alongside came, Death and Life-in-Death have diced for the ship's crew, and she (the latter) winneth the Ancient Mariner.
And the twain were casting dice:
'The game is done. I've won! I've won!'
Quoth she, and whistles thrice.

The Sun's rim dips; the stars rush out; No twilight within the courts of the Sun.
At one stride comes the dark;
With far-heard whisper, o'er the sea,
Off shot the spectre-bark.

We listened and looked sideways up! At the rising of the Moon,
Fear at my heart, as at a cup;
My life-blood seemed to sip!
The stars were dim, and thick the night,
The steersman's face by his lamp gleamed
    white;
From the sails the dew did drip—
Till clombe above the eastern bar,
The hornèd Moon, with one bright star
Within the nether tip.

one after an-
other,

One after one, by the star-dogged Moon,
Too quick for groan or sigh,
Each turned his face with a ghastly pang,
And cursed me with his eye.

his ship-mates
drop down dead.

Four times fifty living men
(And I heard nor sigh nor groan),
With heavy thump, a lifeless lump,
They dropped down one by one.

But Life-in-
Death begins her
work on the An-
cient Mariner.

The souls did from their bodies fly,—
They fled to bliss or woe!
And every soul, it passed me by,
Like the whizz of my cross-bow!"

PART IV.

The Wedding-
Guest feareth
that a spirit is
talking to him ;

"I FEAR thee, Ancient Mariner!
I fear thy skinny hand!
And thou art long, and lank, and brown,
As is the ribbed sea-sand.

I fear thee and thy glittering eye,
And thy skinny hand so brown."—

but the Ancient
Mariner assureth
him of his bodily
life, and pro-
ceedeth to relate
his horrible pen-
ance.

"Fear not, fear not, thou Wedding-Guest!
This body dropt not down.

Alone, alone, all, all alone,
Alone on a wide, wide sea!
And never a saint took pity on
My soul in agony.

He despiseth the
creatures of the
calm ;

The many men so beautiful!
And they all dead did lie :
And a thousand thousand slimy things
Lived on ; and so did I.

I looked upon the rotting sea,
And drew my eyes away ;
I looked upon the rotting deck,
And there the dead men lay.

and envieth that
they should live,
and so many lie
dead.

I looked to heaven, and tried to pray
But, or ever a prayer had gusht,
A wicked whisper came, and made
My heart as dry as dust.

I closed my lids, and kept them close,
And the balls like pulses beat ;
For the sky and the sea, and the sea and
    the sky,
Lay like a load on my weary eye,
And the dead were at my feet.

The cold sweat melted from their limbs,
Nor rot nor reek did they :
The look with which they looked on me
Had never passed away.

But the curse
liveth for him in
the eye of the
dead men.

An orphan's curse would drag to hell
A spirit from on high ;
But oh ! more horrible than that
Is a curse in a dead man's eye !
Seven days, seven nights, I saw that
    curse,
And yet I could not die.

The moving Moon went up the sky,
And nowhere did abide :
Softly she was going up,
And a star or two beside—

In his loneliness
and fixedness he
yearneth to-
wards the jour-
neying Moon,
and the stars
that still sojourn,
yet still move on-
ward ; and every-
where the blue
sky belongs to them, and is their appointed rest, and their native country, and their own
natural homes. which they enter unannounced, as lords that are certainly expected, and
yet there is a silent joy at their arrival.

Her beams bemocked the sultry main,
Like April hoar-frost spread ;
But where the ship's huge shadow lay
The charmèd water burnt alway,
A still and awful red.

Beyond the shadow of the ship
I watched the water-snakes ;
They moved in tracks of shining white ;
And when they reared, the elfish light
Fell off in hoary flakes.

Within the shadow of the ship
I watched their rich attire—
Blue, glossy green, and velvet black,
They coiled and swam ; and every track
Was a flash of golden fire.

O happy living things ! no tongue
Their beauty might declare ;
A spring of love gushed from my heart,
And I blessed them unaware—
Sure my kind saint took pity on me,
And I blessed them unaware.

The selfsame moment I could pray ;
And from my neck so free
The Albatross fell off, and sank
Like lead into the sea.

PART V.

" O sleep ! it is a gentle thing,
Beloved from pole to pole !
To Mary Queen the praise be given !
She sent the gentle sleep from heaven
That slid into my soul.

The silly buckets on the deck,
That had so long remained,
I dreamt that they were filled with dew ;
And when I awoke, it rained.

By grace of the holy Mother, the Ancient Mariner is refreshed with rain.

My lips were wet, my throat was cold,
My garments all were dank ;
Sure I had drunken in my dreams,
And still my body drank.

I moved, and could not feel my limbs ;
I was so light—almost
I thought that I had died in sleep,
And was a blessèd ghost.

And soon I heard a roaring wind—
It did not come anear ;
But with its sound it shook the sails,
That were so thin and sere.

He heareth sounds and seeth strange sights and commotions in the sky and the element.

The upper air burst into life ;
And a hundred fire-flags sheen,
To and fro they were hurried about ;
And to and fro, and in and out,
The wan stars danced between.

And the coming wind did roar more loud,
And the sails did sigh like sedge ;
And the rain poured down from one
    black cloud—
The Moon was at its edge.

The thick black cloud was cleft, and still
The Moon was at its side ;
Like waters shot from some high crag,
The lightning fell with never a jag—
A river steep and wide.

The bodies of the ship's crew are inspired, and the ship moves on ; The loud wind never reached the ship,
Yet now the ship moved on !
Beneath the lightning and the Moon
The dead men gave a groan.

They groaned, they stirred, they all up-
rose—
Nor spake, nor moved their eyes ;
It had been strange, even in a dream,
To have seen those dead men rise.

The helmsman steered, the ship moved
on ;
Yet never a breeze up blew ;
The mariners all 'gan work the ropes,
Where they were wont to do ;
They raised their limbs like lifeless
tools—
We were a ghastly crew.

The Body of my brother's son
Stood by me, knee to knee :
The Body and I pulled at one rope,
But he said naught to me."

but not by the souls of the men, nor by dæmons of earth or middle air, but by a blessed troop of angelic spirits, sent down by the invocation of the guardian saint. " I fear thee, Ancient Mariner ! "
" Be calm, thou Wedding-Guest !
'T was not those souls that fled in pain,
Which to their corses came again,
But a troop of spirits blest :

For when it dawned—they dropped their
arms,
And clustered round the mast ;
Sweet sounds rose slowly through their
mouths,
And from their bodies passed.

Around, around, flew each sweet sound,
Then darted to the Sun;
Slowly the sounds came back again,
Now mixed, now one by one.

Sometimes a-dropping from the sky,
I heard the skylark sing;
Sometimes all little birds that are,
How they seemed to fill the sea and air
With their sweet jargoning!

And now 't was like all instruments,
Now like a lonely flute;
And now it is an angel's song
That makes the heavens be mute.

It ceased; yet still the sails made on
A pleasant noise till noon,
A noise like of a hidden brook
In the leafy month of June,
That to the sleeping woods all night
Singeth a quiet tune.

Till noon we quietly sailed on,
Yet never a breeze did breathe:
Slowly and smoothly went the ship,
Moved onward from beneath.

Under the keel nine fathom deep,
From the land of mist and snow,
The Spirit slid: and it was he
That made the ship to go.
The sails at noon left off their tune,
And the ship stood still also.

The lonesome spirit from the south pole carries on the ship as far as the line, in obedience to the angelic troop, but still requireth vengeance.

The Sun, right up above the mast,
Had fixed her to the ocean :
But in a minute she 'gan stir,
With a short uneasy motion—
Backwards and forwards half her length
With a short uneasy motion.

Then like a pawing horse let go,
She made a sudden bound :
It flung the blood into my head
And I fell down in a swound.

The Polar
Spirit's fellow-
dæmons, the in-
visible inhabi-
tants of the ele-
ment, take part
in his wrong ;
and two of them
relate, one to the
other, that pen-
ance long and
heavy for the
Ancient Mariner
hath been accord-
ed to the Polar
Spirit, who re-
turneth south-
ward.

How long in that same fit I lay,
I have not to declare ;
But ere my living life returned,
I heard, and in my soul discerned
Two voices in the air.

'Is it he ?' quoth one, 'Is this the man?
By Him who died on cross,
With his cruel bow he laid full low
The harmless Albatross !

The Spirit who bideth by himself
In the land of mist and snow,
He loved the bird that loved the man
Who shot him with his bow.'

The other was a softer voice,
As soft as honey-dew :
Quoth he, 'The man hath penance done,
And penance more will do.'

PART VI.

FIRST VOICE.

" 'But tell me, tell me ! speak again,
Thy soft response renewing—

What makes that ship drive on so fast?
What is the ocean doing?'

SECOND VOICE.

' Still as a slave before his lord,
The ocean hath no blast ;
His great bright eye most silently
Up to the Moon is cast—

If he may know which way to go ;
For she guides him smooth or grim.
See, brother, see ! how graciously
She looketh down on him.'

FIRST VOICE.

' But why drives on that ship so fast,
Without or wave or wind?'

> The Mariner hath been cast into a trance ; for the angelic power causeth the vessel to drive northward faster than human life could endure.

SECOND VOICE.

' The air is cut away before,
And closes from behind.

Fly, brother, fly ! more high, more high !
Or we shall be belated ;
For slow and slow that ship will go,
When the Mariner's trance is abated.'

I woke, and we were sailing on
As in a gentle weather ;
'T was night, calm night—the moon was
      high ;
The dead men stood together.

> The supernatural motion is retarded ; the Mariner awakes, and his penance begins anew.

All stood together on the deck,
For a charnel-dungeon fitter ;

All fixed on me their stony eyes,
That in the Moon did glitter.

The pang, the curse, with which they
      died,
Had never passed away;
I could not draw my eyes from theirs,
Nor turn them up to pray.

The curse is fin-
ally expiated. And now this spell was snapt; once
      more
I viewed the ocean green,
And looked far forth, yet little saw
Of what had else been seen—

Like one that on a lonesome road
Doth walk in fear and dread,
And, having once turned round, walks on,
And turns no more his head;
Because he knows a frightful fiend
Doth close behind him tread.

But soon there breathed a wind on me,
Nor sound nor motion made;
Its path was not upon the sea,
In ripple or in shade.

It raised my hair, it fanned my cheek,
Like a meadow-gale of Spring—
It mingled strangely with my fears,
Yet it felt like a welcoming.

Swiftly, swiftly flew the ship,
Yet she sailed softly too;
Sweetly, sweetly blew the breeze—
On me alone it blew.

O dream of joy! is this indeed
The light-house top I see?
Is this the hill? is this the kirk?
Is this mine own countree?

And the Ancient Mariner beholdeth his native country.

We drifted o'er the harbor-bar,
And I with sobs did pray—
O let me be awake, my God!
Or let me sleep alway.

The harbor-bay was clear as glass,
So smoothly it was strewn!
And on the bay the moonlight lay,
And the shadow of the moon.

The rock shone bright, the kirk no less
That stands above the rock;
The moonlight steeped in silentness
The steady weathercock.

And the bay was white with silent light,
Till rising from the same,
Full many shapes, that shadows were,
In crimson colors came.

The angelic spirits leave the dead bodies,

A little distance from the prow
Those crimson shadows were:
I turned my eyes upon the deck—
O Christ! what saw I there!

and appear in their own forms of light.

Each corse lay flat, lifeless and flat,
And, by the holy rood!
A man all light, a seraph man,
On every corse there stood.

This seraph-band, each waved his hand :
It was a heavenly sight !
They stood as signals to the land,
Each one a lovely light ;

This seraph-band, each waved his hand,
No voice did they impart —
No voice ; but oh ! the silence sank
Like music on my heart.

But soon I heard the dash of oars,
I heard the pilot's cheer ;
My head was turned perforce away,
And I saw a boat appear.

The pilot and the pilot's boy,
I heard them coming fast :
Dear Lord in Heaven ! it was a joy
The dead men could not blast.

I saw a third—I heard his voice :
It is the hermit good !
He singeth loud his godly hymns
That he makes in the wood.
He 'll shrieve my soul, he 'll wash away
The Albatross's blood.

PART VII.

The hermit of the wood " THIS hermit good lives in that wood
Which slopes down to the sea.
How loudly his sweet voice he rears !
He loves to talk with marineres
That come from a far countree.

He kneels at morn, and noon, and eve—
He hath a cushion plump :

It is the moss that wholly hides
The rotted old oak-stump.

The skiff-boat neared : I heard them talk,
‘ Why, this is strange, I trow !
Where are those lights so many and fair,
That signal made but now ? ’

‘Strange, by my faith !’ the hermit said— _{approach-}
‘ And they answered not our cheer !
The planks looked warped ! and see those
 sails
How thin they are and sere !
I never saw aught like to them,
Unless perchance it were

approach-
eth the ship with
wonder.

Brown skeletons of leaves that lag
My forest-brook along ;
When the ivy-tod is heavy with snow,
And the owlet whoops to the wolf below,
That eats the she-wolf’s young.’

‘ Dear Lord ! it hath a fiendish look
(The pilot made reply)—
I am a-feared.’—‘ Push on, push on ! ’
Said the hermit cheerily.

The boat came closer to the ship,
But I nor spake nor stirred ;
The boat came close beneath the ship,
And straight a sound was heard.

Under the water it rumbled on, The ship suddenly
Still louder and more dread :   sinketh.
It reached the ship, it split the bay ;
The ship went down like lead.

POEMS OF FANCY.

The Ancient Mariner is saved in the pilot's boat.

Stunned by that loud and dreadful
    sound,
Which sky and ocean smote,
Like one that hath been seven days
    drowned
My body lay afloat ;
But swift as dreams, myself I found
Within the pilot's boat.

Upon the whirl where sank the ship
The boat span round and round ;
And all was still, save that the hill
Was telling of the sound.

I moved my lips—the pilot shrieked
And fell down in a fit ;
The holy hermit raised his eyes,
And prayed where he did sit.

I took the oars ; the pilot's boy,
Who now doth crazy go,
Laughed loud and long ; and all the while
His eyes went to and fro :
'Ha ! ha !' quoth he, 'full plain I see,
The Devil knows how to row.'

And now, all in my own countree,
I stood on the firm land !
The hermit stepped forth from the boat,
And scarcely he could stand.

The Ancient Mariner earnestly entreateth the hermit to shrieve him : and the penance of life falls on him.

'O shrieve me, shrieve me, holy man !'—
The hermit crossed his brow :
'Say quick,' quoth he, 'I bid thee say—
What manner of man art thou ?'

Forthwith this frame of mine was
    wrenched
With a woful agony,
Which forced me to begin my tale—
And then it left me free.

Since then, at an uncertain hour,
That agony returns ;
And till my ghastly tale is told
This heart within me burns.

And ever and anon throughout his future life an agony constraineth him to travel from land to land ;

I pass, like night, from land to land ;
I have strange power of speech ;
That moment that his face I see
I know the man that must hear me—
To him my tale I teach.

What loud uproar bursts from that door !
The wedding-guests are there ;
But in the garden-bower the Bride
And bride-maids singing are ;
And hark the little vesper bell,
Which biddeth me to prayer !

O Wedding-Guest ! this soul hath been
Alone on a wide, wide sea—
So lonely 't was, that God himself
Scarce seemèd there to be.

O sweeter than the marriage-feast,
'T is sweeter far to me,
To walk together to the kirk
With a goodly company !—

To walk together to the kirk,
And all together pray,

While each to his great Father bends—
Old men, and babes, and loving friends,
And youths and maidens gay !

Farewell ! farewell ! but this I tell
To thee, thou Wedding-Guest !
He prayeth well who loveth well
Both man and bird and beast.

He prayeth best who loveth best
All things both great and small ;
For the dear God who loveth us,
He made and loveth all."

The Mariner, whose eye is bright,
Whose beard with age is hoar,
Is gone.　And now the Wedding-Guest
Turned from the Bridegroom's door.

He went like one that hath been stunned,
And is of sense forlorn ;
A sadder and a wiser man
He rose the morrow morn.

　　　　　　SAMUEL TAYLOR COLERIDGE.

ULALUME.

THE skies they were ashen and sober ;
　　The leaves they were crispèd and sere,
　　The leaves they were withering and sere ;
It was night in the lonesome October
　　Of my most immemorial year ;
It was hard by the dim lake of Auber,
　　In the misty mid region of Weir :

It was down by the dank tarn of Auber,
   In the ghoul-haunted woodland of Weir.

Here once, through an alley Titanic
   Of cypress, I roamed with my Soul—
   Of cypress, with Psyche, my Soul.
These were days when my heart was volcanic
   As the scoriac rivers that roll,
   As the lavas that restlessly roll
Their sulphurous currents down Yaanek
   In the ultimate climes of the pole,
That groan as they roll down Mount Yaanek
   In the realms of the boreal pole.

Our talk had been serious and sober,
   But our thoughts they were palsied and sere,
   Our memories were treacherous and sere,
For we knew not the month was October,
   And we marked not the night of the year,
   (Ah, night of all nights in the year!)
We noted not the dim lake of Auber
   (Though once we had journeyed down here),
Remembered not the dank tarn of Auber
   Nor the ghoul-haunted woodland of Weir.

And now, as the night was senescent
   And star-dials pointed to morn,
   As the star-dials hinted of morn,
At the end of our path a liquescent
   And nebulous lustre was born,
Out of which a miraculous crescent
   Arose with a duplicate horn,
Astarte's bediamonded crescent
   Distinct with its duplicate horn.

And I said—" She is warmer than Dian :
    She rolls through an ether of sighs,
    She revels in a region of sighs :
She has seen that the tears are not dry on
    These cheeks, where the worm never dies,
And has come past the stars of the Lion
    To point us the path to the skies,
    To the Lethean peace of the skies :
Come up, in despite of the Lion,
    To shine on us with her bright eyes :
Come up through the lair of the Lion,
    With love in her luminous eyes."

But Psyche, uplifting her finger,
    Said—" Sadly this star I mistrust,
    Her pallor I strangely mistrust :
Oh, hasten !—oh, let us not linger !
    Oh, fly !—let us fly !—for we must."
In terror she spoke, letting sink her
    Wings until they trailed in the dust ;
In agony sobbed, letting sink her
    Plumes till they trailed in the dust,
    Till they sorrowfully trailed in the dust.

I replied—" This is nothing but dreaming :
    Let us on by this tremulous light !
    Let us bathe in this crystalline light !
Its sibyllic splendor is beaming
    With hope and in beauty to-night :
    See, it flickers up the sky through the night !
Ah, we safely may trust to its gleaming,
    And be sure it will lead us aright :
We safely may trust to a gleaming
    That cannot but guide us aright,
    Since it flickers up to Heaven through the night."

Thus I pacified Psyche and kissed her,
   And tempted her out of her gloom,
   And conquered her scruples and gloom;
And we passed to the end of the vista,
   But were stopped by the door of a tomb,
   By the door of a legended tomb;
And I said—" What is written, sweet sister,
   On the door of this legended tomb ? "
   She replied—" Ulalume— Ulalume—
   'T is the vault of thy lost Ulalume ! "

Then my heart it grew ashen and sober
   As the leaves that were crispèd and sere,
   As the leaves that were withering and sere,
And I cried—" It was surely October
   On this very night of last year
   That I journeyed—I journeyed down here,
   That I brought a dread burden down here:
   On this night of all nights in the year,
   Ah, what demon has tempted me here?
Well I know, now, this dim lake of Auber,
   This misty mid region of Weir:
Well I know, now, this dank tarn of Auber,
   This ghoul-haunted woodland of Weir."

EDGAR ALLAN POE.

THE RAVEN.

Once upon a midnight dreary, while I pondered,
   weak and weary,
Over many a quaint and curious volume of forgotten
   lore,—
While I nodded, nearly napping, suddenly there
   came a tapping,

As of some one gently rapping, rapping at my
　　chamber door.
" 'T is some visitor," I muttered, "tapping at my
　　chamber door ;
　　　Only this, and nothing more."

Ah, distinctly I remember, it was in the bleak
　　December,
And each separate dying ember wrought its ghost
　　upon the floor.
Eagerly I wished the morrow ; vainly I had sought
　　to borrow
From my books surcease of sorrow,—sorrow for the
　　lost Lenore,—
For the rare and radiant maiden whom the angels
　　named Lenore,—
　　　Nameless here forevermore.

And the silken, sad, uncertain rustling of each pur-
　　ple curtain
Thrilled me,—filled me with fantastic terrors never
　　felt before ;
So that now, to still the beating of my heart, I stood
　　repeating,
" 'T is some visitor entreating entrance at my cham-
　　ber door,—
Some late visitor entreating entrance at my cham-
　　ber door ;
　　　That it is, and nothing more."

Presently my soul grew stronger ; hesitating then
　　no longer,
" Sir," said I, " or madam, truly your forgiveness I
　　implore ;

But the fact is, I was napping, and so gently you
    came rapping,
And so faintly you came tapping, tapping at my
    chamber door,
That I scarce was sure I heard you "—Here I
    opened wide the door;
    Darkness there, and nothing more.

Deep into that darkness peering, long I stood there,
    wondering, fearing,
Doubting, dreaming dreams no mortal ever dared
    to dream before;
But the silence was unbroken, and the darkness
    gave no token,
And the only word there spoken was the whispered
    word " Lenore ! "
This I whispered, and an echo murmured back the
    word " Lenore ! "
    Merely this, and nothing more.

Back into the chamber turning, all my soul within
    me burning,
Soon again I heard a tapping, something louder than
    before :
" Surely," said I, " surely that is something at my
    window-lattice;
Let me see then what thereat is, and this mystery
    explore,—
Let my heart be still a moment, and this mystery
    explore ;—
    'T is the wind, and nothing more."

Open then I flung the shutter, when, with many a
    flirt and flutter,

In there stepped a stately raven of the saintly days
  of yore.
Not the least obeisance made he; not an instant
  stopped or stayed he;
But, with mien of lord or lady, perched above my
  chamber door,—
Perched upon a bust of Pallas, just above my chamber door,—
  Perched, and sat, and nothing more.

Then this ebony bird beguiling my sad fancy into
  smiling,
By the grave and stern decorum of the countenance
  it wore,
" Though thy crest be shorn and shaven, thou," I
  said, " art sure no craven;
Ghastly, grim, and ancient raven, wandering from
  the nightly shore,
Tell me what thy lordly name is on the night's
  Plutonian shore? "
  Quoth the raven, " Nevermore! "

Much I marvelled this ungainly fowl to hear dis-
  course so plainly,
Though its answer little meaning, little relevancy
  bore;
For we cannot help agreeing that no living human
  being
Ever yet was blessed with seeing bird above his
  chamber door,
Bird or beast upon the sculptured bust above his
  chamber door,
  With such name as " Nevermore! "

But the raven, sitting lonely on the placid bust,
  spoke only

That one word, as if his soul in that one word he
    did outpour.
Nothing further then he uttered,—not a feather
    then he fluttered,—
Till I scarcely more than muttered, "Other
    friends have flown before,—
On the morrow he will leave me, as my hopes
    have flown before."
      Then the bird said, "Nevermore!"

Startled at the stillness, broken by reply so aptly
    spoken,
"Doubtless," said I, "what it utters is its only
    stock and store,
Caught from some unhappy master, whom un-
    merciful disaster
Followed fast and followed faster, till his song one
    burden bore,
Till the dirges of his hope that melancholy burden
    bore,—
      Of 'Nevermore,—nevermore!'"

But the raven still beguiling all my sad soul into
    smiling,
Straight I wheeled a cushioned seat in front of
    bird and bust and door,
Then, upon the velvet sinking, I betook myself to
    linking
Fancy unto fancy, thinking what this ominous
    bird of yore—
What this grim, ungainly, ghastly, gaunt, and
    ominous bird of yore—
      Meant in croaking "Nevermore!"

This I sat engaged in guessing, but no syllable
   expressing
To the fowl whose fiery eyes now burned into my
   bosom's core ;
This and more I sat divining, with my head at ease
   reclining
On the cushion's velvet lining that the lamplight
   gloated o'er,
But whose velvet violet lining, with the lamplight
   gloating o'er,
   She shall press—ah ! nevermore !

Then methought the air grew denser, perfumed
   from an unseen censer,
Swung by seraphim, whose footfalls tinkled on the
   tufted floor.
" Wretch," I cried, " thy God hath lent thee,—by
   these angels he hath sent thee
Respite,—respite and nepenthe from the memories
   of Lenore !
Quaff, O, quaff this kind nepenthe, and forget this
   lost Lenore ! "
   Quoth the raven, " Nevermore ! "

" Prophet ! " said I, " thing of evil !—prophet still,
   if bird or devil !
Whether tempter sent, or whether tempest tossed
   thee here ashore,
Desolate yet all undaunted, on this desert land
   enchanted,—
On this home by horror haunted,—tell me truly, I
   implore,—
Is there—is there balm in Gilead ?—tell me,—tell
   me, I implore ! "
   Quoth the raven, " Nevermore ! "

"Prophet!" said I, "thing of evil!—prophet still if
    bird or devil!
By that heaven that bends above us,—by that
    God we both adore,
Tell this soul with sorrow laden, if, within the
    distant Aidenn,
It shall clasp a sainted maiden, whom the angels
    name Lenore,
Clasp a fair and radiant maiden, whom the angels
    name Lenore!"
    Quoth the raven, "Nevermore!"

"Be that word our sign of parting, bird or fiend!"
    I shrieked, upstarting,—
"Get thee back into the tempest and the night's
    Plutonian shore!
Leave no black plume as a token of that lie thy
    soul hath spoken!
Leave my loneliness unbroken!—quit the bust
    above my door!
Take thy beak from out my heart, and take thy
    form from off my door!"
    Quoth the raven, "Nevermore!"

And the raven, never flitting, still is sitting, still
    is sitting
On the pallid bust of Pallas, just above my chamber
    door;
And his eyes have all the seeming of a demon that
    is dreaming,
And the lamplight o'er him streaming throws his
    shadow on the floor;
And my soul from out that shadow that lies
    floating on the floor
    Shall be lifted—*nevermore!*

                EDGAR ALLAN POE.

KUBLA KHAN.*

In Xanadu did Kubla Khan
A stately pleasure-dome decree
Where Alph, the sacred river, ran,
Through caverns measureless to man,
Down to a sunless sea.

* "In the summer of the year 1797 the author, then in ill-health, had retired to a lonely farmhouse between Porlock and Linton, on the Exmoor confines of Somerset and Devonshire. In consequence of a slight indisposition, an anodyne had been prescribed, from the effect of which he fell asleep in his chair at the moment he was reading the following sentence, or words of the same substance, in Purchas's "Pilgrimage": 'Here the Khan Kubla commanded a palace to be built, and a stately garden thereunto: and thus ten miles of fertile ground were enclosed with a wall.' The author continued for about three hours in a profound sleep, at least of the external senses, during which time he has the most vivid confidence that he could not have composed less than from two to three hundred lines; if that indeed can be called composition in which all the images rose up before him as things, with a parallel production of the correspondent expressions, without any sensation or consciousness of effort. On awaking he appeared to himself to have a distinct recollection of the whole, and, taking his pen, ink, and paper, instantly and eagerly wrote down the lines that are here preserved. At this moment he was unfortunately called out by a person on business from Porlock, and detained by him above an hour, and on his return to his room found, to his no small surprise and mortification, that though he still retained some vague and dim recollection of the general purport of the vision, yet, with the exception of some eight or ten scattered lines and images, all the rest had passed away, like the images on the surface of a stream into which a stone had been cast, but, alas! without the after restoration of the latter."—*The Author*, 1816.

So twice five miles of fertile ground
With walls and towers were girdled round ;
And there were gardens, bright with sinuous rills,
Where blossomed many an incense-bearing tree ;
And here were forests ancient as the hills,
Infolding sunny spots of greenery.

But O that deep romantic chasm, which slanted
Down the green hill athwart a cedarn cover !
A savage place ! as holy and enchanted
As e'er beneath a waning moon was haunted
By woman wailing for her demon-lover !
And from this chasm, with ceaseless turmoil seething,
As if this earth in fast thick pants were breathing,
A mighty fountain momently was forced,
Amid whose swift, half-intermitted burst
Huge fragments vaulted like rebounding hail,
Or chaffy grain beneath the thresher's flail ;
And mid these dancing rocks at once and ever
It flung up momently the sacred river.
Five miles, meandering with a mazy motion
Through wood and dale, the sacred river ran,—
Then reached the caverns measureless to man,
And sank in tumult to a lifeless ocean,
And mid this tumult Kubla heard from far
Ancestral voices prophesying war.

   The shadow of the dome of pleasure
   Floated midway on the waves
   Where was heard the mingled measure
   From the fountain and the caves.
It was a miracle of rare device,—
A sunny pleasure-dome with caves of ice !
   A damsel with a dulcimer
   In a vision once I saw ;

It was an Abyssinian maid,
And on her dulcimer she played,
Singing of Mount Abora.
Could I revive within me
Her symphony and song,
To such a deep delight 't would win me
That, with music loud and long,
I would build that dome in air,—
That sunny dome! those caves of ice!
And all who heard should see them there,
And all should cry, Beware! beware
His flashing eyes, his floating hair!
Weave a circle round him thrice,
And close your eyes with holy dread,
For he on honey-dew hath fed,
And drunk the milk of Paradise.

SAMUEL TAYLOR COLERIDGE.

THE HAUNTED PALACE.

In the greenest of our valleys
    By good angels tenanted,
Once a fair and stately palace—
    Radiant palace—reared its head.
In the monarch Thought's dominion,
    It stood there;
Never seraph spread a pinion
    Over fabric half so fair.

Banners yellow, glorious, golden,
    On its roof did float and flow
(This—all this—was in the olden
    Time long ago),

And every gentle air that dallied,
  In that sweet day,
Along the ramparts plumed and pallid,
  A wingèd odor went away.

Wanderers in that happy valley
  Through two luminous windows saw
Spirits moving musically,
  To a lute's well-tunèd law,
Round about a throne where, sitting,
  Porphyrogene,
In state his glory well befitting,
  The ruler of the realm was seen.

And all with pearl and ruby glowing
  Was the fair palace door,
Through which came flowing, flowing, flowing,
  And sparkling evermore,
A troop of Echoes, whose sweet duty
  Was but to sing,
In voices of surpassing beauty,
  The wit and wisdom of their king.

But evil things, in robes of sorrow,
  Assailed the monarch's high estate;
(Ah, let us mourn, for never morrow
  Shall dawn upon him desolate!)
And round about his home the glory
  That blushed and bloomed,
Is but a dim-remembered story
  Of the old time entombed.

And travellers now within that valley
  Through the red-litten windows see

Vast forms that move fantastically
    To a discordant melody ;
While, like a ghastly rapid river,
    Through the pale door
A hideous throng rush out forever,
    And laugh—but smile no more.

EDGAR ALLAN POE.

THE SUNKEN CITY.

Hark ! the faint bells of the sunken city
    Peal once more their wonted evening chime !
From the deep abysses floats a ditty,
    Wild and wondrous, of the olden time.

Temples, towers, and domes of many stories
    There lie buried in an ocean grave,—
Undescried, save when their golden glories
    Gleam, at sunset, through the lighted wave.

And the mariner who had seen them glisten,
    In whose ears those magic bells do sound,
Night by night bides there to watch and listen,
    Though death lurks behind each dark rock round.

So the bells of memory's wonder-city
    Peal for me their old melodious chime !
So my heart pours forth a changeful ditty,
    Sad and pleasant, from the bygone time.

Domes and towers and castles, fancy-builded,
    There lie lost to daylight's garish beams,—
There lie hidden till unveiled and gilded,
    Glory-gilded, by my nightly dreams !

And then hear I music sweet upknelling
 From many a well-known phantom band,
And, through tears, can see my natural dwelling
 Far off in the spirit's luminous land !

From the German of WILHELM MUELLER.
Translation of JAMES CLARENCE MANGAN.

THE WALKER OF THE SNOW.

SPEED on, speed on, good Master !
 The camp lies far away ;
We must cross the haunted valley
 Before the close of day.

How the snow-blight came upon me
 I will tell you as I go,—
The blight of the Shadow-hunter
 Who walks the midnight snow.

To the cold December heaven
 Came the pale moon and the stars,
As the yellow sun was sinking
 Behind the purple bars.

The snow was deeply drifted
 Upon the ridges drear,
That lay for miles around me
 And the camps for which we steer.

'T was silent on the hill-side,
 And by the solemn wood,
No sound of life or motion
 To break the solitude,

Save the wailing of the moose-bird
  With a plaintive note and low,
And the skating of the red leaf
  Upon the frozen snow.

And said I, " Though dark is falling,
  And far the camp must be,
Yet my heart it would be lightsome
  If I had but company."

And then I sang and shouted,
  Keeping measure, as I sped,
To the harp-twang of the snow-shoe
  As it sprang beneath my tread.

Nor far into the valley
  Had I dipped upon my way,
When a dusky figure joined me,
  In a capuchon of gray,

Bending upon the snow-shoes,
  With a long and limber stride;
And I hailed the dusky stranger
  As we travelled side by side.

But no token of communion
  Gave he by word or look,
And the fear-chill fell upon me,
  At the crossing of the brook.

For I saw by the sickly moonlight
  As I followed, bending low,
That the walking of the stranger
  Left no footmarks on the snow.

Then the fear-chill gathered o'er me,
   Like a shroud around me cast,
As I sank upon the snow-drift
   Where the Shadow-hunter passed.

And the other trappers found me,
   Before the break of day,
With my dark hair blanched and whitened
   As the snow in which I lay.

But they spoke not as they raised me;
   For they knew that in the night
I had seen the Shadow-hunter
   And had withered in his blight.

Sancta Maria speed us!
   The sun is falling low,
Before us lies the valley,
   Of the Walker of the Snow!
              CHARLES DAWSON SHANLY.

THE PIED PIPER OF HAMELIN.

Hamelin Town 's in Brunswick,
   By famous Hanover City;
     The river Weser, deep and wide,
     Washes its wall on the southern side;
   A pleasanter spot you never spied;
   But when begins my ditty,
     Almost five hundred years ago,
     To see the townsfolk suffer so
   From vermin was a pity.

Rats!
They fought the dogs, and killed the cats,
   And bit the babies in the cradles,
And ate the cheeses out of the vats,
   And licked the soup from the cook's own ladles,
Split open the kegs of salted sprats,
Made nests inside men's Sunday hats,
And even spoiled the women's chats,
    By drowning their speaking
    With shrieking and squeaking
In fifty different sharps and flats.

At last the people in a body
   To the Town Hall came flocking:
" 'T is clear," cried they, " our Mayor 's a noddy;
   And as for our Corporation,—shocking
To think we buy gowns lined with ermine
For dolts that can't or won't determine
What 's best to rid us of our vermin!
You hope, because you 're old and obese,
To find in the furry civic robe ease?
Rouse up, Sirs! Give your brains a racking
To find the remedy we 're lacking,
Or, sure as fate, we 'll send you packing!"
At this the Mayor and Corporation
Quaked with a mighty consternation.

An hour they sate in counsel,—
   At length the Mayor broke silence:
" For a guilder I 'd my ermine gown sell;
   I wish I were a mile hence!
It 's easy to bid one rack one's brain,—
I 'm sure my poor head aches again,
I 've scratched it so, and all in vain.

O for a trap, a trap, a trap!"
Just as he said this, what should hap
At the chamber door but a gentle tap?
"Bless us," cried the Mayor, "what's that?"
(With the Corporation as he sat,
Looking little though wondrous fat;
Nor brighter was his eye, nor moister
Then a too-long-opened oyster,
Save when at noon his paunch grew mutinous
For a plate of turtle, green and glutinous,)
"Only a scraping of shoes on the mat?
Anything like the sound of a rat
Makes my heart go pit-a-pat!"
"Come in!"—the Mayor cried, looking bigger;
And in did come the strangest figure:
His queer long coat from heel to head
Was half of yellow and half of red;
And he himself was tall and thin;
With sharp blue eyes, each like a pin;
And light loose hair, yet swarthy skin;
No tuft on cheek nor beard on chin,
But lips where smiles went out and in—
There was no guessing his kith and kin!
And nobody could enough admire
The tall man and his quaint attire.
Quoth one: "It's as my great-grandsire,
Starting up at the trump of doom's tone,
Had walked this way from his painted tombstone!"
He advanced to the council-table:
And, "Please your honors," said he, "I'm able,
By means of a secret charm, to draw
All creatures living beneath the sun,
That creep or swim or fly or run,

After me so as you never saw !
And I chiefly use my charm
On creatures that do people harm—
The mole, and toad, and newt, and viper—
And people call me the Pied Piper."
(And here they noticed round his neck
A scarf of red and yellow stripe,
To match with his coat of the self-same check ;
And at the scarf's end hung a pipe ;
And his fingers, they noticed, were ever straying
As if impatient to be playing
Upon this pipe, as low it dangled
Over his vesture so old-fangled.)
" Yet," said he, " poor piper as I am,
In Tartary I freed the Cham,
Last June, from his huge swarm of gnats ;
I eased in Asia the Nizam
Of a monstrous brood of vampire-bats ;
And as for what your brain bewilders,—
If I can rid your town of rats,
Will you give me a thousand guilders ? "
" One ? fifty thousand ! " was the exclamation
Of the astonished Mayor and Corporation.

Into the street the piper stept,
    Smiling first a little smile,
As if he knew what magic slept
    In his quiet pipe the while ;
Then, like a musical adept,
To blow the pipe his lips he wrinkled,
And green and blue his sharp eyes twinkled,
Like a candle flame were salt is sprinkled ;
And ere three shrill notes the pipe uttered,
You heard as if an army muttered ;

And the muttering grew to a grumbling;
And the grumbling grew to a mighty rumbling;
And out of the houses the rats came tumbling.
Great rats, small rats, lean rats, brawny rats,
Brown rats, black rats, gray rats, tawny rats,
Grave old plodders, gay young friskers,
 Fathers, mothers, uncles, cousins,
Cocking tails and pricking whiskers;
 Families by tens and dozens,
Brothers, sisters, husbands, wives—
Followed the piper for their lives.
From street to street he piped advancing,
And step for step they followed dancing,
Until they came to the river Weser,
Wherein all plunged and perished
—Save one who, stout as Julius Cæsar,
Swam across and lived to carry
(As he the manuscript he cherished)
To Rat-land home his commentary,
Which was: "At the first shrill notes of the pipe,
I heard a sound as of scraping tripe,
And putting apples, wondrous ripe,
Into a cider-press's gripe,—
And a moving away of pickle-tub-boards,
And a leaving ajar of conserve-cupboards,
And a drawing the corks of train-oil-flasks,
And a breaking the hoops of butter-casks;
And it seemed as if a voice
(Sweeter far than by harp or by psaltery
Is breathed) called out, O rats, rejoice!
The world is grown to one vast drysaltery!
So munch on, crunch on, take your nuncheon,
Breakfast, supper, dinner, luncheon!
—And just as a bulky sugar-puncheon,

Already staved, like a great sun shone
Glorious scarce an inch before me,
Just as methought it said, Come, bore me!
—I found the Weser rolling o'er me."

You should have heard the Hamelin people
Ringing the bells till they rocked the steeple;
"Go," cried the Mayor, "and get long poles!
Poke out the nests and block up the holes!
Consult with carpenters and builders,
And leave in our town not even a trace
Of the rats!"—when suddenly, up the face
Of the piper perked in the market-place,
With a "First, if you please, my thousand guilders!"

A thousand guilders! the Mayor looked blue!
So did the Corporation too.
For council-dinners made rare havoc
With Claret, Moselle, Vin-de-Grave, Hock;
And half the money would replenish
Their cellar's biggest butt with Rhenish.
To pay this sum to a wandering fellow
With a gypsy coat of red and yellow!
"Beside," quoth the Mayor, with a knowing wink,
"Our business was done at the river's brink;
We saw with our eyes the vermin sink,
And what's dead can't come to life, I think.
So, friend, we're not the folks to shrink
From the duty of giving you something for drink,
And a matter of money to put in your poke;
But as for the guilders, what we spoke
Of them, as you very well know, was in joke
Beside, our losses have made us thrifty;
A thousand guilders! Come, take fifty!"

The piper's face fell, and he cried,
" No trifling! I can't wait! beside,
I 've promised to visit by dinner time
Bagdat, and accept the prime
Of the head cook's pottage, all he 's rich in,
For having left, in the Caliph's kitchen,
Of a nest of scorpions no survivor,—
With him I proved no bargain-driver;
With you, don't think I 'll bate a stiver!
And folks who put me in a passion
May find me pipe to another fashion."

"How?" cried the Mayor, " d' ye think I 'll brook
Being worse treated than a cook?
Insulted by a lazy ribald
With idle pipe and vesture piebald?
You threaten us, fellow? Do your worst,
Blow your pipe there till you burst!"

Once more he stept into the street;
    And to his lips again
Laid his long pipe of smooth straight cane;
    And ere he blew three notes (such sweet
Soft notes as yet musician's cunning
    Never gave the enraptured air)
There was a rustling that seemed like a bustling
Of merry crowds justling at pitching and hustling;
Small feet were pattering, wooden shoes clattering,
Little hands clapping, and little tongues chattering;
And, like fowls in a farm-yard when barley is scat-
      tering,
Out came the children running:
All the little boys and girls,

With rosy cheeks and flaxen curls,
And sparkling eyes and teeth like pearls,
Tripping and skipping, ran merrily after
The wonderful music with shouting and laughter.

The Mayor was dumb, and the Council stood
As if they were changed into blocks of wood,
Unable to move a step, or cry
To the children merrily skipping by,—
And could only follow with the eye
That joyous crowd at the piper's back.
But how the Mayor was on the rack,
And the wretched Council's bosoms beat,
As the piper turned from the High Street
To where the Weser rolled its waters
Right in the way of their sons and daughters!
However, he turned from south to west,
And to Koppelberg Hill his steps addressed,
And after him the children pressed;
Great was the joy in every breast.
" He never can cross that mighty top!
He 's forced to let the piping drop,
And we shall see our children stop!"
When, lo, as they reached the mountain's side,
A wondrous portal opened wide,
As if a cavern was suddenly hollowed;
And the piper advanced and the children followed;
And when all were in, to the very last,
The door in the mountain-side shut fast.
Did I say all? No! One was lame,
And could not dance the whole of the way;
And in after years, if you would blame
His sadness, he was used to say,—

" It 's dull in our town since my playmates left!
I can't forget that I 'm bereft
Of all the pleasant sights they see,
Which the piper also promised me;
For he led us, he said, to a joyous land,
Joining the town and just at hand,
Where waters gushed, and fruit-trees grew,
And flowers put forth a fairer hue,
And everything was strange and new;
The sparrows were brighter than peacocks here,
And their dogs outran our fallow deer,
And honey-bees had lost their stings,
And horses were born with eagles' wings;
And just as I became assured
My lame foot would be speedily cured,
The music stopped and I stood still,
And found myself outside the Hill,
Left alone against my will,
To go now limping as before,
And never hear of that country more!"

Alas, alas for Hamelin!
There came into many a burgher's pate
A text which says, that Heaven's gate
Opes to the rich at as easy rate
As the needle's eye takes a camel in!
The Mayor sent East, West, North, and South,
To offer the Piper by word of mouth,
    Wherever it was men's lot to find him,
Silver and gold to his heart's content,
If he 'd only return the way he went,
    And bring the children behind him.
But when they saw 't was a lost endeavor,
And piper and dancers were gone for ever,

They made a decree that lawyers never
    Should think their records dated duly
If, after the day of the month and year,
These words did not as well appear,
"And so long after what happened here
    On the Twenty-second of July,
Thirteen Hundred and Seventy-six:"
And the better in memory to fix
The place of the Children's last retreat
They called it the Pied Piper's Street—
Where any one playing on pipe or tabor
Was sure for the future to lose his labor.
Nor suffered they hostelry or tavern
    To shock with mirth a street so solemn;
But opposite the place of the cavern
    They wrote the story on a column,
And on the Great Church window painted
The same, to make the world acquainted
How their children were stolen away;
And there it stands to this very day.
And I must not omit to say
That in Transylvania there 's a tribe
Of alien people that ascribe
The outlandish ways and dress
On which their neighbors lay such stress
To their fathers and mothers having risen
Out of some subterranean prison
Into which they were trepanned
Long time ago, in a mighty band,
Out of Hamelin town in Brunswick land,
But how or why, they don't understand.

So, Willy, let you and me be wipers
Of scores out with all men—especially pipers;

And, whether they pipe us free from rats or from
mice,
If we 've promised them aught, let us keep our
promise.

ROBERT BROWNING.

_____

QUATRAINS.

MOONLIGHT SONG OF THE MOCKING-BIRD.

EACH golden note of music greets
The listening leaves, divinely stirred,
As if the vanished soul of Keats
Had found its new birth in a bird.

NIGHT MISTS.

SOMETIMES, when Nature falls asleep,
    Around her woods and streams
The mists of night serenely creep—
    For they are Nature's dreams.

AN AUTUMN BREEZE.

THIS gentle and half melancholy breeze
Is but a wandering Hamlet of the trees,
Who finds a tongue in every lingering leaf
To voice some subtlety of sylvan grief.

WILLIAM HAMILTON HAYNE.

_____

A YELLOW PANSY.

To the wall of the old green garden
    A butterfly quivering came;
His wings on the sombre lichens
    Played like a yellow flame.

He looked at the gray geraniums,
　And the sleepy four-o'-clocks,
He looked at the low lanes bordered
　With the glossy growing box.

He longed for the peace and the silence
　And the shadows that lengthened there,
And his wild wee heart was weary
　Of skimming the endless air.

And now in the old green garden,—
　I know not how it came,—
A single pansy is blooming,
　Bright as a yellow flame.

And whenever a gay gust passes,
　It quivers as if with pain,
For the butterfly soul within it
　Longs for the winds again.

HELEN GRAY CONE.

ECHO AND SILENCE.*

In eddying course when leaves began to fly,
And Autumn in her lap the store to strew,
As mid wild scenes I chanced the Muse to woo,
Through glens untrod, and woods that frowned on
　　high,
Two sleeping nymphs with wonder mute I spy !
And, lo, she 's gone !—In robe of dark-green hue,
'T was Echo from her sister Silence flew,
For quick the hunter's horn resounded to the sky !
In shade affrighted Silence melts away.
Not so her sister.　Hark ! for onward still,

* Declared by Wordsworth to be the best sonnet in the
English language.

With far-heard step, she takes her listening way,
Bounding from rock to rock, and hill to hill.
Ah, mark the merry maid in mockful play
With thousand mimic tones the laughing forest fill !

SIR SAMUEL EGERTON BRYDGES.

SHERWOOD.

SHERWOOD in the twilight, is Robin Hood awake ?
Gray and ghostly shadows are gliding thro' the brake ;
Shadows of the dappled deer, dreaming of the morn,
Dreaming of a shadowy man that winds a shadowy
 horn.

Robin Hood is here again ; all his merry thieves
Hear a ghostly bugle-note shivering thro' the leaves,
Calling as he used to call, faint and far away,
In Sherwood, in Sherwood, about the break of day.

Merry, merry England has kissed the lips of June :
All the wings of fairyland were here beneath the
 moon ;
Like a flight of rose leaves fluttering in a mist
Of opal and ruby and pearl and amethyst.

Merry, merry England is waking as of old,
With eyes of blither hazel and hair of brighter gold :
For Robin Hood is here again beneath the bursting
 spray
In Sherwood, in Sherwood, about the break of day.

Love is in the greenwood building him a house
Of wild rose and hawthorne and honeysuckle
 boughs :

Love is in the greenwood : Dawn is in the skies;
And Marian is waiting with a glory in her eyes.

Hark ! The dazzled laverock climbs the golden steep ;
Marian is waiting : is Robin Hood asleep ?
Round the fairy grass-rings frolic elf and fay,
In Sherwood, in Sherwood, about the break of day.

Oberon, Oberon, rake away the gold,
Rake away the red leaves, roll away the mold,
Rake away the gold leaves, roll away the red,
And wake Will Scarlett from his leafy forest bed.

Friar Tuck and Little John are riding down together
　　With quarter-staff and drinking-can and gray goose
　　　　feather ;
The dead are coming back again ; the years are
　　　　rolled away
In Sherwood, in Sherwood, about the break of day.

Softly over Sherwood the south wind blows ;
All the heart of England hidden in a rose
Hears across the greenwood the sunny whisper leap,
Sherwood in the red dawn, is Robin Hood asleep ?

Hark, the voice of England wakes him as of old,
And, shattering the silence with a cry of brighter
　　gold,
A bugle in the greenwood echoes from the steep,
Sherwood in the red dawn, is Robin Hood asleep ?

Where the deer are gliding down the shadowy glen
All across the glades of fern he calls his merry men ;
Doublets of the Lincoln green glancing thro' the May
In Sherwood, in Sherwood, about the break of day ;

Calls them and they answer : from aisles of oak and
    ash
Rings the *Follow! Follow!* and the boughs begin
    to crash ;
The ferns begin to waver and the flowers begin to
    fly ;
And through the crimson dawning the robber band
    goes by.

Robin! Robin! Robin! All his merry thieves
Answer as the bugle-note shivers thro' the leaves :
Calling as he used to call, faint and far away,
In Sherwood, in Sherwood, about the break of day.

ALFRED NOYES.

FAR-AWAY.

As chimes that flow o'er shining seas
  When Morn alights on meads of May,
Faint voices fill the western breeze
  With whisp'ring songs from Far-Away.
    Oh, dear the dells of Dunamore,
      A home is odorous Ossory ;
    But sweet as honey, running o'er,
      The Golden Shore of Far-Away !

There grows the Tree whose summer breath
  Perfumes with joy the azure air;
And he who feels it fears not Death,
  Nor longer heeds the hounds of Care.
    Oh, soft the skies of Seskinore,
      And mild is meadowy Mellaray .
    But sweet as honey, running o'er,
      The Golden Shore of Far-Away.

There sings the Voice whose wondrous tune
Falls, like diamond-showers above
That in the radiant day of June
Renew a world of Youth and Love.
Oh, fair the founts of Farranfore,
And bright is billowy Ballintrae ;
But sweet as honey, running o'er,
The Golden Shore of Far-Away.

Come, Fragrance of the Flowering Tree,
Oh, sing, sweet Bird, thy magic lay,
Till all the world be young with me,
And Love shall lead us far away.
Oh, dear the dells of Dunamore,
A home is odorous Ossory ;
But sweet as honey, running o'er
The Golden Shore of Far-Away.

DR. GEORGE SIGERSON.

POEMS OF SENTIMENT.

POEMS OF SENTIMENT.

I.

TIME.

TIME THE SUPREME.

FROM " NIGHT THOUGHTS," NIGHT I.

THE bell strikes one : we take no note of time,
But from its loss.   To give it, then, a tongue,
Is wise in man.   As if an angel spoke,
I feel the solemn sound.   If heard aright,
It is the knell of my departed hours :
Where are they ?   With the years beyond the flood.
It is the signal that demands despatch;
How much is to be done ! my hopes and fears
Start up alarmed, and o'er life's narrow verge
Look down—on what? a fathomless abyss ;
A dread eternity ; how surely mine !
And can eternity belong to me,
Poor pensioner on the bounties of an hour?

 . . . . . .

Time the supreme ! —Time is eternity ;
Pregnant with all eternity can give ;
Pregnant with all that makes archangels smile.

187

Who murders time, he crushes in the birth
A power ethereal, only not adored.
　Ah ! how unjust to Nature and himself,
Is thoughtless, thankless, inconsistent man !
Like children babbling nonsense in their sports,
We censure Nature for a span too short ;
That span too short, we tax as tedious too ;
Torture invention, all expedients tire,
To lash the lingering moments into speed,
And whirl us (happy riddance !) from ourselves.
Art, brainless Art ! our furious charioteer
(For Nature's voice, unstifled, would recall),
Drives headlong towards the precipice of death !
Death, most our dread ; death, thus more dreadful
　　made :
O, what a riddle of absurdity !
Leisure is pain ; takes off our chariot wheels :
How heavily we drag the load of life !
Blest leisure is our curse : like that of Cain,
It makes us wander ; wander earth around
To fly that tyrant, Thought.　As Atlas groaned
The world beneath, we groan beneath an hour.
We cry for mercy to the next amusement :
The next amusement mortgages our fields ;
Slight inconvenience ! prisons hardly frown,
From hateful Time if prisons set us free.
Yet when Death kindly tenders us relief,
We call him cruel ; years to moments shrink,
Ages to years.　The telescope is turned.
To man's false optics (from his folly false)
Time, in advance, behind him hides his wings,
And seems to creep, decrepit with his age ;
Behold him when past by : what then is seen
But his broad pinions, swifter than the winds ?

And all mankind, in contradiction strong,
Rueful, aghast, cry out on his career.

DR. EDWARD YOUNG.

TO–MORROW.

FROM " IRENE."

To-morrow's action! can that hoary wisdom,
Borne down with years, still doat upon to-morrow!
The fatal mistress of the young, the lazy,
The coward and the fool, condemned to lose
An useless life in waiting for to-morrow,
To gaze with longing eyes upon to-morrow,
Till interposing death destroys the prospect.
Strange that this general fraud from day to day
Should fill the world with wretches, undetected!
The soldier, laboring through a winter's march,
Still sees to-morrow drest in robes of triumph ;
Still to the lover's long-expecting arms
To-morrow brings the visionary bride.
But thou, too old to bear another cheat,
Learn that the present hour alone is man's.

SAMUEL JOHNSON.

THREE DAYS.

So much to do : so little done !
Ah ! yesternight I saw the sun
Sink beamless down the vaulted gray,—
The ghastly ghost of YESTERDAY.

So little done : so much to do !
Each morning breaks on conflicts new ;

But eager, brave, I 'll join the fray,
And fight the battle of To-day.

So much to do : so little done !
But when it 's o'er,—the victory won,—
Oh ! then, my soul, this strife and sorrow
Will end in that great, glad To-morrow.

JAMES ROBERTS GILMORE.

PROCRASTINATION.

FROM "NIGHT THOUGHTS," NIGHT I.

Be wise to-day ; 't is madness to defer ;
Next day the fatal precedent will plead ;
Thus on, till wisdom is pushed out of life.
Procrastination is the thief of time ;
Year after year it steals, till all are fled,
And to the mercies of a moment leaves
The vast concerns of an eternal scene.
If not so frequent, would not this be strange?
That 't is so frequent, this is stranger still.
Of man's miraculous mistakes this bears
The palm, " That all men are about to live,"
Forever on the brink of being born.
All pay themselves the compliment to think
They one day shall not drivel : and their pride
On this reversion takes up ready praise ;
At least, their own ; their future selves applaud :
How excellent that life they ne'er will lead !
Time lodged in their own hands is folly's veils ;
That lodged in Fate's, to wisdom they consign ;
The thing they can't but purpose, they postpone :

'T is not in folly not to scorn a fool,
And scarce in human wisdom to do more.
All promise is poor dilatory man,
And that through every stage. When young, in-
 deed,
In full content we sometimes nobly rest,
Unanxious for ourselves, and only wish,
As duteous sons, our fathers were more wise,
At thirty, man suspects himself a fool ;
Knows it at forty, and reforms his plan ;
At fifty, chides his infamous delay,
Pushes his prudent purpose to resolve ;
In all the magnanimity of thought,
Resolves, and re-resolves ; then dies the same.
 And why ? Because he thinks himself immortal.
All men think all men mortal but themselves ;
Themselves, when some alarming shock of fate
Strikes through their wounded hearts the sudden
 dread ;
But their hearts wounded, like the wounded air,
Soon close; where passed the shaft, no trace is
 found.
As from the wing no scar the sky retains,
The parted wave no furrow from the keel,
So dies in human hearts the thought of death :
Even with the tender tears which Nature sheds
O'er those we love, we drop it in their grave.
DR. EDWARD YOUNG.

AVE ATQUE VALE.

FAREWELL, my Youth ! for now we needs must part,
For here the paths divide ;

Here hand from hand must sever, heart from heart,—
Divergence deep and wide.

You 'll wear no withered roses for my sake,
Though I go mourning for you all day long,
Finding no magic more in bower or brake,
     No melody in song.

Gray Eld must travel in my company
To seal this severance more fast and sure.
A joyless fellowship, i'faith, 't will be,
Yet must we fare together, I and he,
Till I shall tread the footpath way no more.

But when a blackbird pipes among the boughs,
On some dim, iridescent day in spring,
Then I may dream you are remembering
     Our ancient vows.

Or when some joy foregone, some fate forsworn,
Looks through the dark eyes of the violet,
I may re-cross the set, forbidden bourne,
     I may forget
Our long, long parting for a little while,
Dream of the golden splendors of your smile,
Dream you remember yet.

                    ROSAMUND MARRIOTT WATSON.

THE BALLAD OF DEAD LADIES.

TELL me now in what hidden way is
     Lady Flora the lovely Roman?
Where 's Hipparchia, and where is Thais,
     Neither of them the fairer woman?

Where is Echo, beheld of no man,
Only heard on river and mere,—
　　She whose beauty was more than human?
But where are the snows of yester-year?

Where 's Heloise, the learned nun,
　For whose sake Abeillard, I ween,
Lost manhood and put priesthood on?
　　(From love he won such dule and teen!)
　And where, I pray you, is the Queen
Who willed that Buridan should steer
　Sewed in a sack's mouth down the Seine?
But where are the snows of yester-year?

White Queen Blanche, like a queen of lilies,
　With a voice like any mermaiden,—
Bertha Broadfoot, Beatrice, Alice,
　And Ermengarde the lady of Maine,—
　And that good Joan whom Englishmen
At Rouen doomed and burned her there,—
　Mother of God, where are they then?
But where are the snows of yester-year?

Nay, never ask this week, fair lord,
　Where they are gone, nor yet this year,
Except with this for an overword,—
　But where are the snows of yester-year?

From the French of FRANÇOIS VILLON.
Translation of DANTE GABRIEL ROSSETTI.

THE APPROACH OF AGE.

SONNET XII.

When I do count the clock that tells the time,
And see the brave day sunk in hideous night;
When I behold the violet past prime,
And sable curls all silvered o'er with white;
When lofty trees I see barren of leaves,
Which erst from heat did canopy the herd,
And summer's green all girded up in sheaves,
Borne on the bier with white and bristly beard;
Then of thy beauty do I question make,
That thou among the wastes of time must go,
Since sweets and beauties do themselves forsake,
And die as fast as they see others grow;
    And nothing 'gainst Time's scythe can make de-
      fence,
    Save breed, to brave him when he takes thee
      hence.

                       SHAKESPEARE.

THE OLD YEAR AND THE NEW.

Last night at twelve, amid the knee-deep snows,
A child of Time accepted his repose,—
The eighteen hundred fifty-sixth of grace,
With sudden chance, fell forward on his face.

Solemn and slow the winter sun had gone,
Sailing full early for the port of dawn;
Across broad zones of the ethereal sea,
With even rate he voyaged far and free,
While the cone-shadow of the earth swept round

The other half of heaven's embracing bound—
A weird and mystic dial-hand to mark,
From orb to orb, along the shuddering arc,
Measured to music of the sphery chime,
The noiseless process of eternal time.

I walked in doubt and dread—as if the weight
Of all the impending heaven upon me sate:
The crisp snow creaked, my breath pushed stiffly out,
And keen frost-sparkles merrily glanced about;
The clear cold stars reached down a frory ray,
Like a fine icicle accrete of spray,
That pricked my blood with many a light attack
Of Lilliput lances in my front and back,
For every several nerve alive to feel
The eager season had some shrewd appeal.

And so the fields I gained, and there I found
The fresh dry snow laid by that querulous sound,
And all grew still as death. Within my breast
Hushing the noisy heart-beat, on I pressed.

The punctual shadow to the summit drew;
Twelve strokes of lighter silence fell like dew,
Audible to the spirit, and behold,
The vision of the Dead Year was unrolled.
Full length he leaned aslant the slumbering snow,
Which clad all things in Chinese weeds of woe,
Easing his fall—that not a breath might mar
The listening awe that yearned from snow to star.

But over him a spirit fair doth smile,
As fain all grief with gladness to beguile;
A torch he bears to light the world anew—
O blithe Young Year, but keep thy promise true!

WILLIAM CLEAVER WILKINSON.

THE DEATH OF THE OLD YEAR.

FULL knee-deep lies the winter snow,
And the winter winds are wearily sighing:
Toll ye the church-bell sad and slow,
And tread softly and speak low,
For the old year lies a-dying.
  Old year, you must not die;
  You came to us so readily,
  You lived with us so steadily,
  Old year, you shall not die.

He lieth still: he doth not move:
He will not see the dawn of day.
He hath no other life above.
He gave me a friend, and a true true-love,
And the New-year will take 'em away.
  Old year, you must not go;
  So long as you have been with us,
  Such joy as you have seen with us,
  Old year, you shall not go.

He frothed his bumpers to the brim;
A jollier year we shall not see.
But, though his eyes are waxing dim,
And though his foes speak ill of him,
He was a friend to me.
  Old year, you shall not die;
  We did so laugh and cry with you,
  I 've half a mind to die with you,
  Old year, if you must die.

He was full of joke and jest,
But all his merry quips are o'er.
To see him die, across the waste
His son and heir doth ride post-haste,
But he 'll be dead before.
   Every one for his own.
   The night is starry and cold, my friend,
   And the New-year, blithe and bold, my friend,
   Comes up to take his own.

How hard he breathes! over the snow
I heard just now the crowing cock.
The shadows flicker to and fro:
The cricket chirps: the light burns low:
'T is nearly twelve o'clock.
Shake hands before you die.
Old year, we 'll dearly rue for you:
What is it we can do for you?
Speak out before you die.

His face is growing sharp and thin.
Alack! our friend is gone.
Close up his eyes: tie up his chin:
Step from the corpse, and let him in
That standeth there alone,
   And waiteth at the door.
   There 's a new foot on the floor, my friend,
   And a new face at the door, my friend,
   A new face at the door.

          ALFRED, LORD TENNYSON.

A FANCY FROM FONTENELLE.

" De mémoires de Roses on n'a point vu mourir le Jardinier."

THE Rose in the garden slipped her bud,
And she laughed in the pride of her youthful blood,
As she thought of the Gardener standing by—
" He is old—so old!   And he soon must die ! "

The full Rose waxed in the warm June air,
And she spread and spread till her heart lay bare ;
And she laughed once more as she heard his tread—
" He is older now !   He will soon be dead ! "

But the breeze of the morning blew, and found
That the leaves of the blown Rose strewed the
     ground ;
And he came at noon, that Gardener old,
And he raked them gently under the mold.

And I wove the thing to a random rhyme:
For the Rose is Beauty ; the Gardener, Time.
                              AUSTIN DOBSON.

WHAT IS THE GRASS ?

FROM " THE SONG OF MYSELF."

A CHILD said *What is the grass ?* fetching it to me
     with full hands ;
How could I answer the child ?   I do not know
     what it is any more than he.

I guess it must be the flag of my disposition, out of
     hopeful green stuff woven.

Or I guess it is the handkerchief of the Lord,
A scented gift and remembrancer designedly dropped,
Bearing the owner's name someway in the corners,
    that we may see and remark, and say *Whose?*

Or I guess the grass is itself a child, the produced
    babe of the vegetation.

Or I guess it is a uniform hieroglyphic,
And it means, Sprouting alike in broad zones and
    narrow zones,
Growing among black folks as among white,
Kanuck, Tuckahoe, Congressman, Cuff, I give them
    the same, I receive them the same.

And now it seems to me the beautiful uncut hair of
    graves.

Tenderly will I use you curling grass,
It may be you transpire from the breasts of young
    men,
It may be if I had known them I would have loved
    them,
It may be you are from old people, or from offspring
    taken soon out of their mothers' laps,
And here you are the mothers' laps.

This grass is very dark to be from the white heads
    of old mothers,
Darker than the colorless beards of old men,
Dark to come from under the faint red roofs of
    mouths.

O I perceive after all so many uttering tongues,
And I perceive they do not come from the roofs of
    mouths for nothing.

I wish I could translate the hints about the dead
    young men and women,
And the hints about old men and mothers, and the
    offspring taken soon out of their laps.

What do you think has become of the young and
    old men?
And what do you think has become of the women
    and children?

They are alive and well somewhere,
The smallest sprout shows there is really no death,
And if ever there was it led forward life, and does
    not wait at the end to arrest it,
And ceased the moment life appeared.

All goes onward and outward, nothing collapses,
And to die is different from what any one supposed,
    and luckier.
Has any one supposed it lucky to be born?
I hasten to inform him or her, it is just as lucky to
    die, and I know it.

.   .   .   .

My foothold is tenoned and mortised in granite,
I laugh at what you call dissolution,
And I know the amplitude of time.

WALT WHITMAN.

THE PETRIFIED FERN.

In a valley, centuries ago,
    Grew a little fern-leaf, green and slender,
Veining delicate and fibres tender;

Waving when the wind crept down so low.
Rushes tall, and moss, and grass grew round it,
Playful sunbeams darted in and found it,
Drops of dew stole in by night, and crowned it,
But no foot of man e'er trod that way ;
Earth was young, and keeping holiday.

Monster fishes swam the silent main,
Stately forests waved their giant branches,
Mountains hurled their snowy avalanches,
Mammoth creatures stalked across the plain ;
Nature revelled in grand mysteries,
But the little fern was not of these,
Did not number with the hills and trees ;
Only grew and waved its wild sweet way,
No one came to note it day by day.

Earth, one time, put on a frolic mood,
Heaved the rocks and changed the mighty motion
Of the deep, strong currents of the ocean ;
Moved the plain and shook the haughty wood,
Crushed the little fern in soft moist clay,—
Covered it, and hid it safe away.
O, the long, long centuries since that day !
O, the changes ! O, life's bitter cost,
Since that useless little fern was lost !

Useless ? Lost ? There came a thoughtful man
Searching Nature's secrets, far and deep ;
From a fissure in a rocky steep
He withdrew a stone, o'er which there ran
Fairy pencillings, a quaint design,
Veinings, leafage, fibres clear and fine.
And the fern's life lay in every line !

So, I think, God hides some souls away,
Sweetly to surprise us, the last day.

MARY L. BOLLES BRANCH.

THE MAKING OF MAN.

As the insect from the rock
    Takes the color of its wing ;
As the boulder from the shock
    Of the ocean's rhythmic swing
Makes itself a perfect form,
    Learns a calmer front to raise ;
As the shell, enamelled warm
    With the prism's mystic rays,
Praises wind and wave that make
    All its chambers fair and strong ;
As the mighty poets take
    Grief and pain to build their song :
Even so for every soul,
    Whatsoe'er its lot may be,—
Building, as the heavens roll,
    Something large and strong and free,—
Things that hurt and things that mar
    Shape the man for perfect praise ;
Shock and strain and ruin are
    Friendlier than the smiling days.

JOHN WHITE CHADWICK.

THE ASCENT OF MAN.

He stood upon the earth, and turned
    To gaze on sky and land and sea,

While in his ear the whisper burned,
　"Behold, these all belong to thee!"

O wondrous call to conquests new!
　O thrill of blood! O joy of Soul!
O peaks with ever-widening view!
　O race, with still-receding goal!

He heard; he followed, evermore
　Stumbling and falling, wandering far,
Yet still advancing, while before
　His footsteps shone the guiding star.

He cleft the seas; the torrent loud
　He harnessed to his need or whim;
He bade the lightning of the cloud
　Run with his words, and toil for him.

He pierced the rock; he scaled the steep;
　Destroyed; created; brought to light
The secrets of the deepest deep,
　The glories of the highest height!

The future and the past he scanned;
　With sense refined and vision keen,
Explored, beyond this lower land,
　The treasures of a realm unseen.

Until he stood with regal brow,—
　No more, as on the primal sod,
A creature yet ungrown, but now
　Lord of two worlds, and child of God!

　　　　　　　　ROSSITER W. RAYMOND.

RUBÁIYÁT.

I.

W<small>AKE</small>! for the Sun, who scattered into flight
The Stars before him from the Field of Night,
    Drives Night along with them from Heaven, and
      strikes
The Sultan's Turret with a Shaft of Light.

II.

Before the phantom of False morning died,
Methought a Voice within the Tavern cried,
    " When all the Temple is prepared within,
Why nods the drowsy Worshiper outside?"

III.

And as the Cock crew, those who stood before
The Tavern shouted—" Open then the Door!
    You know how little while we have to stay,
And once departed, may return no more."

IV.

Now the New Year reviving old Desires,
The thoughtful Soul to Solitude retires,
    Where the White Hand of Moses on the Bough
Puts out, and Jesus from the Ground suspires.

V.

Iram indeed is gone with all his Rose,
And Jamshyd's Seven-ringed Cup where no one
      knows;
    But still a Ruby kindles in the Vine,
And many a Garden by the Water blows.

VI.

And David's lips are lockt; but in divine
High-piping Pehleví, with " Wine! Wine! Wine!
Red Wine!"—the Nightingale cries to the Rose,
That sallow cheek of hers t' incarnadine.

VII.

Come, fill the Cup, and in the fire of Spring
Your Winter garment of Repentance fling :
  The Bird of Time has but a little way
To flutter—and the Bird is on the Wing.

VIII.

Whether at Naishápúr or Babylon,
Whether the Cup with sweet or bitter run,—
  The Wine of Life keeps oozing drop by drop,
The Leaves of Life keep falling one by one.

IX.

Each Morn a thousand Roses brings, you say :
Yes, but where leaves the Rose of Yesterday?
  And this first Summer month that brings the
    Rose
Shall take Jamshyd and Kaikobád away.

X.

Well, let it take them ! What have we to do
With Kaikobád the Great, or Kaikhosrú?
  Let Zál and Rustum bluster as they will,
Or Hátim call to Supper—heed not you.

XI.

With me along the strip of Herbage strown
That just divides the desert from the sown,
　Where name of Slave and Sultán is forgot—
And Peace to Mahmúd on his golden Throne !

XII.

A Book of Verses underneath the Bough,
A Jug of Wine, a Loaf of Bread—and Thou
　Beside me singing in the Wilderness—
Oh, Wilderness were Paradise enow !

XIII.

Some for the Glories of This World ; and some
Sigh for the Prophet's Paradise to come :
　Ah, take the Cash, and let the Credit go,
Nor heed the rumble of a distant Drum !

XIV.

Look to the blowing Rose about us—" Lo,
Laughing," she says, " into the world I blow,
　At once the silken tassel of my Purse
Tear, and its Treasure on the Garden throw."

XV.

And those who husbanded the Golden grain,
And those who flung it to the winds like Rain,
　Alike to no such aureate Earth are turned
As, buried once, Men want dug up again.

XVI.

The Worldly Hope men set their Hearts upon
Turns Ashes—or it prospers ; and anon,
  Like Snow upon the Desert's dusty Face,
Lighting a little hour or two—is gone.

XVII.

Think, in this battered Caravanserai
Whose Portals are alternate Night and Day,
  How Sultán after Sultán with his Pomp
Abode his destined Hour, and went his way.

XVIII.

They say the Lion and the Lizard keep
The Courts where Jamshyd gloried and drank deep :
  And Bahrám, that great Hunter—the Wild Ass
Stamps o'er his Head, but cannot break his Sleep.

XIX.

I sometimes think that never blows so red
The Rose as where some buried Cæsar bled ;
  That every Hyacinth the Garden wears
Dropt in her Lap from some once lovely Head.

XX.

And this reviving Herb whose tender Green
Fledges the River-Lip on which we lean—
  Ah, lean upon it lightly ! for who knows
From what once lovely Lip it springs unseen !

XXI.

Ah, my Belovèd, fill the Cup that clears
To-day of past Regrets and future Fears:
 To-morrow!—Why, To-morrow I may be
Myself with Yesterday's Seven thousand Years.

XXII.

For some we loved, the loveliest and the best
That from his Vintage rolling Time hath prest,
 Have drunk their Cup a Round or two before,
And one by one crept silently to rest.

XXIII.

And we, that now make merry in the Room
They left, and Summer dresses in new bloom,
 Ourselves must we beneath the Couch of Earth
Descend—ourselves to make a Couch—for whom?

XXIV.

Ah, make the most of what we yet may spend,
Before we too into the Dust descend;
 Dust into Dust, and under Dust to lie,
Sans Wine, sans Song, sans Singer, and—sans End!

XXV.

Alike for those who for *To-day* prepare,
And those that after some *To-morrow* stare,
 A Muezzín from the Tower of Darkness cries,
"Fools! your Reward is neither Here nor There."

XXVI.

Why, all the Saints and Sages who discussed
Of the Two Worlds so wisely—they are thrust
   Like foolish Prophets forth ; their Words to Scorn
Are scattered, and their Mouths are stopt with Dust.

XXVII.

Myself when young did eagerly frequent
Doctor and Saint, and heard great argument
   About it and about ; but evermore
Came out by the same door wherein I went.

XXVIII.

With them the seed of Wisdom did I sow,
And with mine own hand wrought to make it grow ;
   And this was all the Harvest that I reaped—
" I came like Water, and like Wind I go."

XXIX.

Into this Universe, and *Why* not knowing,
Nor *Whence*, like Water willy-nilly flowing ;
   And out of it, as Wind along the Waste,
I know not *Whither*, willy-nilly blowing.

XXX.

What, without asking, hither hurried *Whence ?*
And, without asking, *Whither* hurried hence !
   Oh, many a Cup of this forbidden Wine
Must drown the memory of that insolence !

XXXI.

Up from Earth's Centre through the Seventh Gate
I rose, and on the Throne of Saturn sate:
    And many a Knot unravelled by the Road;
But not the Master-knot of Human Fate.

XXXII.

There was the Door to which I found no Key;
There was the Veil through which I might not see:
    Some little talk awhile of *Me* and *Thee*
There was—and then no more of *Thee* and *Me.*

XXXIII.

Earth could not answer; nor the Seas that mourn
In flowing Purple, of their Lord forlorn;
    Nor rolling Heaven, with all his Signs revealed
And hidden by the sleeve of Night and Morn.

XXXIV.

Then of the THEE IN ME who works behind
The Veil, I lifted up my hands to find
    A lamp amid the Darkness; and I heard,
As from Without—" The Me within Thee Blind!"

XXXV.

Then to the Lip of this poor earthen Urn
I leaned, the Secret of my Life to learn;
    And Lip to Lip it murmured—" While you live,
Drink!—for once dead, you never shall return."

XXXVI.

I think the Vessel, that with fugitive
Articulation answered, once did live,
    And drink ; and Ah ! the passive Lip I kissed,
How many Kisses might it take—and give !

XXXVII.

For I remember stopping by the way
To watch a Potter thumping his wet Clay :
    And with its all-obliterated Tongue
It murmured—" Gently, Brother, gently, pray ! "

XXXVIII.

And has not such a Story from of Old
Down Man's successive generations rolled
    Of such a clod of saturated Earth
Cast by the Maker into Human mould ?

XXXIX.

And not a drop that from our Cups we throw
For Earth to drink of, but may steal below
    To quench the fire of Anguish in some Eye
There hidden—far beneath, and long ago.

XL.

As then the Tulip for her morning sup
Of Heavenly Vintage from the soil looks up,
    Do you devoutly do the like, till Heaven
To Earth invert you—like an empty Cup.

XLI.

Perplext no more with Human or Divine,
To-morrow's tangle to the winds resign,
   And lose your fingers in the tresses of
The Cypress-slender Minister of Wine.

XLII.

And if the Wine you drink, the Lip you press,
End in what All begins and ends in—Yes;
   Think then you are *To-day* what *Yesterday*
You were—*To-morrow* you shall not be less.

XLIII.

So when that Angel of the darker Drink
At last shall find you by the river-brink,
   And, offering his Cup, invite your Soul
Forth to your Lips to quaff—you shall not shrink.

XLIV.

Why, if the Soul can fling the Dust aside,
And naked on the Air of Heaven ride,
   Were 't not a Shame—were 't not a Shame for him
In this clay carcass crippled to abide?

XLV.

'T is but a Tent where takes his one day's rest
A Sultán to the realm of Death addrest;
   The Sultán rises, and the dark Ferrásh
Strikes and prepares it for another Guest.

XLVI.

And fear not lest Existence, closing your
Account, and mine, should know the like no more;
   The Eternal Sákí from that Bowl has poured
Millions of Bubbles like us, and will pour.

XLVII.

When You and I behind the Veil are past,
Oh, but the long, long while the World shall last,
   Which of our Coming and Departure heeds
As the Sea's self should heed a pebble-cast.

XLVIII.

A Moment's Halt—a momentary taste
Of *Being* from the Well amid the Waste—
   And Lo!—the phantom Caravan has reached
The *Nothing* it set out from—Oh, make haste!

XLIX.

Would you that spangle of Existence spend
About *the secret*—quick about it, Friend!
   A Hair perhaps divides the False and True—
And upon what, prithee, may life depend?

L.

A Hair perhaps divides the False and True;
Yes; and a single Alif were the clue—
   Could you but find it—to the Treasure-house
And peradventure to *The Master* too;

LI.

Whose secret Presence, through Creation's veins
Running Quicksilver-like, eludes your pains ;
    Taking all shapes from Máh to Máhi ; and
They change and perish all—but He remains :

LII.

A moment guessed—then back behind the Fold
Immerst of Darkness round the Drama rolled
    Which, for the Pastime of Eternity,
He doth Himself contrive, enact, behold.

LIII.

But if in vain, down on the stubborn floor
Of Earth, and up to Heaven's unopening Door,
    You gaze *To-day*, while You are You—how then
To-morrow, when You shall be You no more ?

LIV.

Waste not your Hour, nor in the vain pursuit
Of This and That endeavor and dispute ;
    Better be jocund with the fruitful Grape
Than sadden after none, or bitter, Fruit.

LV.

You know, my Friends, with what a brave Carouse
I made a Second Marriage in my house ;
    Divorced old barren Reason from my Bed,
And took the Daughter of the Vine to Spouse.

LVI.

For " *Is* " and " *Is-not* " though with Rule and
   Line
And " *Up-and-Down* " by Logic I define,
  Of all that one should care to fathom, I
Was never deep in anything but—Wine.

LVII.

Ah, but my Computations, People say,
Reduced the Year to better reckoning?—Nay,
  'T was only striking from the Calendar
Unborn To-morrow, and dead Yesterday.

LVIII.

And lately, by the Tavern Door agape,
Came shining through the Dusk an Angel Shape
  Bearing a Vessel on his Shoulder ; and
He bid me taste of it ; and 't was—the Grape !

LIX.

The Grape, that can with Logic absolute
The Two-and-Seventy jarring Sects confute ;
  The sovereign Alchemist that in a trice
Life's leaden metal into Gold transmute ;

LX.

The mighty Mahmúd, Allah-breathing Lord,
That all the misbelieving and black Horde
  Of Fears and Sorrows that infest the Soul
Scatters before him with his whirlwind Sword.

LXI.

Why, be this Juice the growth of God, who dare
Blaspheme the twisted tendril as a Snare?
   A Blessing, we should use it, should we not?
And if a Curse—why, then, Who set it there?

LXII.

I must abjure the Balm of Life, I must,
Scared by some After-reckoning ta'en on trust,
   Or lured with Hope of some Diviner Drink,
To fill the Cup—when crumbled into Dust!

LXIII.

Oh, threats of Hell and Hopes of Paradise!
One thing at least is certain—This Life flies;
   One thing is certain and the rest is Lies:
The Flower that once has blown forever dies.

LXIV.

Strange, is it not? that of the myriads who
Before us passed the door of Darkness through,
   Not one returns to tell us of the Road,
Which to discover we must travel too.

LXV.

The Revelations of Devout and Learned
Who rose before us, and as Prophets burned,
   Are all but Stories, which awoke from Sleep
They told their comrades, and to Sleep returned.

LXVI.

I sent my Soul through the Invisible,
Some letter of that After-life to spell;
   And by-and-by my Soul returned to me,
And answered, "I Myself am Heaven and Hell:"

LXVII.

Heaven but the Vision of fulfilled Desire,
And Hell the Shadow from a Soul on fire,
   Cast on the Darkness into which Ourselves,
So late emerged from, shall so soon expire.

LXVIII.

We are no other than a moving row
Of Magic Shadow-shapes that come and go
   Round with the Sun-illumined Lantern held
In Midnight by the Master of the Show;

LXIX.

But helpless Pieces of the Game He plays
Upon this Chequer-board of Nights and Days;
   Hither and thither moves, and checks, and slays,
And one by one back in the Closet lays.

LXX.

The Ball no question makes of Ayes and Noes,
But Here or There as strikes the Player goes;
   And he that tossed you down into the Field,
He knows about it all—HE knows—HE knows!

LXXI.

The Moving Finger writes ; and having writ,
Moves on : nor all your Piety nor Wit
   Shall lure it back to cancel half a Line,
Nor all your Tears wash out a Word of it.

LXXII.

And that inverted Bowl they call the Sky,
Whereunder crawling cooped we live and die,
   Lift not your hands to *It* for help—for It
As impotently moves as you or I.

LXXIII.

With Earth's first Clay They did the Last Man knead,
And there of the Last Harvest sowed the Seed ;
   And the first Morning of Creation wrote
What the Last Dawn of Reckoning shall read.

LXXIV.

Yesterday This Day's Madness did prepare ;
To-morrow's Silence, Triumph, or Despair :
   Drink ! for you know not whence you came, nor
      why ;
Drink ! for you know not why you go, nor where.

LXXV.

I tell you this—When, started from the Goal,
Over the flaming shoulders of the Foal
   Of Heaven Parwín and Mushtarí they flung,
In my predestined Plot of Dust and Soul

LXXVI.

The Vine had struck a fibre ; which about
If clings my Being—let the Dervish flout :
  Of my Base metal may be filed a Key
That shall unlock the Door he howls without.

LXXVII.

And this I know : whether the one True Light
Kindle to Love, or Wrath consume me quite,
  One Flash of It within the Tavern caught
Better than in the Temple lost outright.

LXXVIII.

What ! out of senseless Nothing to provoke
A conscious Something to resent the yoke
  Of unpermitted Pleasure, under pain
Of Everlasting Penalties, if broke !

LXXIX.

What ! from his helpless Creature be repaid
Pure Gold for what He lent him dross-allayed—
  Sue for a Debt he never did contract,
And cannot answer—Oh the sorry trade !

LXXX.

Oh Thou, who didst with pitfall and with gin
Beset the Road I was to wander in,
  Thou wilt not with Predestined Evil round
Enmesh, and then impute my Fall to Sin !

LXXXI.

Oh Thou, who Man of baser Earth didst make,
And e'en with Paradise devise the Snake:
   For all the Sin wherewith the Face of Man
Is blackened—Man's forgiveness give—and take!

      *   *   *   *

LXXXII.

As under cover of departing Day
Slunk hunger-stricken Ramazán away,
   Once more within the Potter's house alone
I stood, surrounded by the Shapes of Clay.

LXXXIII.

Shapes of all Sorts and Sizes, great and small,
That stood along the floor and by the wall:
   And some loquacious Vessels were; and some
Listened, perhaps, but never talked at all.

LXXXIV.

Said one among them—" Surely not in vain
My substance of the common Earth was ta'en
   And to this Figure moulded, to be broke,
Or trampled back to shapeless Earth again."

LXXXV.

Then said a Second—" Ne'er a peevish Boy
Would break the Bowl from which he drank in joy;
   And He that with his hand the Vessel made
Will surely not in after Wrath destroy."

LXXXVI.

After a momentary silence spake
Some Vessel of a more ungainly Make :—
    " They sneer at me for leaning all awry :
What ! did the Hand then of the Potter shake ? "

LXXXVII.

Whereat some one of the loquacious Lot—
I think a Súfi pipkin—waxing hot—
    " All this of Pot and Potter—Tell me, then,
Who is the Potter, pray, and who the Pot ? "

LXXXVIII.

" Why," said another, " Some there are who tell
Of one who threatens he will toss to Hell
    The luckless Pots he marred in making—Pish !
He's a Good Fellow, and 't will all be well."

LXXXIX.

" Well," murmured one, " Let whoso make or buy,
My Clay with long Oblivion is gone dry ;
    But fill me with the old familiar Juice,
Methinks I might recover by-and-by."

XC.

So while the Vessels one by one were speaking
The little Moon looked in that all were seeking :
    And then they jogged each other, " Brother !
      Brother !
Now for the Porter's shoulder-knot a-creaking ! "

XCI.

Ah, with the Grape my fading life provide,
And wash the Body whence the Life has died,
    And lay me, shrouded in the living Leaf,
By some not unfrequented Garden-side.

XCII.

That e'en my buried Ashes such a snare
Of Vintage shall fling up into the Air,
    As not a True-believer passing by
But shall be overtaken unaware.

XCIII.

Indeed, the Idols I have loved so long
Have done my credit in this World much wrong :
    Have drowned my Glory in a shallow Cup,
And sold my Reputation for a Song.

XCIV.

Indeed, indeed, Repentance oft before,
I swore—but was I sober when I swore ?
    And then and then came Spring, and Rose-in-hand
My threadbare Penitence apieces tore.

XCV.

And much as Wine has played the Infidel,
And Robbed me of my Robe of Honor—Well,
    I wonder often what the Vintners buy
One half so precious as the stuff they sell.

XCVI.

Yet Ah, that Spring should vanish with the Rose !
That Youth's sweet-scented manuscript should close !
   The Nightingale that in the branches sang,
Ah whence, and whither flown again, who knows !

XCVII.

Would but the Desert of the Fountain yield
One glimpse—if dimly, yet indeed revealed,
   To which the fainting Traveller might spring,
As springs the trampled herbage of the field !

XCVIII.

Would but some wingèd Angel ere too late
Arrest the yet unfolded Roll of Fate,
   And make the stern Recorder otherwise
Enregister, or quite obliterate !

XCIX.

Ah Love ! could you and I with Him conspire
To grasp this sorry Scheme of Things entire,
   Would not we shatter it to bits—and then
Remould it nearer to the Heart's Desire !

     *   *   *   *

C.

Yon rising Moon that looks for us again—
How oft hereafter will she wax and wane ;
   How oft hereafter rising look for us
Through this same Garden—and for *one* in vain !

CI.

And when like her, O Sákí, you shall pass
Among the Guests Star-scattered on the Grass,
    And in your joyous errand reach the spot
Where I made One—turn down an empty Glass !

From the Persian of OMAR KHAYYÁM.
Paraphrased version of EDWARD FITZGERALD.

TIME.

AN ENIGMA.

EVER eating, never cloying,
All-devouring, all-destroying,
Never finding full repast
Till I eat the world at last.

JONATHAN SWIFT.

II.

LIFE.

THIS LIFE.

This Life, which seems so fair,
Is like a bubble blown up in the air
By sporting children's breath,
Who chase it everywhere
And strive who can most motion it bequeath.
And though it sometimes seem of its own might
Like to an eye of gold to be fixed there,
And firm to hover in that empty height,
That only is because it is so light.
—But in that pomp it doth not long appear;
For when 't is most admired, in a thought,
Because it erst was nought, it turns to nought.
                              WILLIAM DRUMMOND.

THE CHARACTER OF A HAPPY LIFE.

How happy is he born and taught
    That serveth not another's will;
Whose armor is his honest thought,
    And simple truth his utmost skill!

Whose passions not his masters are;
    Whose soul is still prepared for death,

Not tied unto the world with care
  Of public fame or private breath ;

Who envies none that chance doth raise,
  Or vice ; who never understood
How deepest wounds are given by praise,
  Nor rules of state, but rules of good ;

Who hath his life from rumors freed ;
  Whose conscience is his strong retreat ;
Whose state can neither flatterers feed,
  Nor ruin make accusers great ;

Who God doth late and early pray
  More of his grace than gifts to lend,
And entertains the harmless day
  With a well-chosen book or friend,—

This man is freed from servile bands
  Of hope to rise, or fear to fall ;
Lord of himself, though not of lands ;
  And, having nothing, yet hath all.

SIR HENRY WOTTON.

RETRIBUTION.

'Οψὲ θεῶν ἀλέουσι μύλοι, ἀλέουσι δὲ λεπτά.

(" The mills of the gods grind late, but they grind fine.")
—*Greek Poet.*

THOUGH the mills of God grind slowly, yet they
  grind exceeding small;
Though with patience he stands waiting, with ex-
  actness grinds he all.

From the German of F. VON LOGAU.
Translation of H. W. LONGFELLOW.

THE LYE

Goe, soule, the bodie's guest,
  Upon a thanklesse arrant;
Feare not to touche the best—
    The truth shall be thy warrant;
      Goe, since I needs must dye,
      And give the world the lye.

Goe tell the court it glowes
  And shines like rotten wood ;
Goe tell the church it showes
    What 's good, and doth no good;
      If church and court reply,
      Then give them both the lye.

Tell potentates they live
  Acting by others' actions—
Not loved unlesse they give,
    Not strong but by their factions ;
      If potentates reply,
      Give potentates the lye.

Tell men of high condition,
  That rule affairs of state,
Their purpose is ambition,
    Their practice only hate ;
      And if they once reply,
      Then give them all the lye.

Tell them that brave it most
  They beg for more by spending,

Who in their greatest cost
  Seek nothing but commending;
  And if they make reply,
  Spare not to give the lye.

Tell zeale it lacks devotion;
  Tell love it is but lust;
Tell time it is but motion;
  Tell flesh it is but dust;
    And wish them not reply,
    For thou must give the lye.

Tell age it daily wasteth;
  Tell honor how it alters;
Tell beauty how she blasteth;
  Tell favor how she falters;
    And as they then reply,
    Give each of them the lye.

Tell wit how much it wrangles
  In tickle points of nicenesse;
Tell wisedome she entangles
  Herselfe in over wisenesse;
    And if they doe reply,
    Straight give them both the lye.

Tell physicke of her boldnesse;
  Tell skill it is pretension;
Tell charity of coldnesse;
  Tell law it is contention;
    And as they yield reply,
    So give them still the lye.

Tell fortune of her blindnesse;
  Tell nature of decay;

Tell friendship of unkindnesse ;
  Tell justice of delay ;
    And if they dare reply,
    Then give them all the lye.

Tell arts they have no soundnesse,
  But vary by esteeming ;
Tell schooles they want profoundnesse,
  And stand too much on seeming ;
    If arts and schooles reply,
    Give arts and schooles the lye.

Tell faith it 's fled the citie ;
  Tell how the country erreth ;
Tell, manhood shakes off pitie ;
  Tell, vertue least preferreth ;
    And if they doe reply,
    Spare not to give the lye.

So, when thou hast, as I
  Commanded thee, done blabbing—
Although to give the lye
  Deserves no less then stabbing—
    Yet stab at thee who will,
    No stab the soule can kill.

               SIR WALTER RALEIGH.

THE GENEROUS AIR.

BREATHING the thin breath through our nostrils, we
Live, and a little space the sunlight see—
Even all that live—each being an instrument
To which the generous air its life has lent.

If with the hand one quench our draught of breath,
He sends the stark soul shuddering down to death.
We that are nothing on our pride are fed,
Seeing, but for a little air, we are as dead.

From the Greek of PALLADAS.
Translation of WILLIAM M. HARDINGE.

GOOD LIFE, LONG LIFE.

It is not growing like a tree
In bulk, doth make man better be ;
Or standing long an oak, three hundred year,
To fall a log at last, dry, bald, and sear :
A lily of a day
Is fairer far in May,
Although it fall and die that night,—
It was the plant and flower of Light.
In small proportions we just beauties see,
And in short measures life may perfect be.

BEN JONSON.

LIFE.

My life is like the summer rose,
That opens to the morning sky,
But, ere the shades of evening close,
Is scattered on the ground—to die !
Yet on the rose's humble bed
The sweetest dews of night are shed,
As if she wept the waste to see,—
But none shall weep a tear for me !

My life is like the autumn leaf
That trembles in the moon's pale ray ;
Its hold is frail,—its date is brief,
Restless, and soon to pass away !
Yet, ere that leaf shall fall and fade,
The parent tree will mourn its shade,
The winds bewail the leafless tree,—
But none shall breathe a sigh for me !

My life is like the prints which feet
Have left on Tampa's desert strand ;
Soon as the rising tide shall beat,
All trace will vanish from the sand ;
Yet, as if grieving to efface
All vestige of the human race,
On that lone shore loud moans the sea,—
But none, alas ! shall mourn for me !

RICHARD HENRY WILDE.

WHERE LIES THE LAND?

WHERE lies the land to which the ship would go ?
Far, far ahead, is all her seamen know.
And where the land she travels from ? Away,
Far, far behind, is all that they can say.

On sunny noons upon the deck's smooth face,
Linked arm in arm, how pleasant here to pace !
Or o'er the stern reclining, watch below
The foaming wake far widening as we go.

On stormy nights, when wild northwesters rave,
How proud a thing to fight with wind and wave !

The dripping sailor on the reeling mast
Exults to bear, and scorns to wish it past.

Where lies the land to which the ship would go?
Far, far ahead, is all her seamen know.
And where the land she travels from? Away,
Far, far behind, is all that they can say.

ARTHUR HUGH CLOUGH.

LIFE.

I MADE a posie, while the day ran by:
" Here will I smell my remnant out, and tie
    My life within this band."
But Time did beckon to the flowers, and they
By noon most cunningly did steal away,
    And withered in my hand.

My hand was next to them, and then my heart;
I took, without more thinking, in good part
    Time's gentle admonition;
Who did so sweetly death's sad taste convey,
Making my minde to smell my fatall day,
    Yet sug'ring the suspicion.

Farewell, dear flowers! sweetly your time ye spent;
Fit, while ye lived, for smell or ornament,
    And after death for cures.
I follow straight without complaints or grief;
Since, if my scent be good, I care not if
    It be as short as yours.

GEORGE HERBERT.

LIFE.

Life, like a romping school-boy full of glee,
  Doth bear us on his shoulders for a time:
  There is no path too steep for him to climb,
With strong lithe limbs, as agile and as free
As some young roe, he speeds by vale and sea,
By flowery mead, by mountain-peak sublime,
And all the world seems motion set to rhyme,
Till, tired out, he cries, " Now carry me ! "
  In vain we murmur. " Come," Life says, " Fair
    play ! "
And seizes on us. God ! He goads us so.
He does not let us sit down all the day.
At each new step we feel the burden grow,
Till our bent backs seem breaking as we go,
  Watching for Death to meet us on the way.

ELLA WHEELER WILCOX.

THE ROSE-BUSH.

A Child sleeps under a rose-bush fair,
The buds swell out in the soft May air ;
Sweetly it rests, and on dream-wings flies
To play with the angels in Paradise.
  And the years glide by.

A Maiden stands by the rose-bush fair,
The dewy blossoms perfume the air ;
She presses her hand to her throbbing breast,
With love's first wonderful rapture blest.
  And the years glide by.

A Mother kneels by the rose-bush fair,
Soft sigh the leaves in the evening air;
Sorrowing thoughts of the past arise,
And tears of anguish bedim her eyes.
    And the years glide by.

Naked and lone stands the rose-bush fair,
Whirled are the leaves in the autumn air,
Withered and dead they fall to the ground,
And silently cover a new-made mound.
    And the years glide by.

From the German.
Translation of WILLIAM W. CALDWELL.

HISTORY OF A LIFE.

DAY dawned ;—within a curtained room,
Filled to faintness with perfume,
A lady lay at point of doom.

Day closed ;—a Child had seen the light:
But, for the lady fair and bright,
She rested in undreaming night.

Spring rose ;—the lady's grave was green ;
And near it, oftentimes, was seen
A gentle Boy with thoughtful mien.

Years fled ;—he wore a manly face,
And struggled in the world's rough race,
And won at last a lofty place.

And then he died ! Behold before ye
Humanity's poor sum and story ;
Life,—Death,—and all that is of Glory.

BRYAN WALLER PROCTER (*Barry Cornwall*).

MY QUAKER GRANDMOTHERS.

LIKE two little doves in gray
  On the boughs of a greenwood tree,
My two Quaker grandmothers sit
  In my gay genealogy.

The Cavalier struts in my heart,
  The Puritan tugs at my will,
But the Quaker faces say " Peace,"
  And passion and pride are still.

Dear faces of infinite calm,
  Ye have wrought a spell in my blood
That maketh the world seem wise
  And sweet with the sunshine of God.

OLIVER HUCKEL.

ADDRESS TO THE MUMMY AT BELZONI'S EXHIBITION.

AND thou hast walked about (how strange a story !
  In Thebes's streets three thousand years ago,
When the Memnonium was in all its glory,
  And time had not begun to overthrow
Those temples, palaces, and piles stupendous,
Of which the very ruins are tremendous.

Speak ! for thou long enough hast acted dummy ;
  Thou hast a tongue,—come, let us hear its tune ;
Thou 'rt standing on thy legs, above ground, mum-
    my !
  Revisiting the glimpses of the moon,—

Not like thin ghosts or disembodied creatures,
But with thy bones and flesh and limbs and features.

Tell us—for doubtless thou canst recollect—
    To whom should we assign the Sphinx's fame?
Was Cheops or Cephrenes architect
    Of either pyramid that bears his name?
Is Pompey's Pillar really a misnomer?
Had Thebes a hundred gates, as sung by Homer?

Perhaps thou wert a Mason, and forbidden
    By oath to tell the secrets of thy trade,—
Then say what secret melody was hidden
    In Memnon's statue, which at sunrise played?
Perhaps thou wert a priest,—if so, my struggles
Are vain, for priestcraft never owns its juggles.

Perhaps that very hand, now pinioned flat,
    Has hob-a-nobbed with Pharaoh, glass to glass;
Or dropped a halfpenny in Homer's hat;
    Or doffed thine own to let Queen Dido pass;
Or held, by Solomon's own invitation,
A torch at the great temple's dedication.

I need not ask thee if that hand, when armed,
    Has any Roman soldier mauled and knuckled;
For thou wert dead and buried and embalmed
    Ere Romulus and Remus had been suckled:
Antiquity appears to have begun
Long after thy primeval race was run.

Thou couldst develop—if that withered tongue
    Might tell us what those sightless orbs have seen—
How the world looked when it was fresh and young,
    And the great deluge still had left it green;

Or was it then so old that history's pages
Contained no record of its early ages?

Still silent! incommunicative elf!
    Art sworn to secrecy? then keep thy vows;
But prithee tell us something of thyself,
    Reveal the secrets of thy prison-house;
Since in the world of spirits thou hast slumbered,
What hast thou seen, what strange adventures
      numbered?

Since first thy form was in this box extended
    We have, above ground, seen some strange muta-
      tions:
The Roman empire has begun and ended,
    New worlds have risen, we have lost old nations;
And countless kings have into dust been humbled,
While not a fragment of thy flesh has crumbled.

Didst thou not hear the pother o'er thy head,
    When the great Persian conqueror, Cambyses,
Marched armies o'er thy tomb with thundering
      tread,—
    O'erthrew Osiris, Orus, Apis, Isis; '
And shook the pyramids with fear and wonder,
When the gigantic Memnon fell asunder?

If the tomb's secrets may not be confessed,
    The nature of thy private life unfold:
A heart has throbbed beneath that leathern breast,
    And tears adown that dusty cheek have rolled;
Have children climbed those knees, and kissed that
      face?
What was thy name and station, age and race?

Statue of flesh,—immortal of the dead!
  Imperishable type of evanescence!
Posthumous man,—who quit'st thy narrow bed,
  And standest undecayed within our presence!
Thou wilt hear nothing till the judgment morning,
When the great trump shall thrill thee with its
    warning.

Why should this worthless tegument endure,
  If its undying guest be lost forever?
O, let us keep the soul embalmed and pure
  In living virtue, that when both must sever,
Although corruption may our frame consume,
The immortal spirit in the skies may bloom!

HORACE SMITH.

LONDON BRIDGE.

PROUD and lowly, beggar and lord,
  Over the bridge they go;
Rags and velvet, fetter and sword,
  Poverty, pomp, and woe.
Laughing, weeping, hurrying ever,
  Hour by hour they crowd along,
While, below, the mighty river
  Sings them all a mocking song,
    Hurry along, sorrow and song,
      All is vanity 'neath the sun;
    Velvet and rags, so the world wags,
      Until the river no more shall run.

Dainty, painted, powdered and gay,
  Rolleth my lady by;

Rags-and-tatters, over the way,
  Carries a heart as high.
Flowers and dreams from country meadows,
  Dust and din through city skies,
Old men creeping with their shadows,
  Children with their sunny eyes,—
    Hurry along, sorrow and song,
      All is vanity 'neath the sun;
      Velvet and rags, so the world wags,
        Until the river no more shall run.

Storm and sunshine, peace and strife,
  Over the bridge they go;
Floating on in the tide of life,
  Whither no man shall know.
Who will miss them there to-morrow,
  Waifs that drift to the shade or sun?
Gone away with their songs and sorrow;
  Only the river still flows on.
    Hurry along, sorrow and song,
      All is vanity 'neath the sun;
      Velvet and rags, so the world wags,
        Until the river no more shall run.

FREDERIC EDWARD WEATHERLY.

THE CROWDED STREET.

LET me move slowly through the street,
  Filled with an ever-shifting train,
Amid the sound of steps that beat
  The murmuring walks like autumn rain.

How fast the flitting figures come!
  The mild, the fierce, the stony face——

Some bright with thoughtless smiles, and some
  Where secret tears have left their trace.

They pass to toil, to strife, to rest—
  To halls in which the feast is spread—
To chambers where the funeral guest
  In silence sits beside the dead.

And some to happy homes repair,
  Where children, pressing cheek to cheek,
With mute caresses shall declare
  The tenderness they cannot speak.

And some, who walk in calmness here,
  Shall shudder as they reach the door
Where one who made their dwelling dear,
  Its flower, its light, is seen no more.

Youth, with pale cheek and slender frame,
  And dreams of greatness in thine eye !
Go'st thou to build an early name,
  Or early in the task to die ?

Keen son of trade, with eager brow !
  Who is now fluttering in thy snare ?
Thy golden fortunes, tower they now,
  Or melt the glittering spires in air ?

Who of this crowd to-night shall tread
  The dance till daylight gleam again ?
Who sorrow o'er the untimely dead ?
  Who writhe in throes of mortal pain ?

Some, famine-struck, shall think how long
  The cold, dark hours, how slow the light ;

And some, who flaunt amid the throng,
   Shall hide in dens of shame to-night.

Each where his tasks or pleasures call,
   They pass, and heed each other not.
There is who heeds, who holds them all
   In His large love and boundless thought.

These struggling tides of life, that seem
   In wayward, aimless course to tend,
Are eddies of the mighty stream
   That rolls to its appointed end.

                WILLIAM CULLEN BRYANT.

L' ALLEGRO.

HENCE, loathed Melancholy,
   Of Cerberus and blackest Midnight born,
   In Stygian cave forlorn,
'Mongst horrid shapes, and shrieks, and sights un-
      holy !
Find out some uncouth cell,
Where brooding Darkness spreads his jealous wings,
And the night-raven sings ;
There under ebon shades, and low-browed rocks,
As ragged as thy locks,
   In dark Cimmerian desert ever dwell.
But come, thou goddess fair and free,
In heaven ycleped Euphrosyne,
And, by men, heart-easing Mirth ;
Whom lovely Venus, at a birth,
With two sister Graces more,
To ivy-crownèd Bacchus bore ;

Or whether (as some sager sing)
The frolic wind that breathes the spring,
Zephyr, with Aurora playing,—
As he met her once a-Maying,—
There, on beds of violets blue
And fresh-blown roses washed in dew,
Filled her with thee, a daughter fair,
So buxom, blithe, and debonair.

Haste thee, nymph, and bring with thee
Jest, and youthful Jollity,—
Quips and cranks and wanton wiles,
Nods and becks and wreathèd smiles,
Such as hang on Hebe's cheek,
And love to live in dimple sleek,—
Sport, that wrinkled Care derides,
And Laughter, holding both his sides.
Come! and trip it, as you go,
On the light fantastic toe;
And in thy right hand lead with thee
The mountain nymph, sweet Liberty;
And if I give thee honor due,
Mirth, admit me of thy crew,
To live with her, and live with thee,
In unreprovèd pleasures free,—
To hear the lark begin his flight,
And singing startle the dull Night,
From his watch-tower in the skies,
Till the dappled dawn doth rise;
Then to come, in spite of sorrow,
And at my window bid good morrow,
Through the sweet-brier, or the vine,
Or the twisted eglantine;

While the cock with lively din
Scatters the rear of darkness thin,
And to the stack, or the barn door,
Stoutly struts his dames before ;
Oft listening how the hounds and horn
Cheerly rouse the slumbering Morn,
From the side of some hoar hill
Through the high wood echoing shrill ;
Sometime walking, not unseen,
By hedgerow elms, on hillocks green,
Right against the eastern gate,
Where the great Sun begins his state,
Robed in flames, and amber light,
The clouds in thousand liveries dight;
While the ploughman, near at hand,
Whistles o'er the furrowed land,
And the milkmaid singeth blithe,
And the mower whets his scythe,
And every shepherd tells his tale
Under the hawthorn in the dale.

Straight mine eye hath caught new pleasures,
Whilst the landscape round it measures
Russet lawns, and fallows gray,
Where the nibbling flocks do stray,—
Mountains, on whose barren breast
The laboring clouds do often rest,—
Meadows trim with daisies pied,
Shallow brooks, and rivers wide.
Towers and battlements it sees
Bosomed high in tufted trees,
Where perhaps some beauty lies,
The cynosure of neighboring eyes.

Hard by, a cottage chimney smokes
From betwixt two aged oaks,
Where Corydon and Thyrsis, met,
Are at their savory dinner set
Of herbs, and other country messes,
Which the neat-handed Phillis dresses :
And then in haste her bower she leaves,
With Thestylis to bind the sheaves ;
Or, if the earlier season lead,
To the tanned haycock in the mead.
Sometimes with secure delight
The upland hamlets will invite,
When the merry bells ring round,
And the jocund rebecks sound
To many a youth and many a maid,
Dancing in the checkered shade ;
And young and old come forth to play
On a sunshine holiday,
Till the livelong daylight fail ;
Then to the spicy nut-brown ale
With stories told of many a feat :
How fairy Mab the junkets eat,—
She was pinched and pulled, she said,
And he, by friar's lantern led ;
Tells how the drudging goblin sweat
To earn his cream-bowl duly set,
When in one night, ere glimpse of morn,
His shadowy flail had thrashed the corn
That ten day-laborers could not end ;
Then lies him down the lubber fiend,
And, stretched out all the chimney's length,
Basks at the fire his hairy strength,
And, crop-full, out of doors he flings
Ere the first cock his matin rings.

Thus done the tales, to bed they creep,
By whispering winds soon lulled asleep.

Towered cities please us then,
And the busy hum of men,
Where throngs of knights and barons bold
In weeds of peace high triumphs hold,—
With store of ladies, whose bright eyes
Rain influence, and judge the prize
Of wit or arms, while both contend
To win her grace whom all commend.
There let Hymen oft appear
In saffron robe, with taper clear,
And pomp and feast and revelry,
With masque, and antique pageantry,—
Such sights as youthful poets dream
On summer eves by haunted stream;
Then to the well-trod stage anon,
If Jonson's learnèd sock be on,
Or sweetest Shakespeare, Fancy's child,
Warble his native wood-notes wild.

And ever, against eating cares,
Lap me in soft Lydian airs,
Married to immortal verse,—
Such as the meeting soul may pierce,
In notes with many a winding bout
Of linkèd sweetness long drawn out,
With wanton heed and giddy cunning
The melting voice through mazes running,
Untwisting all the chains that tie
The hidden soul of harmony,—
That Orpheus' self may heave his head
From golden slumber on a bed

Of heaped Elysian flowers, and hear
Such strains as would have won the ear
Of Pluto, to have quite set free
His half-regained Eurydice.

These delights if thou canst give,
Mirth, with thee I mean to live.

MILTON.

DINING.

FROM " LUCILE."

O HOUR of all hours, the most blest upon earth,
Blest hour of our dinners!
            The land of his birth;
The face of his first love; the bills that he owes;
The twaddle of friends, and venom of foes;
The sermon he heard when to church he last went;
The money he borrowed, the money he spent;
All of these things a man, I believe, may forget,
And not be the worse for forgetting; but yet
Never, never, oh, never! earth's luckiest sinner
Hath unpunished forgotten the hour of his dinner!
Indigestion, that conscience of every bad stomach,
Shall relentlessly gnaw and pursue him with some
            ache
Or some pain; and trouble, remorseless, his best
            ease,
As the Furies once troubled the sleep of Orestes.

We may live without poetry, music, and art;
We may live without conscience, and live without
            earth;

We may live without friends; we may live without
  books;
But civilized men cannot live without cooks.
He may live without books,—what is knowledge
  but grieving?
He may live without hope,—what is hope but de-
  ceiving?
He may live without love,—what is passion but
  pining?
But where is the man that can live without dining?

ROBERT, EARL OF LYTTON (*Owen Meredith*).

THE FAMILY SKELETON.

FROM " MODERN LOVE."

AT dinner she is hostess, I am host.
Went the feast ever cheerfuller?   She keeps
The topic over intellectual deeps
In buoyancy afloat.   They see no ghost.
With sparkling surface-eyes we ply the ball:
It is in truth a most contagious game;
HIDING THE SKELETON shall be its name.
Such play as this the devils might appall!
But here 's the greater wonder; in that we,
Enamored of our acting and our wits,
Admire each other like true hypocrites.
Warm-lighted glances, Love's Ephemeræ,
Shoot gayly o'er the dishes and the wine.
We waken envy of our happy lot.
Fast, sweet, and golden, shows our marriage-knot.
Dear guests, you now have seen Love's corpse-light
  shine!

GEORGE MEREDITH.

THE EPICURE.

Fill the bowl with rosy wine!
Around our temples roses twine!
And let us cheerfully awhile,
Like the wine and roses, smile.
Crowned with roses, we contemn
Gyges' wealthy diadem.
To-day is ours, what do we fear?
To-day is ours; we have it here:
Let 's treat it kindly, that it may
Wish, at least, with us to stay.
Let 's banish business, banish sorrow;
To the gods belongs to-morrow.

———

Underneath this myrtle shade,
On flowery beds supinely laid,
With odorous oils my head o'erflowing,
And around it roses growing,
What should I do but drink away
The heat and troubles of the day?
In this more than kingly state
Love himself shall on me wait.
Fill to me, Love, nay fill it up;
And, mingled, cast into the cup
Wit, and mirth, and noble fires,
Vigorous health, and gay desires.
The wheel of life no less will stay
In a smooth than rugged way:
Since it equally doth flee,
Let the motion pleasant be.

Why do we precious ointments show'r ?
Noble wines why do we pour ?
Beauteous flowers why do we spread,
Upon the monuments of the dead ?
Nothing they but dust can show,
Or bones that hasten to be so.
Crown me with roses while I live,
Now your wines and ointments give ;
After death I nothing crave.
Let me alive my pleasures have ;
All are Stoics in the grave.

From the Greek of ANACREON.
Translation of ABRAHAM COWLEY

THE INDIAN WEED.

This Indian weed, now withered quite,
Though green at noon, cut down at night,
 Shows thy decay,—
 All flesh is hay :
Thus think, and drink * tobacco.

The pipe, so lily-like and weak,
Does thus thy mortal state bespeak ;
 Thou art e'en such,—
 Gone with a touch :
Thus think, and drink tobacco.

And when the smoke ascends on high,
Then thou behold'st the vanity
 Of worldly stuff,—
 Gone with a puff :
Thus think, and drink tobacco.

* The current phrase for smoking, in the XVII. Century.

And when the pipe grows foul within,
Think on thy soul defiled with sin ;
    For then the fire
    It does require :
Thus think, and drink tobacco.

And seest the ashes cast away,
Then to thyself thou mayest say
    That to the dust
    Return thou must :
Thus think, and drink tobacco.
        ANONYMOUS (*Seventeenth Century*).

SMOKING SPIRITUALIZED.

Was this small plant for thee cut down ?
So was the plant of great renown,
    Which Mercy sends
    For nobler ends.
Thus think, and smoke tobacco.

Doth juice medicinal proceed
From such a naughty foreign weed ?
    Then what 's the power
    Of Jesse's flower ?
Thus think, and smoke tobacco.

The promise, like the pipe, inlays,
And by the mouth of faith conveys
    What virtue flows
    From Sharon's rose :
Thus think, and smoke tobacco.

In vain the unlighted pipe you blow—
Your pains in outward means are so,
    Till heavenly fire
    Your heart inspire :
Thus think, and smoke tobacco.

The smoke like burning incense towers ;
So should a praying heart of yours
    With ardent cries
    Surmount the skies :
Thus think, and smoke tobacco.

RALPH ERSKINE.

WITHOUT AND WITHIN.

IF every man's internal care
    Were written on his brow,
How many would our pity share
    Who raise our envy now ?

The fatal secret, when revealed,
    Of every aching breast,
Would prove that only while concealed
    Their lot appeared the best.

From the Italian of METASTASIO.

IL PENSEROSO.

HENCE, vain deluding joys,
    The brood of Folly without father bred !
    How little you bestead,
Or fill the fixèd mind with all your toys !
    Dwell in some idle brain,
And fancies fond with gaudy shapes possess,
As thick and numberless
As the gay motes that people the sunbeams,—
Or likest hovering dreams,
    The fickle pensioners of Morpheus' train.

But hail, thou goddess, sage and holy !
Hail, divinest Melancholy !
Whose saintly visage is too bright
To hit the sense of human sight,
And therefore, to our weaker view,
O'erlaid with black, staid Wisdom's hue,—
Black, but such as in esteem
Prince Memnon's sister might beseem,
Or that starred Ethiop queen that strove
To set her beauty's praise above
The Sea-Nymphs, and their powers offended.
Yet thou art higher far descended;
Thee bright-haired Vesta, long of yore,
To solitary Saturn bore,—
His daughter she (in Saturn's reign
Such mixture was not held a stain).
Oft in glimmering bowers and glades
He met her, and in secret shades
Of woody Ida's inmost grove,
While yet there was no fear of Jove.

Come, pensive nun, devout and pure,
Sober, steadfast, and demure,
All in a robe of darkest grain
Flowing with majestic train,
And sable stole of cyprus-lawn
Over thy decent shoulders drawn.
Come but keep thy wonted state,
With even step, and musing gait,
And looks commercing with the skies,
Thy rapt soul sitting in thine eyes ;
There held in holy passion still,
Forget thyself to marble, till

With a sad, leaden, downward cast
Thou fix them on the earth as fast;
And join with thee calm Peace, and Quiet,—
Spare Fast, that oft with gods doth diet,
And hears the Muses in a ring
Aye round about Jove's altar sing;
And add to these retirèd Leisure,
That in trim gardens takes his pleasure:
But first and chiefest, with thee bring
Him that yon soars on golden wing,
Guiding the fiery-wheelèd throne,—
The cherub Contemplation;
And the mute Silence hist along,
'Less Philomel will deign a song
In her sweetest, saddest plight,
Smoothing the rugged brow of Night,
While Cynthia checks her dragon yoke
Gently o'er the accustomed oak.
Sweet bird, that shun'st the noise of folly,—
Most musical, most melancholy!
Thee, chantress, oft, the woods among,
I woo, to hear thy even-song.
And, missing thee, I walk unseen
On the dry, smooth-shaven green,
To behold the wandering moon
Riding near her highest noon,
Like one that had been led astray
Through the heaven's wide pathless way;
And oft, as if her head she bowed,
Stooping through a fleecy cloud.
Oft, on a plat of rising ground,
I hear the far-off curfew sound
Over some wide-watered shore,
Swinging slow with sullen roar;

Or if the air will not permit,
Some still removèd place will fit,
Where glowing embers through the room
Teach light to counterfeit a gloom,—
Far from all resort of mirth,
Save the cricket on the hearth,
Or the bellman's drowsy charm,
To bless the doors from nightly harm ;
Or let my lamp at midnight hour
Be seen in some high lonely tower,
Where I may oft out-watch the Bear
With thrice-great Hermes, or unsphere
The spirit of Plato, to unfold
What worlds or what vast regions hold
The immortal mind that hath forsook
Her mansion in this fleshly nook ;
And of those demons that are found
In fire, air, flood, or under ground,
Whose power hath a true consent
With planet or with element.
Sometime let gorgeous Tragedy
In sceptred pall come sweeping by,
Presenting Thebes, or Pelops' line,
Or the tale of Troy divine,
Or what (though rare) of later age
Ennobled hath the buskined stage.

But, O sad Virgin, that thy power
Might raise Musæus from his bower !
Or bid the soul of Orpheus sing
Such notes as, warbled to the string,
Drew iron tears down Pluto's cheek,
And made hell grant what love did seek !

Or call up him that left half told
The story of Cambuscan bold,—
Of Camball, and of Algarsife,—
And who had Canacè to wife,
That owned the virtuous ring and glass,—
And of the wondrous horse of brass,
On which the Tartar king did ride !
And, if aught else great bards beside
In sage and solemn tunes have sung,—
Of tourneys and of trophies hung,
Of forests, and enchantments drear,
Where more is meant than meets the ear.

Thus, Night, oft see me in thy pale career,
Till civil-suited Morn appear,—
Not tricked and frounced, as she was wont
With the Attic boy to hunt,
But kerchiefed in a comely cloud,
While rocking winds are piping loud,
Or ushered with a shower still
When the gust hath blown his fill,
Ending on the rustling leaves,
With minute drops from off the eaves.
And when the sun begins to fling
His flaring beams, me, goddess, bring
To archèd walks of twilight groves,
And shadows brown, that Sylvan loves,
Of pine, or monumental oak, .
Where the rude axe with heavèd stroke
Was never heard the Nymphs to daunt,
Or fright them from their hallowed haunt.
There in close covert by some brook,
Where no profaner eye may look,

Hide me from day's garish eye,
While the bee with honeyed thigh,
That at her flowery work doth sing,
And the waters murmuring
With such consort as they keep,
Entice the dewy-feathered Sleep ;
And let some strange mysterious dream
Wave at his wings, in airy stream
Of lively portraiture displayed,
Softly on my eyelids laid ;
And, as I wake, sweet music breathe
Above, about, or underneath,
Sent by some spirit to mortals good,
Or the unseen Genius of the wood.

But let my due feet never fail
To walk the studious cloister's pale,
And love the high embowèd roof,
With antique pillars massy proof,
And storied windows, richly dight,
Casting a dim religious light.
There let the pealing organ blow
To the full-voiced quire below,
In service high and anthems clear,
As may with sweetness, through mine ear,
Dissolve me into ecstasies,
And bring all heaven before mine eyes.

And may at last my weary age
Find out the peaceful hermitage,
The hairy gown and mossy cell,
Where I may sit and rightly spell
Of every star that heaven doth shew,
And every herb that sips the dew ;

Till old experience do attain
To something like prophetic strain.

These pleasures, Melancholy, give,
And I with thee will choose to live.

MILTON.

EXCELSIOR.

THE shades of night were falling fast,
As though an Alpine village passed
A youth, who bore, 'mid snow and ice,
A banner with the strange device—
  Excelsior!

His brow was sad; his eye beneath
Flashed like a falchion from its sheath;
And like a silver clarion rung
The accents of that unknown tongue—
  Excelsior!

In happy homes he saw the light
Of household fires gleam warm and bright;
Above, the spectral glaciers shone,
And from his lips escaped a groan—
  Excelsior!

"Try not the pass," the old man said:
"Dark lowers the tempest overhead;
The roaring torrent is deep and wide!"
And loud that clarion voice replied,
  Excelsior!

"O stay," the maiden said, "and rest
Thy weary head upon this breast!"

A tear stood in his bright blue eye,
But still he answered, with a sigh,
 Excelsior!

" Beware the pine-tree's withered branch!
Beware the awful avalanche!"
This was the peasant's last good-night:
A voice replied, far up the height,
 Excelsior!

At break of day, as heavenward
The pious monks of Saint Bernard
Uttered the oft-repeated prayer,
A voice cried, through the startled air,
 Excelsior!

A traveller, by the faithful hound,
Half buried in the snow was found,
Still grasping in his hand of ice
That banner with the strange device—
 Excelsior!

There in the twilight cold and gray,
Lifeless, but beautiful, he lay,
And from the sky, serene and far,
A voice fell, like a falling star—
 Excelsior!

   HENRY WADSWORTH LONGFELLOW.

THE WILD RIDE.

I hear in my heart, I hear in its ominous pulses,
All day, the commotion of sinewy, mane-tossing horses;
All night, from their cells, the importunate tramping
 and neighing.

Cowards and laggards fall back; but alert to the
   saddle,
Straight, grim, and abreast, vault our weather-worn,
   galloping legion,
With stirrup-cup each to the one gracious woman
   that loves him.

The road is through dolor and dread, over crags and
   morasses ;
There are shapes by the way, there are things that
   appall or entice us :
What odds ?   We are knights, and our souls are but
   bent on the riding !

Thought's self is a vanishing wing, and joy is a cob-
   web,
And friendship a flower in the dust, and glory a
   sunbeam :
Not here is our prize, nor, alas ! after these our
   pursuing.

A dipping of plumes, a tear, a shake of the bridle,
A passing salute to this world, and her pitiful
   beauty !
We hurry with never a word in the track of our
   fathers.

I hear in my heart, I hear in its ominous pulses,
All day, the commotion of sinewy, mane-tossing horses,
All night, from their cells, the importunate tramping
   and neighing.

We spur to a land of no name, outracing the storm-
   wind ;

We leap to the infinite dark, like the sparks from
    the anvil.
Thou leadest, O God! All 's well with Thy troopers
    that follow!
LOUISE IMOGEN GUINEY.

THE VAGABONDS.

We are two travellers, Roger and I.
  Roger 's my dog:—come here, you scamp!
Jump for the gentlemen,—mind your eye!
  Over the table,—look out for the lamp!—
The rogue is growing a little old;
    Five years we 've tramped through wind and
      weather,
And slept out-doors when nights were cold,
    And ate and drank—and starved together.

We 've learned what comfort is, I tell you!
  A bed on the floor, a bit of rosin,
A fire to thaw our thumbs (poor fellow!
  The paw he holds up there 's been frozen),
Plenty of catgut for my fiddle
  (This out-door business is bad for the strings),
Then a few nice buckwheats hot from the griddle,
  And Roger and I set up for kings!

No, thank ye, sir,—I never drink;
  Roger and I are exceedingly moral,—
Aren't we, Roger?—see him wink!—
  Well, something hot, then—we won't quarrel.
He 's thirsty too,—see him nod his head?
  What a pity, sir, that dogs can't talk!

He understands every word that's said,—
And he knows good milk from water-and-chalk.

The truth is, sir, now I reflect,
I've been so sadly given to grog,
I wonder I've not lost the respect
(Here's to you, sir!) even of my dog.
But he sticks by through thick and thin;
And this old coat, with its empty pockets,
And rags that smell of tobacco and gin,
He'll follow while he has eyes in his sockets.

There isn't another creature living
Would do it, and prove, through every disaster,
So fond, so faithful, and so forgiving
To such a miserable, thankless master!
No, sir!—see him wag his tail and grin!
By George! it makes my old eyes water!—
That is, there's something in this gin
That chokes a fellow. But no matter!

We'll have some music, if you're willing,
And Roger (hem! what a plague a cough is, sir!)
Shall march a little. Start, you villain!
Stand straight! 'Bout face! Salute your officer!
Put up that paw! Dress! Take your rifle!
(Some dogs have arms, you see!) Now hold your
Cap while the gentlemen give a trifle,
To aid a poor old patriot soldier!

March! Halt! Now show how the rebel shakes
When he stands up to hear his sentence.
Now tell us how many drams it takes
To honor a jolly new acquaintance.

Five yelps,—that's five; he's mighty knowing!
  The night's before us, fill the glasses!—
Quick, sir! I'm ill,—my brain is going!
  Some brandy,—thank you,—there!—it passes!

Why not reform? That's easily said,
  But I've gone through such wretched treatment,
Sometimes forgetting the taste of bread,
  And scarce remembering what meat meant,
That my poor stomach's past reform;
  And there are times when, mad with thinking,
I'd sell out heaven for something warm
  To prop a horrible inward sinking.

Is there a way to forget to think?
  At your age, sir, home, fortune, friends,
A dear girl's love,—but I took to drink,—
  The same old story; you know how it ends.
If you could have seen these classic features,—
  You needn't laugh, sir; they were not then
Such a burning libel on God's creatures;
  I was one of your handsome men!

If you had seen her, so fair and young,
  Whose head was happy on this breast!
If you could have heard the songs I sung
  When the wine went round, you wouldn't have
      guessed
That ever I, sir, should be straying
  From door to door, with fiddle and dog,
Ragged and penniless, and playing
  To you to-night for a glass of grog!

She's married since,—a parson's wife;
  'T was better for her that we should part,—

Better the soberest, prosiest life
   Than a blasted home and a broken heart.
I have seen her? Once: I was weak and spent
   On the dusty road; a carriage stopped;
But little she dreamed, as on she went,
   Who kissed the coin that her fingers dropped!

You 've set me talking, sir; I 'm sorry;
   It makes me wild to think of the change!
What do you care for a beggar's story?
   Is it amusing? you find it strange?
I had a mother so proud of me!
   'T was well she died before— Do you know
If the happy spirits in heaven can see
   The ruin and wretchedness here below?

Another glass, and strong, to deaden
   This pain; then Roger and I will start.
I wonder, has he such a lumpish, leaden,
   Aching thing in place of a heart?
He is sad sometimes, and would weep, if he could,
   No doubt, remembering things that were,—
A virtuous kennel, with plenty of food,
   And himself a sober, respectable cur.

I 'm better now; that glass was warming.
   You rascal! limber your lazy feet!
We must be fiddling and performing
   For supper and bed, or starve in the street.
Not a very gay life to lead, you think?
   But soon we shall go where lodgings are free,
And the sleepers need neither victuals nor drink;—
   The sooner the better for Roger and me!

                JOHN TOWNSEND TROWBRIDGE.

FAME.

FROM "AN ESSAY ON MAN," EPISTLE IV.

What 's fame ?—a fancied life in others' breath,
A thing beyond us, e'en before our death.
Just what you hear, you have ; and what 's unknown
The same (my lord) if Tully's, or your own.
All that we feel of it begins and ends
In the small circle of our foes or friends ;
To all beside, as much an empty shade
A Eugene living as a Cæsar dead ;
Alike or when or where they shone or shine,
Or on the Rubicon, or on the Rhine.
A wit 's a feather, and a chief a rod ;
An honest man 's the noblest work of God.
Fame but from death a villain's name can save,
As justice tears his body from the grave ;
When what to oblivion better were resigned
Is hung on high, to poison half mankind.
All fame is foreign, but of true desert ;
Plays round the head, but comes not to the heart :
One self-approving hour whole years outweighs
Of stupid starers and of loud huzzas ;
And more true joy Marcellus exiled feels
Than Cæsar with a senate at his heels.

ALEXANDER POPE.

PELTERS OF PYRAMIDS.

A shoal of idlers, from a merchant craft
Anchored off Alexandria, went ashore,

And mounting asses in their headlong glee,
Round Pompey's Pillar rode with hoots and taunts,
As men oft say, " What art thou more than we ? "
Next in a boat they floated up the Nile,
Singing and drinking, swearing senseless oaths,
Shouting, and laughing most derisively
At all majestic scenes.   A bank they reached,
And clambering up, played gambols among tombs ;
And in portentous ruins (through whose depths,
The mighty twilight of departed Gods,
Both sun and moon glanced furtive, as in awe)
They hid, and whooped, and spat on sacred things.

   At length, beneath the blazing sun they lounge
Near a great Pyramid.   Awhile they stood,
With stupid stare, until resentment grew,
In the recoil of meanness from the vast ;
And gathering stones, they with coarse oaths and
      jibes
(As they would say, " What art thou more than
      we ? ")
Pelted the Pyramid !   But soon these men,
Hot and exhausted, sat them down to drink—
Wrangled, smoked, spat, and laughed, and drowsily
Cursed the bald Pyramid, and fell asleep.

   Night came :—a little sand went drifting by—
And morn again was in the soft blue heavens.
The broad slopes of the shining Pyramid
Looked down in their austere simplicity
Upon the glistening silence of the sands
Whereon no trace of mortal dust was seen.

                    RICHARD HENRY HENGIST HORNE.

ENID'S SONG.

FROM "IDYLS OF THE KING."

TURN, Fortune, turn thy wheel and lower the proud;
Turn thy wild wheel through sunshine, storm, and
    cloud;
Thy wheel and thee we neither love nor hate.

Turn, Fortune, turn thy wheel with smile or frown;
With that wild wheel we go not up or down;
Our hoard is little, but our hearts are great.

Smile and we smile, the lords of many lands;
Frown and we smile, the lords of our own hands;
For man is man and master of his fate.

Turn, turn thy wheel above the staring crowd;
Thy wheel and thou are shadows in the cloud;
Thy wheel and thee we neither love nor hate.

ALFRED, LORD TENNYSON.

FORTUNE.

FROM "FANNY."

BUT Fortune, like some others of her sex,
    Delights in tantalizing and tormenting.
One day we feed upon their smiles,—the next
    Is spent in swearing, sorrowing, and repenting.

  .   .   .   .   .   .

Eve never walked in Paradise more pure
    Than on that morn when Satan played the devil

With her and all her race. A lovesick wooer
Ne'er asked a kinder maiden, or more civil,
Than Cleopatra was to Antony
The day she left him on the Ionian sea.

The serpent—loveliest in his coilèd ring,
With eye that charms, and beauty that outvies
The tints of the rainbow—bears upon his sting
The deadliest venom. Ere the dolphin dies
Its hues are brightest. Like an infant's breath
Are tropic winds before the voice of death

Is heard upon the waters, summoning
The midnight earthquake from its sleep of years
To do its task of woe. The clouds that fling
The lightning brighten ere the bolt appears;
The pantings of the warrior's heart are proud
Upon that battle-morn whose night-dews wet his
    shroud;
The sun is loveliest as he sinks to rest;
The leaves of autumn smile when fading fast;
The swan's last song is sweetest.

FITZ-GREENE HALLECK.

OPPORTUNITY.

HE who bends to himself a joy
Does the wingèd life destroy;
But he who kisses the joy as it flies
Lives in eternity's sunrise.

If you trap the moment before it is ripe,
The tears of repentance you 'll certainly wipe;
But if once you let the ripe moment go,
You can never wipe off the tears of woe.

WILLIAM BLAKE.

OPPORTUNITY.

MASTER of human destinies am I.
Fame, love, and fortune on my footsteps wait.
Cities and fields I walk ; I penetrate
Deserts and seas remote, and passing by
Hovel, and mart, and palace—soon or late
I knock unbidden once at every gate !

If sleeping, wake—if feasting, rise before
I turn away. It is the hour of fate,
And they who follow me reach every state
Mortals desire, and conquer every foe
Save death ; but those who doubt or hesitate,
Condemned to failure, penury, and woe,
Seek me in vain and uselessly implore—
I answer not, and I return no more.

JOHN JAMES INGALLS.

UNDEVELOPED LIVES.

NOT every thought can find its words,
    Not all within is known ;
For minds and hearts have many chords
    That never yield their tone.

Tastes, instincts, feelings, passions, powers,
    Sleep there, unfelt, unseen ;
And other lives lie hid in ours—
    The lives that might have been ;

Affections whose transforming force
    Could mould the heart anew ;

Strong motives that might change the course
　　Of all we think and do.

Upon the tall cliff's cloud-wrapt verge
　　The lonely shepherd stands,
And hears the thundering ocean surge
　　That sweeps the far-off strands ;

And thinks in peace of raging storms
　　Where he will never be—
Of life in all its unknown forms
　　In lands beyond the sea.

So in our dreams some glimpse appears,
　　Though soon it fades again,
How other lands or times or spheres
　　Might make us other men ;

How half our being lies in trance,
　　Nor joy nor sorrow brings,
Unless the hand of circumstance
　　Can touch the latent strings.

We know not fully what we are,
　　Still less what we might be ;
But hear faint voices from the far
　　Dim lands beyond the sea.

　　　　　　　　　　WILLIAM E. H. LECKY.

AUGURY.

I.

A HORSE-SHOE nailed, for luck, upon a mast ;
That mast, wave-bleached, upon the shore was cast !
I saw, and thence no fetich I revered,
But safe, through tempest, to my haven steered.

II.

The place with rose and myrtle was o'ergrown,
Yet Fear and Sorrow held it for their own.
A garden then I sowed without one fear,—
Sowed fennel, yet lived griefless all the year.

III.

Brave lines, long life, did my friend's hand display.
Not so mine own; yet mine is quick to-day.
Once more in his I read Fate's idle jest,
Then fold it down forever on his breast.

EDITH M. THOMAS.

"KEEP SWEET AND KEEP MOVIN'."

HOMELY phrase of our southland bright—
    Keep steady step to the flam of the drum;
Touch to the left—eyes to the right—
    Sing with the soul tho' the lips be dumb.
Hard to be good when the wind's in the east;
    Hard to be gay when the heart is down;
When "they that trouble you are increased,"
    When you look for a smile and see a frown.
        But
        "Keep sweet and keep movin'."

Sorrow will shade the blue sky gray—
    Gray is the color our brothers wore;
Sunshine will scatter the clouds away;
    Azure will gleam in the skies once more.
Colors of Patience and Hope are they—
    Always at even in one they blend;

Tinting the heavens by night and day,
  Over our hearts to the journey's end.
        Just
    " Keep sweet and keep movin'."

Hard to be sweet when the throng is dense,
  When elbows jostle and shoulders crowd ;
Easy to give and to take offence
  When the touch is rough and the voice is loud ;
" Keep to the right " in the city's throng ;
  " Divide the road " on the broad highway ;
There 's one way right when everything 's wrong ;
  " Easy and fair goes far in a day."
        Just
    " Keep sweet and keep movin'."

The quick taunt answers the hasty word—
  The lifetime chance for a " help " is missed ;
The muddiest pool is a fountain stirred,
  A kind hand clenched makes an ugly fist.
When the nerves are tense and the mind is vexed,
  The spark lies close to the magazine ;
Whisper a hope to the soul perplexed—
  Banish the fear with a smile serene —
        Just
    " Keep sweet and keep movin'."

                    ROBERT J. BURDETTE.

A TEAR.

O THAT the chemist's magic art
  Could crystallize this sacred treasure !
Long should it glitter near my heart,
  A secret source of pensive pleasure.

The little brilliant, ere it fell,
　Its lustre caught from Chloe's eye ;
Then, trembling, left its coral cell,—
　The spring of Sensibility !

Sweet drop of pure and pearly light !
　In thee the rays of Virtue shine,
More calmly clear, more mildly bright,
　Than any gem that gilds the mine.

Benign restorer of the soul !
　Who ever fliest to bring relief,
When first we feel the rude control
　Of Love or Pity, Joy or Grief.

The sage's and the poet's theme,
　In every clime, in every age,
Thou charm'st in Fancy's idle dream,
　In Reason's philosophic page.

That very law which moulds a tear,
　And bids it trickle from its source,—
That law preserves the earth a sphere,
　And guides the planets in their course.

　　　　　　　　　SAMUEL ROGERS.

THE JESTER'S SERMON.

The Jester shook his hood and bells, and leaped
　upon a chair ;
The pages laughed, the women screamed, and tossed
　their scented hair ;
The falcon whistled, staghounds bayed, the lapdog
　barked without,
The scullion dropped the pitcher brown, the cook
　railed at the lout ;

The steward, counting out his gold, let pouch and
    money fall,—
And why? because the Jester rose to say grace in
    the hall!

The page played with the heron's plume, the stew-
    ard with his chain;
The butler drummed upon the board, and laughed
    with might and main;
The grooms beat on their metal cans, and roared
    till they were red,—
But still the Jester shut his eyes and rolled his
    witty head,
And when they grew a little still, read half a yard
    of text,
And, waving hand, struck on the desk, then frowned
    like one perplexed.

"Dear sinners all," the fool began, "man's life is but
    a jest,
A dream, a shadow, bubble, air, a vapor at the best.
In a thousand pounds of law I find not a single
    ounce of love;
A blind man killed the parson's cow in shooting at
    the dove;
The fool that eats till he is sick must fast till he is
    well;
The wooer who can flatter most will bear away the
    belle.

" Let no man halloo he is safe till he is through the
    wood;
He who will not when he may, must tarry when he
    should;

He who laughs at crooked men should need walk
  very straight;
O, he who once has won a name may lie abed till
  eight;
Make haste to purchase house and land, be very
  slow to wed;
True coral needs no painter's brush, nor need be
  daubed with red.

" The friar, preaching, cursed the thief (the pudding
  in his sleeve);
To fish for sprats with golden hooks is foolish, by
  your leave;
To travel well,—an ass's ears, hog's mouth, and
  ostrich legs;
He does not care a pin for thieves who limps about
  and begs;
Be always first man at a feast and last man at a
  fray;
The short way round, in spite of all, is still the
  longest way;
When the hungry curate licks the knife, there's not
  much for the clerk;
When the pilot, turning pale and sick, looks up—
  the storm grows dark."

Then loud they laughed; the fat cook's tears ran
  down into the pan;
The steward shook, that he was forced to drop the
  brimming can;
And then again the women screamed, and every
  staghound bayed,—
And why? because the motley fool so wise a sermon made.
                    GEORGE WALTER THORNBURY.

THE FOOL'S PRAYER.

THE royal feast was done ; the King
  Sought some new sport to banish care,
And to his jester cried : " Sir Fool,
  Kneel now, and make for us a prayer ! "

The jester doffed his cap and bells,
  And stood the mocking court before ;
They could not see the bitter smile
  Behind the painted grin he wore.

He bowed his head, and bent his knee
  Upon the monarch's silken stool ;
His pleading voice arose : " O Lord,
  Be merciful to me, a fool !

" No pity, Lord, could change the heart
  From red with wrong to white as wool :
The rod must heal the sin ; but, Lord,
  Be merciful to me, a fool !

" 'T is not by guilt the onward sweep
  Of truth and right, O Lord, we stay ;
'T is by our follies that so long
  We hold the earth from heaven away.

" These clumsy feet, still in the mire,
  Go crushing blossoms without end ;
These hard, well-meaning hands we thrust
  Among the heart-strings of a friend.

" The ill-timed truth we might have kept—
  Who knows how sharp it pierced and stung !

The word we had not sense to say—
　Who knows how grandly it had rung!

" Our faults no tenderness should ask,
　The chastening stripes must cleanse them all ;
But for our blunders—oh, in shame
　Before the eyes of heaven we fall.

" Earth bears no balsam for mistakes ;
　Men crown the knave, and scourge the tool
That did his will ; but Thou, O Lord,
　Be merciful to me, a fool."

The room was hushed ; in silence rose
　The King, and sought his gardens cool,
And walked apart, and murmured low,
　" Be merciful to me, a fool! "
　　　　　　　　　　EDWARD ROWLAND SILL.

AT MIDSUMMER.

THE spacious Noon enfolds me with its peace—
　The affluent Midsummer wraps me round—
　So still the earth and air, that scarce a sound
Affronts the silence, and the swift caprice
Of one stray bird's lone call does but increase
　The sense of some compelling hush profound,
　Some spell by which the whole vast world is bound,
Till star-crowned Night smile downward its release.

I sit and dream—midway of the long day—
　Midway of the glad year—midway of life—
　　My whole world seems, indeed, to hold its
　　　　breath :—

For me the sun stands still upon his way—
　The winds for one short hour remit their strife—
　　Then Day, and Year, and Life whirl on toward
　　　Death.

LOUISE CHANDLER MOULTON.

A SUNRISE SONG.

YOUNG palmer sun, that to the shining sands
　Pourest thy pilgrim's tale, discoursing still
Thy silver passages of sacred lands,
　With news of Sepulchre and Dolorous Hill,

Canst thou be he that, Yester-Sunset warm,
　Purple with Paynim rage and wrack-desire,
Dashed ravening out of a dusty lair of storm,
　Harried the west, and set the world on fire?

Hast thou perchance repented, Saracen Sun?
　Wilt warm the world with peace and dove-desire?
Or wilt thou, ere this very day be done,
　Blaze Saladin still, with unforgiving fire?

SIDNEY LANIER.

ILLUSIONS.

Go stand at night upon an ocean craft,
And watch the folds of its imperial train
Catching in fleecy foam a thousand glows—
A miracle of fire unquenched by sea.
There in bewildering turbulence of change
Whirls the whole firmament, till as you gaze,

All else unseen, it is as heaven itself
Had lost its poise, and each unanchored star
In phantom haste flees to the horizon line.

What dupes we are of the deceiving eye!
How many a light men wonderingly acclaim
Is but the phosphor of the path Life makes
With its own motion, while above, forgot,
Sweep on serene the old unenvious stars!

ROBERT UNDERWOOD JOHNSON.

PROEM.

FROM "THE ISLES OF THE AMAZONS," PART III.

Come, lovers, come, forget your pains!
　　I know upon this earth a spot
Where clinking coins, that clank as chains
　　Upon the souls of men, are not;
Nor man is measured for his gains
Of gold that stream with crimson stains.

There snow-topped towers crush the clouds,
　　And break the still abode of stars,
Like sudden ghosts in snowy shrouds,
　　New broken through their earthly bars,
And condors whet their crooked beaks
On lofty limits of the peaks.

O men that fret as frets the main!
　　You irk me with your eager gaze
　　Down in the earth for fat increase—
Eternal talks of gold and gain,
　　Your shallow wit, your shallow ways,

And breaks my soul across the shoal
As breakers break on shallow seas.

JOAQUIN MILLER.

A CALIFORNIA CHRISTMAS.

BEHOLD where Beauty walks with Peace!
Behold where Plenty pours her horn
Of fruits, of flowers, fat increase,
As generous as light of morn.

Green Shasta, San Diego, seas
Of bloom and green between them rolled.
Great herds in grasses to their knees,
And green earth garmented in gold.

White peaks that prop the sapphire blue
Look down on Edens, such as when
That fair, first spot perfection knew
And God walked perfect earth with men.

I say God's kingdom is at hand
Right here, if we but lift our eyes ;
I say there lies no line or land
Between this land and Paradise.

JOAQUIN MILLER.

YUSSOUF.

A STRANGER came one night to Yussouf's tent,
Saying, " Behold one outcast and in dread,
Against whose life the bow of power is bent,
Who flies, and hath not where to lay his head ;

I come to thee for shelter and for food,
To Yussouf, called through all our tribes 'The
  Good.'"

"This tent is mine," said Yussouf, "but no more
Than it is God's; come in, and be at peace;
Freely shalt thou partake of all my store
As I of his who buildeth over these
Oûr tents his glorious roof of night and day,
And at whose door none ever yet heard Nay."

So Yussouf entertained his guest that night,
And, waking him ere day, said: "Here is gold,
My swiftest horse is saddled for thy flight,
Depart before the prying day grow bold."
As one lamp lights another, nor grows less,
So nobleness enkindleth nobleness.

That inward light the stranger's face made grand,
Which shines from all self-conquest; kneeling low,
He bowed his forehead upon Yussouf's hand,
Sobbing: "O Sheik, I cannot leave thee so;
I will repay thee; all this thou hast done
Unto that Ibrahim who slew thy son!"

"Take thrice the gold," said Yussouf, "for with thee
Into the desert, never to return,
My one black thought shall ride away from me;
First-born, for whom by day and night I yearn,
Balanced and just are all of God's decrees;
Thou art avenged, my first-born, sleep in peace!"

JAMES RUSSELL LOWELL.

BEAUTY.

FROM "AN HYMNE IN HONOR OF BEAUTIE."

So every spirit, as it is most pure,
And hath in it the more of heavenly light,
So it the fairer bodie doth procure
To habit in, and it more fairly dight
With cheerfull grace and amiable sight ;
For of the soule the bodie forme doth take ;
For soule is forme, and doth the bodie make.

Therefore whenever that thou dost behold
A comely corpse, with beauty fair endued,
Know this for certaine, that the same doth hold
A beauteous soule, with fair conditions thewed,
Fit to receive the seed of virtue strewed ;
For all that faire is, is by nature good ;
That is a signe to know the gentle blood.

Yet oft it falls that many a gentle minde
Dwells in deformèd tabernacle drowned,
Either by chance, against the course of kinde,
Or through unaptnesse in the substance found,
Which it assumèd of some stubborne ground,
That will not yield unto her forme's direction,
But is performed with some foul imperfection.

And oft it falls (aye me, the more to rue !)
That goodly beautie, albeit heavenly borne,
Is foul abused, and that celestial hue,
Which doth the world with her delight adorne,
Made but the bait of sin, and sinners' scorne,

Whilst every one doth seek and sue to have it,
But every one doth seek but to deprave it.

Yet nathèmore is that faire beautie's blame,
But theirs that do abuse it unto ill:
Nothing so goode, but that through guilty shame
May be corrupt, and wrested unto will:
Natheless the soule is faire and beauteous stille,
However fleshe's fault it filthy make;
For things immortal no corruption take.

EDMUND SPENSER.

BEAUTY UNADORNED.

FROM " ELEGIES " BOOK I. II.

DEAR girl, what boots it thus to dress thy hair,
Or flaunt in silken garment rich and rare,
To reek of perfume from a foreign mart,
And pass thyself for other than thou art—
Thus Nature's gift of beauty to deface
And rob thy own fair form of half its grace?
Trust me, no skill can greater charms impart:
Love is a naked boy and scorns all art.
Bears not the sod unbidden blossoms rare?
The untrained ivy, is it not most fair?
Greenest the shrub on rocks untended grows,
Brightest the rill in unhewn channel flows.
The beach is with unpolished pebbles gay,
And birds untutored trill the sweetest lay.
Not thus the damsels of the golden age
Were wont the hearts of heroes to engage:
Their loveliness was to no jewels due,
But to such tints as once Apelles drew.

From vain coquettish arts they all were free,
Content to charm with simple modesty.
By thee despite to me will ne'er be done;
The woman pleases well who pleases one.

From the Latin of PROPERTIUS.
Translation of GOLDWIN SMITH.

FORTUNE.

'TWIXT good and ill my wavering fortune see
Swayed in capricious instability,
Most like the moon, whose ceaseless wax and wane
Cannot two nights the self-same form retain;
Viewless at first, then a dim streak revealed,
Then slow augmenting to an argent shield;
And when at length to fair perfection brought,
Diminishing and dwindling quite to nought.

From the Greek of SOPHOCLES.
Translation of RICHARD GARNETT.

GREATNESS.

FROM "AN ESSAY ON MAN," EPISTLE IV.

HONOR and shame from no condition rise;
Act well your part, there all the honor lies.
Fortune in men has some small difference made,
One flaunts in rags, one flutters in brocade;
The cobbler aproned, and the parson gowned,
The friar hooded, and the monarch crowned.
" What differ more (you cry) than crown and cowl?"
I 'll tell you, friend; a wise man and a fool.

You 'll find, if once the monarch acts the monk,
Or, cobbler-like, the parson will be drunk,
Worth makes the man, and want of it the fellow ;
The rest is all but leather or prunella.
  Stuck o'er with titles, and hung round with strings,
That thou mayst be by kings, or whores of kings ;
Boast the pure blood of an illustrious race,
In quiet flow from Lucrece to Lucrece ;
But by your fathers' worth if yours you rate,
Count me those only who were good and great.
Go ! if your ancient but ignoble blood
Has crept through scoundrels ever since the flood,
Go ! and pretend your family is young,
Nor own your fathers have been fools so long.
What can ennoble sots, or slaves, or cowards ?
Alas ! not all the blood of all the Howards.

.   .   .   .   .   .

Who wickedly is wise, or madly brave,
Is but the more a fool, the more a knave.
Who noble ends by noble means obtains,
Or, failing, smiles in exile or in chains,
Like good Aurelius let him reign, or bleed
Like Socrates, that man is great indeed.

                              ALEXANDER POPE.

PERSEVERANCE.

In facile natures fancies quickly grow,
But such quick fancies have but little root.
Soon the narcissus flowers and dies, but slow
The tree whose blossoms shall mature to fruit.

Grace is a moment's happy feeling, Power
A life's slow growth; and we for many an hour
Must strain and toil, and wait and weep, if we
The perfect fruit of all we are would see.

From the Italian of LEONARDO DA VINCI.
Translation of WILLIAM WETMORE STORY.

THE ONE WHITE HAIR.

THE wisest of the wise
Listen to pretty lies,
   And love to hear them told ;
Doubt not that Solomon
Listened to many a one,—
Some in his youth, and more when he grew old.

I never sat among
The choir of Wisdom's song,
   But pretty lies loved I
As much as any king,—
When youth was on the wing,
And (must it then be told ?) when youth had quite
      gone by.

Alas ! and I have not
The pleasant hour forgot,
   When one pert lady said,—
"O Landor ! I am quite
Bewildered with affright ;
I see (sit quiet now !) a white hair on your head ! "

Another, more benign,
Drew out that hair of mine,
   And in her own dark hair

Pretended she had found
That one, and twirled it round.—
Fair as she was, she never was so fair.

WALTER SAVAGE LANDOR.

———

GROWING GRAY.

"On a l'âge de son cœur."—A. D'HOUDETOT.

A LITTLE more toward the light.
Me miserum.   Here's one that's white,
      And one that's turning;
Adieu to song and "salad days."
My Muse, let's go at once to Jay's
      And order mourning.

We must reform our rhymes, my dear,
Renounce the gay for the severe,—
      Be grave, not witty;
We have no more the right to find
That Pyrrha's hair is neatly twined,
      That Chloe 's pretty.

Young Love 's for us a farce that 's played;
Light canzonet and serenade
      No more may tempt us;
Gray hairs but ill accord with dreams;
From aught but sour didactic themes
      Our years exempt us.

"*À la bonne heure!*"   You fancy so?
You think for one white streak we grow
      At once satiric?

A fiddlestick ! Each hair 's a string
To which our graybeard Muse shall sing
    A younger lyric.

Our heart 's still sound. Shall " cakes and ale "
Grow rare to youth because we rail
    At school-boy dishes ?
Perish the thought ! 'T is ours to sing,
Though neither Time nor Tide can bring
    Belief with wishes.

AUSTIN DOBSON.

HEALTHFUL OLD AGE.

FROM " AS YOU LIKE IT," ACT II. SC. 2.

ADAM.—Let me be your servant ;
Though I look old, yet am I strong and lusty :
For in my youth I never did apply
Hot and rebellious liquors in my blood ;
Nor did not with unbashful forehead woo
The means of weakness and debility.
Therefore my age is as a lusty winter,
Frosty, but kindly : let me go with you ;
I 'll do the service of a younger man
In all your business and necessities.

SHAKESPEARE.

QUACK MEDICINES.

FROM " THE BOROUGH."

BUT now our Quacks are gamesters, and they play
With craft and skill to ruin and betray ;

With monstrous promise they delude the mind,
And thrive on all that tortures human-kind.
  Void of all honor, avaricious, rash,
The daring tribe compound their boasted trash,—
Tincture or syrup, lotion, drop or pill ;
All tempt the sick to trust the lying bill ;
And twenty names of cobblers turned to squires
Aid the bold language of these blushless liars.
There are among them those who cannot read,
And yet they 'll buy a patent, and succeed ;
Will dare to promise dying sufferers aid,
For who, when dead, can threaten or upbraid ?
With cruel avarice still they recommend
More draughts, more syrup, to the journey's end.
" I feel it not."   " Then take it every hour."
" It makes me worse."   " Why, then it shows its
    power "
" I fear to die."   " Let not your spirits sink,
You 're always safe while you believe and drink."

        .   .   .   .   .

  Troubled with something in your bile or blood,
You think your doctor does you little good ;
And, grown impatient, you require in haste
The nervous cordial, nor dislike the taste ;
It comforts, heals, and strengthens ; nay, you think
It makes you better every time you drink ;
Who tipples brandy will some comfort feel,
But will he to the medicine set his seal ?

        .   .   .   .   .

No class escapes them—from the poor man's pay
The nostrum takes no trifling part away ;
See ! those square patent bottles from the shop
Now decoration to the cupboard's top ;

And there a favorite hoard you 'll find within,
Companions meet! the julep and the gin.

.   .   .   .

Observe what ills to nervous females flow,
When the heart flutters and the pulse is low ;
If once induced these cordial sips to try,
All feel the ease, and few the danger fly ;
For, while obtained, of drams they 've all the force,
And when denied, then drams are the resource.
Who would not lend a sympathizing sigh,
To hear yon infant's pity-moving cry ?
Then the good nurse (who, had she borne a brain,
Had sought the cause that made her babe complain)
Has all her efforts, loving soul ! applied
To set the cry, and not the cause, aside ;
She gave her powerful sweet without remorse,
The sleeping cordial,—she had tried its force,
Repeating oft; the infant, freed from pain,
Rejected food, but took the dose again,
Sinking to sleep, while she her joy expressed,
That her dear charge could sweetly take his rest.
Soon may she spare her cordial; not a doubt
Remains but quickly he will rest without.

GEORGE CRABBE.

THE THREE WARNINGS.

THE tree of deepest root is found
Least willing still to quit the ground ;
'T was therefore said by ancient sages,
That love of life increased with years
So much, that in our latter stages,
When pains grow sharp and sickness rages,
The greatest love of life appears.

This great affection to believe,
Which all confess, but few perceive,
If old assertions can't prevail,
Be pleased to hear a modern tale.

When sports went round, and all were gay,
On neighbor Dodson's wedding-day,
Death called aside the jocund groom
With him into another room,
And, looking grave, " You must," says he,
" Quit your sweet bride, and come with me."
" With you ! and quit my Susan's side ?
With you !" the hapless husband cried ;
" Young as I am, 't is monstrous hard !
Besides, in truth, I 'm not prepared :
My thoughts on other matters go ;
This is my wedding-day, you know."

What more he urged I have not heard,
    His reasons could not well be stronger ;
So Death the poor delinquent spared,
    And left to live a little longer.
Yet calling up a serious look,
His hour-glass trembled while he spoke—
" Neighbor," he said, " farewell ! no more
Shall Death disturb your mirthful hour ;
And further, to avoid all blame
Of cruelty upon my name,
To give you time for preparation,
And fit you for your future station,
Three several warnings you shall have,
Before you 're summoned to the grave ;
Willing for once I 'll quit my prey,
    And grant a kind reprieve,

In hopes you 'll have no more to say,
But when I call again this way,
　Well pleased the world will leave."
To these conditions both consented,
And parted perfectly contented.

What next the hero of our tale befell,
How long he lived, how wise, how well,
How roundly he pursued his course,
And smoked his pipe, and stroked his horse,
The willing muse shall tell:
He chaffered then, he bought and sold,
Nor once perceived his growing old,
Nor thought of Death as near:
His friends not false, his wife no shrew,
Many his gains, his children few,
　He passed his hours in peace.
But while he viewed his wealth increase,
While thus along life's dusty road
The beaten track content he trod,
Old Time, whose haste no mortal spares,
Uncalled, unheeded, unawares,
　Brought on his eightieth year.
And now, one night, in musing mood,
　As all alone he sate,
The unwelcome messenger of Fate
　Once more before him stood.

Half killed with anger and surprise,
" So soon returned!" Old Dodson cries.
" So soon, d' ye call it!" Death replies;
" Surely, my friend, you 're but in jest!
　Since I was here before

'T is six-and-thirty years at least,
And you are now fourscore."

" So much the worse," the clown rejoined ;
" To spare the aged would be kind :
However, see your search be legal ;
And your authority,—is 't regal ?
Else you are come on a fool's errand,
With but a secretary's warrant.
Beside, you promised me three warnings,
Which I have looked for nights and mornings ;
But for that loss of time and ease
I can recover damages."

" I know," cries Death, " that at the best
I seldom am a welcome guest ;
But don't be captious, friend, at least :
I little thought you 'd still be able
To stump about your farm and stable :
Your years have run to a great length ;
I wish you joy, though, of your strength ! "

" Hold," says the farmer, " not so fast !
I have been lame these four years past."
" And no great wonder," Death replies :
" However, you still keep your eyes ;
And sure, to see one's loves and friends
For legs and arms would make amends."
" Perhaps," says Dodson, " so it might,
But latterly I 've lost my sight."
" This is a shocking tale, 't is true ;
But still there 's comfort left for you :
Each strives your sadness to amuse ;
I warrant you hear all the news."

" There 's none," cries he ; " and if there were,
I 'm grown so deaf, I could not hear."
    " Nay, then," the spectre stern rejoined,
" These are unjustifiable yearnings :
If you are lame and deaf and blind,
You 've had your three sufficient warnings ;
So come along, no more we 'll part."
He said, and touched him with his dart.
And now, Old Dodson, turning pale,
Yields to his fate,—so ends my tale.

HESTER LYNCH THRALE.

OLD AGE AND DEATH

FROM "VERSES UPON HIS DIVINE POESY."

The seas are quiet when the winds give o'er ;
So calm are we when passions are no more.
For then we know how vain it was to boast
Of fleeting things, too certain to be lost.
Clouds of affection from our younger eyes
Conceal that emptiness which age descries.

The soul's dark cottage, battered and decayed,
Lets in new light through chinks that time has made :
Stronger by weakness, wiser men become,
As they draw near to their eternal home.
Leaving the old, both worlds at once they view,
That stand upon the threshold of the new.

EDMUND WALLER.

THE RULING PASSION.

FROM "MORAL ESSAYS," EPISTLE I.

SEARCH thou the ruling passion; there, alone,
The wild are constant, and the cunning known;
The fool consistent and the false sincere;
Priests, princes, women, no dissemblers here.

. . . . . .

In this the lust, in that the avarice,
Were means, not ends; ambition was the vice.

. . . . . .

In this one passion man can strength enjoy,
As fits give vigor just when they destroy.
Time, that on all things lays his lenient hand,
Yet tames not this; it sticks to our last sand.
Consistent in our follies and our sins,
Here honest Nature ends as she begins.
    Old politicians chew on wisdom past,
And totter on in business to the last;
As weak, as earnest; and as gravely out,
As sober Lanesborough dancing in the gout.
    Behold a reverend sire, whom want of grace
Has made the father of a nameless race,
Shoved from the wall perhaps, or rudely pressed
By his own son, that passes by unblessed:
Still to his wench he crawls on knocking knees,
And envies every sparrow that he sees.
    A salmon's belly, Helluo, was thy fate.
The doctor, called, declares all help too late.
"Mercy!" cries Helluo, "mercy on my soul!
Is there no hope?—Alas!—then bring the jowl."

The frugal crone, whom praying priests attend,
Still tries to save the hallowed taper's end,
Collects her breath, as ebbing life retires,
For one puff more, and in that puff expires.
"Odious! in woollen! 't would a saint provoke,"
Were the last words that poor Narcissa spoke;
" No, let a charming chintz and Brussels lace
Wrap my cold limbs, and shade my lifeless face:
One would not, sure, be frightful when one 's dead,—
And—Betty—give this cheek a little red."
The courtier smooth, who forty years had shined
An humble servant to all human-kind,
Just brought out this, when scarce his tongue could
 stir,
" If—where I 'm going—I could serve you, sir?"
" I give and I devise" (old Euclio said,
And sighed) " my lands and tenements to Ned."
Your money, sir? " My money, sir! what, all?
Why—if I must " (then wept)—" I give it Paul."
The manor, sir? " The manor, hold! " he cried,
" Not that,—I cannot part with that,"—and died.
And you, brave Cobham! to the latest breath
Shall feel your ruling passion strong in death;
Such in those moments as in all the past,
" O, save my country, Heaven! " shall be your last.
       ALEXANDER POPE.

THE WILL.

Before I sigh my last gasp, let me breathe,
Great Love, some legacies: here I bequeathe
Mine eyes to Argus, if mine eyes can see,
If they be blind, then, Love, I give them thee;

My tongue to Fame, to embassadors my ears ;
    To women, or the sea, my tears ;
    Thou, Love, hast taught me heretofore
By making me serve her who had twenty more,
That I should give to none, but such as had too
    much before.

My constancy I to the planets give ;
My truth to them who at the court do live ;
Mine ingenuity and openness
To Jesuits ; to buffoons my pensiveness ;
My silence to any who abroad have been ;
    My money to a Capuchin.
    Thou, Love, taught'st me, by appointing me
    To love there, where no love received can be,
Only to give to such as have an incapacity.

My faith I give to Roman Catholics ;
All my good works unto the schismatics
Of Amsterdam ; my best civility
And courtship to an University ;
My modesty I give to shoulders bare ;
    My patience let gamesters share.
    Thou, Love, taught'st me, by making me
    Love her, that holds my love disparity,
Only to give to those that count my gifts indignity.

I give my reputation to those
Which were my friends ; mine industry to foes ;
To schoolmen I bequeathe my doubtfulness ;
My sickness to physicians, or excess ;
To Nature all that I in rhyme have writ ;
    And to my company my wit.
    Thou, Love, by making me adore

Her, who begot this love in me before,
Taught'st me to make, as though I gave, when I do
   but restore.

To him, for whom the passing-bell next tolls,
I give my physic-books ; my written rolls
Of moral counsels I to Bedlam give :
My brazen medals unto them which live
In want of bread ; to them which pass among
      All foreigners, mine English tongue.
   Thou, Love, by making me love one
   Who thinks her friendship a fit portiòn
For younger lovers, dost my gifts thus dispropor-
      tion.

Therefore I 'll give no more, but I 'll undo
The world by dying ; because Love dies too.
Then all your beauties will be no more worth
Than gold in mines, where none doth draw it forth ;
And all your graces no more use shall have,
      Than a sun-dial in a grave.
   Thou, Love, taught'st me, by making me
   Love her, who doth neglect both me and thee,
To invent and practise this one way to annihilate all
      three.

DR. JOHN DONNE.

TO A SKELETON.

[The MS. of this poem, which appeared in 1820, was said to have been found in the Museum of the Royal College of Surgeons, in London, near a perfect human skeleton. It was published in the *Morning Chronicle.* The author was never discovered, although a reward of fifty guineas was offered.]

BEHOLD this ruin !   'T was a skull
Once of ethereal spirit full.
This narrow cell was Life's retreat ;
This space was Thought's mysterious seat.
What beauteous visions filled this spot !
What dreams of pleasure long forgot !
Nor hope, nor joy, nor love, nor fear
Has left one trace of record here.

Beneath this moldering canopy
Once shone the bright and busy eye :
But start not at the dismal void,—
If social love that eye employed,
If with no lawless fire it gleamed,
But through the dews of kindness beamed,
That eye shall be forever bright
When stars and sun are sunk in night.

Within this hollow cavern hung
The ready, swift, and tuneful tongue :
If Falsehood's honey it disdained,
And when it could not praise was chained ;
If bold in Virtue's cause it spoke,
Yet gentle concord never broke,—

This silent tongue shall plead for thee
When Time unveils Eternity !

Say, did these fingers delve the mine,
Or with the envied rubies shine ?
To hew the rock, or wear a gem,
Can little now avail to them ;
But if the page of Truth they sought,
Or comfort to the mourner brought,
These hands a richer meed shall claim
Than all that wait on Wealth and Fame.

Avails it whether bare or shod
These feet the paths of duty trod ?
If from the bowers of Ease they fled,
To seek Affliction's humble shed ;
If Grandeur's guilty bribe they spurned,
And home to Virtue's cot returned,—
These feet with angel wings shall vie,
And tread the palace of the sky !

ANONYMOUS.

THE TRUE PHILOSOPHY OF LIFE.

Full oft I muse and hes in thocht.

THE passage of the speeding year,
And Fortune with her changing cheer,
   Are ills on ilka hand confest ;
We will not mourn for that, my dear,
   But to be blythe we 'll count it best.

Fast as this warld fleets awa'
As fast her wheel does Fortune ca',
   At no time tired or takin' rest :
What then ? the limmer 's owre us a',
   And to be blythe, I think it best.

Would pampered man consider weel,
Ere Fortune on him turn her wheel,
  That earthly honour canna lest,
His fa' less painfu' he would feel:
  But to be blythe I think it best.

Wha would wi' this dour warld strive
Will a' his days in dolour drive,
  An', tho' he stood o' lands possest,
He couldna weel be said to live,
  He 's only *tholin'* at the best.

Wi' a' the treasure i' the earth
What profit is there, wantin' mirth?
  Wi' a' the craps o' east an' west,
Without contentment there is dearth:
  So to be blythe is surely best.

Let nane for tinsel droop an' dee,
The thing is but a vanitee;
  And to the life that aye shall lest
Here 's out the twinkling of an ee:
  So to be blythe I think it best.

Had I, because my lot is puir,
Tint heart an' hope, an' harboured fear,
  An' been wi' carried cares opprest,
I had been dead langsyne, I 'm sure;
  But to be blythe I think it best.

However Fortune change an' veer,
Let 's blythely live as lang 's we 're here;
  An' yet be ready and addrest
To pass content, without a tear,
  Believin' a' thing for the best.

WILLIAM DUNBAR.
Modernized by HUGH HALIBURTON.

III.

MEMORY.

———

BLEST MEMORY.

FROM "THE PLEASURES OF MEMORY."

ETHEREAL power! who at the noon of night
Recall'st the far fled spirit of delight;
From whom that musing, melancholy mood
Which charms the wise, and elevates the good;
Blest Memory, hail! O grant the grateful muse,
Her pencil dipped in nature's living hues,
To pass the clouds that round thy empire roll,
And trace its airy precincts in the soul.
  Lulled in the countless chambers of the brain,
Our thoughts are linked by many a hidden chain.
Awake but one, and lo, what myriads rise!
Each stamps its image as the other flies!
Each, as the various avenues of sense
Delight or sorrow to the soul dispense,
Brightens or fades; yet all, with magic art,
Control the latent fibres of the heart.
As studious Prospero's mysterious spell
Drew every subject spirit to his cell,
Each, at thy call, advances or retires,
As judgment dictates, or the scene inspires.

301

Each thrills the seat of sense, that sacred source
Whence the fine nerves direct their mazy course,
And through the frame invisibly convey
The subtle, quick vibrations as they play.

Hail, Memory, hail! in thy exhaustless mine
From age to age unnumbered treasures shine!
Thought and her shadowy brood thy call obey,
And place and time are subject to thy sway!
Thy pleasures most we feel when most alone;
The only pleasures we can call our own.
Lighter than air, hope's summer visions die,
If but a fleeting cloud obscure the sky;
If but a beam of sober reason play,
Lo, fancy's fairy frost-work melts away!
But can the wiles of art, the grasp of power,
Snatch the rich relics of a well spent hour?
These, when the trembling spirit wings her flight
Pour round her path a stream of living light;
And gild those pure and perfect realms of rest,
Where virtue triumphs, and her sons are blest!

SAMUEL ROGERS.

SUDDEN LIGHT.

I HAVE been here before,
    But when or how I cannot tell:
I know the grass beyond the door,
    The sweet keen smell,
The sighing sound, the lights around the shore.

You have been mine before,—
    How long ago I may not know:

But just when at that swallow's soar
  Your neck turned so,
Some veil did fall,—I knew it all of yore.

Has this been thus before?
  And shall not thus time's eddying flight
Still with our lives our love restore
  In death's despite,
And day and night yield one delight once more?

DANTE GABRIEL ROSSETTI.

PRE–EXISTENCE.

WHILE sauntering through the crowded street,
Some half-remembered face I meet,

Albeit upon no mortal shore
That face, methinks, has smiled before.

Lost in a gay and festal throng,
I tremble at some tender song,—

Set to an air whose golden bars
I must have heard in other stars.

In sacred aisles I pause to share
The blessings of a priestly prayer,—

When the whole scene which greets mine eyes
In some strange mode I recognize

As one whose every mystic part
I feel prefigured in my heart.

At sunset, as I calmly stand,
A stranger on an alien strand,

Familiar as my childhood's home
Seems the long stretch of wave and foam.

One sails toward me o'er the bay,
And what he comes to do and say

I can foretell.   A prescient lore
Springs from some life outlived of yore.

O swift, instinctive, startling gleams
Of deep soul-knowledge! not as *dreams*

For aye ye vaguely dawn and die,
But oft with lightning certainty

Pierce through the dark, oblivious brain,
To make old thoughts and memories plain,

Thoughts which perchance must travel back
Across the wild, bewildering track

Of countless æons ; memories far,
High-reaching as yon pallid star,

Unknown, scarce seen, whose flickering grace
Faints on the outmost rings of space !

PAUL HAMILTON HAYNE.

ONCE BEFORE.

ONCE before, this self-same air
Passed me, though I know not where.

Strange ! how very like it came !
Touch and fragrance were the same ;
Sound of mingled voices, too,
With a light laugh ringing through ;
Some one moving,—here or there,—
Some one passing up the stair,
Some one calling from without,
Or a far-off childish shout,—
Simple, home-like, nothing more,
Yet it all hath been before !

No : not to-day, nor yesterday,
Nor any day ! But far away—
So long ago, so very far,
It might have been on other star.
How was it spent ? and where ? and when ?
This life that went, yet comes again ?
Was sleep its world, or death its shore ?
I still the silent Past implore.
Ah ! never dream had power to show
Such vexing glimpse of Long Ago.
Never a death could follow death
With love between, and home, and breath.

The spell has passed. What spendthrifts we,
Of simple, household certainty !
What golden grain we trample low
Searching for flowers that never grow !
Why, home is real, and love is real ;
Nor false our honest high ideal.
Life,—it is bounding, warm, and strong,—
And all my heart resounds with song.
It must be true, whate'er befall,
This and the world to come are all.

And yet it puzzles me—alack!—
When life that could not be, comes back!

MARY MAPES DODGE.

A LOST CHORD.

SEATED one day at the organ,
    I was weary and ill at ease,
And my fingers wandered idly
    Over the noisy keys.

I do not know what I was playing,
    Or what I was dreaming then,
But I struck one chord of music,
    Like the sound of a great Amen.

It flooded the crimson twilight,
    Like the close of an angel's psalm,
And it lay on my fevered spirit,
    With a touch of infinite calm.

It quieted pain and sorrow,
    Like love overcoming strife;
It seemed the harmonious echo
    From our discordant life.

It linked all perplexed meanings
    Into one perfect peace,
And trembled away into silence,
    As if it were loath to cease.

I have sought, but I seek it vainly,
    That one lost chord divine,

That came from the soul of the organ,
   And entered into mine.

It may be that Death's bright angel
   Will speak in that chord again ;
It may be that only in heaven
   I shall hear that grand Amen.

                ADELAIDE ANNE PROCTER.

THE CLOSING YEAR.

'T is midnight's holy hour,—and silence now
Is brooding like a gentle spirit o'er
The still and pulseless world. Hark ! on the winds
The bell's deep tones are swelling,—'t is the knell
Of the departed year. No funeral train
Is sweeping past ; yet, on the stream and wood,
With melancholy light, the moonbeams rest
Like a pale, spotless shroud ; the air is stirred
As by a mourner's sigh ; and on yon cloud
That floats so still and placidly through heaven,
The spirits of the seasons seem to stand,—
Young Spring, bright Summer, Autumn's solemn
    form,
And Winter with its aged locks,—and breathe,
In mournful cadences that come abroad
Like the far wind-harp's wild and touching wail,
A melancholy dirge o'er the dead year,
Gone from the earth forever.

                    'T is a time
For memory and for tears. Within the deep,
Still chambers of the heart, a spectre dim,

Whose tones are like the wizard's voice of Time
Heard from the tomb of ages, points its cold
And solemn finger to the beautiful
And holy visions that have passed away,
And left no shadow of their loveliness
On the dead waste of life. That spectre lifts
The coffin-lid of Hope and Joy and Love,
And bending mournfully above the pale,
Sweet forms that slumber there, scatters dead
    flowers
O 'er what has passed to nothingness.

                              The year
Has gone, and with it, many a glorious throng
Of happy dreams. Its mark is on each brow,
Its shadow in each heart. In its swift course
It waved its sceptre o'er the beautiful,
And they are not. It laid its pallid hand
Upon the strong man, and the haughty form
Is fallen, and the flashing eye is dim.
It trod the hall of revelry, where thronged
The bright and joyous, and the tearful wail
Of stricken ones is heard where erst the song
And reckless shout resounded.

                           It passed o'er
The battle-plain where sword and spear and shield
Flashed in the light of midday, and the strength
Of serried hosts is shivered, and the grass,
Green from the soil of carnage, waves above
The crushed and moldering skeleton. It came,
And faded like a wreath of mist at eve ;
Yet ere it melted in the viewless air
It heralded its millions to their home
In the dim land of dreams.

Remorseless Time !
Fierce spirit of the glass and scythe !—what power
Can stay him in his silent course, or melt
His iron heart to pity ? On, still on,
He presses, and forever. The proud bird,
The condor of the Andes, that can soar
Through heaven's unfathomable depths, or brave
The fury of the northern hurricane,
And bathe his plumage in the thunder's home,
Furls his broad wings at nightfall, and sinks down
To rest upon his mountain crag,—but Time
Knows not the weight of sleep or weariness,
And night's deep darkness has no chain to bind
His rushing pinions.

Revolutions sweep
O'er earth, like troubled visions o'er the breast
Of dreaming sorrow ; cities rise and sink
Like bubbles on the water ; fiery isles
Spring blazing from the ocean, and go back
To their mysterious caverns ; mountains rear
To heaven their bald and blackened cliffs, and bow
Their tall heads to the plain ; new empires rise,
Gathering the strength of hoary centuries,
And rush down like the Alpine avalanche,
Startling the nations ; and the very stars,
Yon bright and burning blazonry of God,
Glitter awhile in their eternal depths,
And, like the Pleiads, loveliest of their train,
Shoot from their glorious spheres, and pass away
To darkle in the trackless void,—yet Time,
Time the tomb-builder, holds his fierce career,
Dark, stern, all-pitiless, and pauses not
Amid the mighty wrecks that strew his path

To sit and muse, like other conquerors,
Upon the fearful ruin he has wrought.

GEORGE DENISON PRENTICE.

ROMA.

FROM "POESIE."

GIVE to the wind thy locks; all glittering
Thy sea-blue eyes, and thy white bosom bared,
Mount to thy chariot, while in speechless roaring
Terror and Force before thee clear the way!
The shadow of thy helmet, like the flashing
Of brazen star, strikes through the trembling air.
The dust of broken empires, cloud-like rising,
Follows the awful rumbling of thy wheels.
So once, O Rome, beheld the conquered nations
Thy image, object of their ancient dread.
To-day a mitre they would place upon
Thy head, and fold a rosary between
Thy hands. O name! again to terrors old
Awake the tired ages and the world!

From the Italian of GIOSUE CARDUCCI.
Translation of FRANK SEWALL.

THERE IS SUCH POWER.

FROM "SONNETS IN SHADOW."

THERE is such power even in smallest things
To bring the dear past back; a flower's tint,
A snatch of some old song, the fleeting glint
Of sunbeams on the wave—each vivid brings

The lost days up, as from the idle strings
  Of wind-harp sad a breeze evokes the hint
  Of antique tunes. A glove which keeps imprint
Of a loved hand the heart with torture wrings

By memory of a clasp meant more than speech ;
  A face seen in the crowd with curve of cheek
Or sweep of eyelash our woe's core can reach.

How strong is love to yearn, and yet how weak
  To strive with fate : the lesson all things teach,
As of the past in myriad ways they speak.

                        ARLO BATES.

VERSES

SUPPOSED TO BE WRITTEN BY ALEXANDER SELKIRK
DURING HIS SOLITARY ABODE IN THE ISLAND OF JUAN
FERNANDEZ.

    I AM monarch of all I survey,—
      My right there is none to dispute ;
    From the centre all round to the sea,
      I am lord of the fowl and the brute.
    O Solitude ! where are the charms
      That sages have seen in thy face ?
    Better dwell in the midst of alarms
      Than reign in this horrible place.

    I am out of humanity's reach ;
      I must finish my journey alone,
    Never hear the sweet music of speech,—
      I start at the sound of my own.
    The beasts that roam over the plain
      My form with indifference see ;

They are so unacquainted with man,
   Their tameness is shocking to me.

Society, friendship, and love,
   Divinely bestowed upon man!
O, had I the wings of a dove,
   How soon would I taste you again!
My sorrows I then might assuage
   In the ways of religion and truth,—
Might learn from the wisdom of age,
   And be cheered by the sallies of youth.

Religion! what treasure untold
   Resides in that heavenly word!—
More precious than silver and gold,
   Or all that this earth can afford;
But the sound of the church-going bell
   These valleys and rocks never heard,
Never sighed at the sound of a knell,
   Or smiled when a Sabbath appeared.

Ye winds that have made me your sport,
   Convey to this desolate shore
Some cordial, endearing report
   Of a land I shall visit no more!
My friends,—do they now and then send
   A wish or a thought after me?
O, tell me I yet have a friend,
   Though a friend I am never to see.

How fleet is a glance of the mind!
   Compared with the speed of its flight,
The tempest itself lags behind,
   And the swift-wingèd arrows of light.

When I think of my own native land,
  In a moment I seem to be there ;
But, alas ! recollection at hand
  Soon hurries me back to despair.

But the sea-fowl is gone to her nest,
  The beast is laid down in his lair ;
Even here is a season of rest,
  And I to my cabin repair.
There 's mercy in every place,
  And mercy—encouraging thought !—
Gives even affliction a grace,
  And reconciles man to his lot.

WILLIAM COWPER.

MIGNON'S SONG.

FROM "WILHELM MEISTER."

" Know'st thou the land where citron-apples bloom,
And oranges like gold in leafy gloom,
A gentle wind from deep-blue heaven blows,
The myrtle thick, and high the laurel grows ?
Know'st thou it then ?
            'T is there ! 'T is there,
O my true loved one, thou with me must go !

" Know'st thou the house, its porch with pillars tall ?
The rooms do glitter, glitters bright the hall,
And marble statues stand, and look each one :
What 's this, poor child, to thee they 've done ?
Know'st thou it then ?
            'T is there ! 'T is there,
O my protector, thou with me must go !

" Know'st thou the hill, the bridge that hangs on
    cloud ?
The mules in mist grope o'er the torrent loud,
In caves lie coiled the dragon's ancient brood,
The crag leaps down, and over it the flood :
Know'st thou it then ?
                    'T is there ! 'T is there
Our way runs : O my father, wilt thou go ? "

From the German of GOETHE.
Translation of THOMAS CARLYLE.

OFT IN THE STILLY NIGHT.

OFT in the stilly night,
    Ere slumber's chain has bound me,
Fond Memory brings the light
    Of other days around me :
        The smiles, the tears,
        Of boyhood's years,
    The words of love then spoken ;
        The eyes that shone,
        Now dimmed and gone,
    The cheerful hearts now broken.
Thus in the stilly night,
    Ere slumber's chain has bound me,
Sad Memory brings the light
    Of other days around me.

When I remember all
    The friends so linked together
I 've seen around me fall,
    Like leaves in wintry weather,
        I feel like one
        Who treads alone

Some banquet-hall deserted,
　　Whose lights are fled,
　　Whose garlands dead,
And all but he departed.
Thus in the stilly night,
　Ere slumber's chain has bound me,
Sad Memory brings the light
　Of other days around me.

THOMAS MOORE.

ON THE RUINS OF A COUNTRY INN.

WHERE now these mingled ruins lie
　A temple once to Bacchus rose,
Beneath whose roof, aspiring high,
　Full many a guest forgot his woes.

No more this dome, by tempests torn,
　Affords a social safe retreat ;
But ravens here, with eye forlorn,
　And clustering bats henceforth will meet.

The Priestess of this ruined shrine,
　Unable to survive the stroke,
Presents no more the ruddy wine,—
　Her glasses gone, her china broke.

The friendly Host, whose social hand
　Accosted strangers at the door,
Has left at length his wonted stand,
　And greets the weary guest no more.

Old creeping Time, that brings decay,
　Might yet have spared these moldering walls,

Alike beneath whose potent sway
A temple or a tavern falls.

Is this the place where mirth and joy,
Coy nymphs, and sprightly lads were found ?
Indeed ! no more the nymphs are coy,
No more the flowing bowls go round.

Is this the place where festive song
Deceived the wintry hours away ?
No more the swains the tune prolong,
No more the maidens join the lay.

Is this the place where Nancy slept
In downy beds of blue and green ?
Dame Nature here no vigils kept,
No cold unfeeling guards were seen.

'T is gone !—and Nancy tempts no more ;
Deep, unrelenting silence reigns ;
Of all that pleased, that charmed before,
The tottering chimney scarce remains.

Ye tyrant winds, whose ruffian blast
Through doors and windows blew too strong,
And all the roof to ruin cast,—
The roof that sheltered us so long,—

Your wrath appeased, I pray be kind
If Mopsus should the dome renew,
That we again may quaff his wine,
Again collect our jovial crew.

PHILIP FRENEAU.

'T IS BUT A LITTLE FADED FLOWER.

'T is but a little faded flower,
    But oh, how fondly dear!
'T will bring me back one golden hour,
    Through many a weary year.
I may not to the world impart
    The secret of its power,
But treasured in my inmost heart,
    I keep my faded flower.

Where is the heart that doth not keep,
    Within its inmost core,
Some fond remembrance, hidden deep,
    Of days that are no more?
Who hath not saved some trifling thing
    More prized than jewels rare—
A faded flower, a broken ring,
    A tress of golden hair?

ELLEN CLEMENTINE HOWARTH.

THE BRIER-WOOD PIPE.

Ha! bully for me again, when my turn for picket
    is over,
And now for a smoke as I lie, with the moonlight,
    out in the clover.

My pipe, it 's only a knot from the root of a brier-
    wood tree,
But it turns my heart to the Northward—Harry
    gave it to me.

And I 'm but a rough at best, bred up to the row
    and the riot;
But a softness comes over my heart, when all are
    asleep and quiet.

For, many a time, in the night, strange things ap-
    pear to my eye,
As the breath from my brier-wood pipe curls up
    between me and the sky.

Last night a beautiful spirit arose with the wisping
    smoke;
O, I shook, but my heart felt good, as it spread out
    its hands and spoke;

Saying, "I am the soul of the brier; we grew at
    the root of a tree
Where lovers would come in the twilight, two ever,
    for company.

" Where lovers would come in the morning—ever
    but two, together;
When the flowers were full in their blow; the
    birds, in their song and feather.

" Where lovers would come in the noontide, loiter-
    ing—never but two,
Looking in each other's eyes, like pigeons that kiss
    and coo.

" And O, the honeyed words that came when the
    lips were parted,
And the passion that glowed in the eyes, and the
    lightning looks that darted!

" Enough : Love dwells in the pipe—so ever it
  glows with fire !
I am the soul of the bush, and the spirits call me
  Sweet Brier."

That 's what the brier-wood said, as nigh as my
  tongue can tell,
And the words went straight to my heart, like the
  stroke of the fire-bell.

To-night I lie in the clover, watching the blossomy
  smoke ;
I 'm glad the boys are asleep, for I ain't in the
  humor to joke.

I lie in the hefty clover : up between me and the
  moon
The smoke of my pipe arises ; my heart will be
  quiet, soon.

My thoughts are back in the city, I 'm everything
  I 've been ;
I hear the bell from the tower, I run with the swift
  machine,

I see the red shirts crowding around the engine-
  house door,
The foreman's hail through the trumpet comes with
  a hollow roar.

The reel in the Bowery dance-house, the row in
  the beer-saloon,
Where I put in my licks at Big Paul, come between
  me and the moon.

I hear the drum and the bugle, the tramp of the
  cow-skin boots,
We are marching on our muscle, the Fire-Zouave
  recruits !

White handkerchiefs wave before me—O, but the
  sight is pretty
On the white marble steps, as we march through
  the heart of the city.

Bright eyes and clasping arms, and lips that bade
  us good hap ;
And the splendid lady who gave me the havelock
  for my cap.

O, up from my pipe-cloud rises, there between me
  and the moon,
A beautiful white-robed lady ; my heart will be
  quiet, soon.

The lovely golden-haired lady ever in dreams I
  see,
Who gave me the snow-white havelock—but what
  does she care for me ?

Look at my grimy features ; mountains between us
  stand :
I with my sledge-hammer knuckles, she with her
  jewelled hand !

What care I ?—the day that 's dawning may see
  me, when all is over,
With the red stream of my life-blood staining the
  hefty clover.

Hark! the reveille sounding out on the morning
    air ;
Devils are we for the battle— Will there be
    angels there ?

Kiss me again, Sweet Brier, the touch of your lip
    to mine
Brings back the white-robed lady with hair like the
    golden wine !

CHARLES DAWSON SHANLY.

MEMORY AND OBLIVION.

ALL hail, Remembrance and Forgetfulness!
    Trace, Memory, trace whate'er is sweet or kind:
When friends forsake us or misfortunes press,
    Oblivion, 'rase the record from our mind.

From the Greek of MACEDONIUS.
Translation of ROBERT BLAND.

IV.

THOUGHT : POETRY : BOOKS.

THE INNER VISION.

Most sweet it is with unuplifted eyes
To pace the ground, if path there be or none,
While a fair region round the traveller lies
Which he forbears again to look upon ;
Pleased rather with some soft ideal scene,
The work of fancy, or some happy tone
Of meditation, slipping in between
The beauty coming and the beauty gone.
If Thought and Love desert us, from that day
Let us break off all commerce with the Muse :
With Thought and Love companions of our way,—
Whate'er the senses take or may refuse,—
The mind's internal Heaven shall shed her dews
Of inspiration on the humblest lay.

WILLIAM WORDSWORTH.

THOUGHT.

Thought is deeper than all speech,
Feeling deeper than all thought;
Souls to souls can never teach
What unto themselves was taught.

We are spirits clad in veils;
  Man by man was never seen;
All our deep communing fails
  To remove the shadowy screen.

Heart to heart was never known;
  Mind with mind did never meet;
We are columns left alone
  Of a temple once complete.

Like the stars that gem the sky,
  Far apart, though seeming near,
In our light we scattered lie;
  All is thus but starlight here.

What is social company
  But a babbling summer stream?
What our wise philosophy
  But the glancing of a dream?

Only when the sun of love
  Melts the scattered stars of thought,
Only when we live above
  What the dim-eyed world hath taught,

Only when our souls are fed
  By the fount which gave them birth,
And by inspiration led
  Which they never drew from earth,

We, like parted drops of rain,
  Swelling till they meet and run,
Shall be all absorbed again,
  Melting, flowing into one.

                CHRISTOPHER PEARSE CRANCH.

DREAM-LIFE.

FROM "SUCH STUFF AS DREAMS ARE MADE OF."

AND yet—and yet—in these our ghostly lives,
Half night, half day, half sleeping, half awake,
How if our waking life, like that of sleep,
Be all a dream in that eternal life
To which we wake not till we sleep in death?
How if, I say, the senses we now trust
For date of sensible comparison,—
Ay, ev'n the Reason's self that dates with them,
Should be in essence of intensity
Hereafter so transcended, and awoke
To a perceptive subtlety so keen
As to confess themselves befooled before,
In all that now they will avouch for most?
One man—like this—but only so much longer
As life is longer than a summer's day,
Believed himself a king upon his throne,
And played at hazard with his fellows' lives,
Who cheaply dreamed away their lives to him.
The sailor dreamed of tossing on the flood:
The soldier, of his laurels grown in blood:
The lover, of the beauty that he knew
Must yet dissolve to dusty residue:
The merchant and the miser of his bags
Of fingered gold; the beggar of his rags:
And all this stage of earth on which we seem
Such busy actors, and the parts we played
Substantial as the shadow of a shade,
And Dreaming but a dream within a dream!

From the Spanish of PEDRO CALDERON.
Translation of EDWARD FITZGERALD.

MY MINDE TO ME A KINGDOM IS.

My minde to me a kingdom is;
  Such perfect joy therein I finde
As farre exceeds all earthly blisse
  That God or nature hath assignde;
Though much I want that most would have,
Yet still my minde forbids to crave.

Content I live; this is my stay,—
  I seek no more than may suffice.
I presse to beare no haughtie sway;
  Look, what I lack my mind supplies.
Loe, thus I triumph like a king,
Content with that my minde doth bring.

I see how plentie surfets oft,
  And hastie clymbers soon do fall;
I see that such as sit aloft
  Mishap doth threaten most of all.
These get with toile, they keepe with feare;
Such cares my minde could never beare.

No princely pompe nor welthie store,
  No force to win the victorie,
No wylie wit to salve a sore,
  No shape to winne a lover's eye,—
To none of these I yeeld as thrall;
For why, my mind despiseth all.

Some have too much, yet still they crave;
  I little have, yet seek no more.
They are but poore, though much they have,
  And I am rich with little store.

They poor, I rich ; they beg, I give ;
They lacke, I lend ; they pine, I live.

I laugh not at another's losse,
   I grudge not at another's gaine ;
No worldly wave my mind can tosse ;
   I brooke that is another's bane.
I feare no foe, I fawne no friend ;
I lothe not life, nor dread mine end.

I joy not in no earthly blisse ;
   I weigh not Crœsus' wealth a straw ;
For care, I care not what it is ;
   I feare not fortune's fatal law ;
My minde is such as may not move
For beautie bright, or force of love.

I wish but what I have at will ;
   I wander not to seeke for more ;
I like the plaine, I clime no hill ;
   In greatest stormes I sitte on shore,
And laugh at them that toile in vaine
To get what must be lost againe.

I kisse not where I wish to kill ;
   I feigne not love where most I hate ;
I breake no sleepe to winne my will ;
   I wayte not at the mightie's gate.
I scorne no poore, I feare no rich ;
I feele no want, nor have too much.

The court ne cart I like ne loath,—
   Extreames are counted worst of all ;
The golden meane betwixt them both
   Doth surest sit, and feares no fall ;

This is my choyce; for why, I finde
No wealth is like a quiet minde.

My wealth is health and perfect ease;
   My conscience clere my chiefe defence;
I neither seeke by bribes to please,
   Nor by desert to breed offence.
Thus do I live; thus will I die;
Would all did so as well as I!

SIR EDWARD DYER.

TO ONE WHO HAD SCOFFED AT THE POET'S POVERTY.

Yes,—I am poor, Callistratus! I own;
And so was ever; yet not quite unknown,
Graced with a knight's degree; nor this alone:
But through the world my verse is often sung;
And "That is he!" sounds buzzed from every
     tongue;
And what to few, when dust, the Fates assign,
In bloom and freshness of my days is mine.
Thy ceilings on a hundred columns rest;
Wealth as of upstart freedman bursts thy chest;
Nile flows in fatness o'er thy ample fields;
Cisalpine Gaul thy silky fleeces yields.
Lo! Such thou art, and such am I: like me,
Callistratus! thou canst not hope to be;
A hundred of the crowd resemble thee!

From the Latin of MARTIAL.

OF A CONTENTED SPIRIT.

When all is done and said, in the end this shall you
    find :
He most of all doth bathe in bliss that hath a quiet
    mind ;
And, clear from worldly cares, to dream can be
    content
The sweetest time in all this life in thinking to be
    spent.

The body subject is to fickle Fortune's power,
And to a million of mishaps is casual every hour ;
And death in time doth change it to a clod of clay ;
Whenas the mind, which is divine, runs never to
    decay.

Companion none is like unto the mind alone,
For many have been harmed by speech,—through
    thinking, few or none ;
Fear oftentimes restraineth words, but makes not
    thought to cease ;
And he speaks best that hath the skill when for to
    hold his peace.

Our wealth leaves us at death, our kinsmen at the
    grave ;
But virtues of the mind unto the heavens with us we
    have :
Wherefor, for Virtue's sake, I can be well content
The sweetest time of all my life to deem in thinking
    spent.

                   THOMAS, LORD VAUX.

A THING OF BEAUTY IS A JOY FOREVER.

FROM "ENDYMION," BOOK I.

A THING of beauty is a joy forever:
Its loveliness increases; it will never
Pass into nothingness; but still will keep
A bower quiet for us, and a sleep
Full of sweet dreams, and health, and quiet breathing.
Therefore, on every morrow, are we wreathing
A flowery band to bind us to the earth,
Spite of despondence, of the inhuman dearth
Of noble natures, of the gloomy days,
Of all the unhealthy and o'er-darkened ways
Made for our searching: yes, in spite of all,
Some shape of beauty moves away the pall
From our dark spirits. Such the sun, the moon,
Trees old and young, sprouting a shady boon
For simple sheep; and such are daffodils
With the green world they live in; and clear rills
That for themselves a cooling covert make
'Gainst the hot season; the mid-forest brake,
Rich with a sprinkling of fair musk-rose blooms:
And such too is the grandeur of the dooms
We have imagined for the mighty dead;
All lovely tales that we have heard or read:
An endless fountain of immortal drink,
Pouring unto us from the heaven's brink.

JOHN KEATS.

THE SOWER AND HIS SEED.

HE planted an oak in his father's park
    And a thought in the minds of men,
And he bade farewell to his native shore,
    Which he never will see again.
Oh merrily stream the tourist throng
    To the glow of the Southern sky ;
A vision of pleasure beckons them on,
    But he went there to die.

The oak will grow and its boughs will spread,
    And many rejoice in its shade,
But none will visit the distant grave,
    Where a stranger youth is laid ;
And the thought will live when the oak has died,
    And quicken the minds of men,
But the name of the thinker has vanished away,
    And will never be heard again.
                WILLIAM E. H. LECKY.

ÆSOP.

HE sat among the woods ; he heard
    The sylvan merriment ; he saw
The pranks of butterfly and bird,
    The humors of the ape, the daw.

And in the lion or the frog,—
    In all the life of moor and fen,—
In ass and peacock, stork and dog,
    He read similitudes of men.

" Of these, from those," he cried, " we come,
   Our hearts, our brains descend from these."
And, lo ! the Beasts no more were dumb,
   But answered out of brakes and trees :

" Not ours," they cried ; " Degenerate,
   If ours at all," they cried again,
" Ye fools, who war with God and Fate,
   Who strive and toil ; strange race of men.

" For *we* are neither bond nor free,
   For *we* have neither slaves nor kings ;
But near to Nature's heart are we,
   And conscious of her secret things.

" Content are we to fall asleep,
   And well content to wake no more ;
We do not laugh, we do not weep,
   Nor look behind us and before :

" But were there cause for moan or mirth,
   'T is *we*, not you, should sigh or scorn,
Oh, latest children of the Earth,
   Most childish children Earth has born."

   .   .   .   .   .

They spoke, but that misshapen slave
   Told never of the thing he heard,
And unto men their portraits gave,
   In likenesses of beast and bird !

                              REW LANG.

INDIRECTION.

Fair are the flowers and the children, but their
    subtle suggestion is fairer;
Rare is the roseburst of dawn, but the secret that
    clasps it is rarer;
Sweet the exultance of song, but the strain that
    precedes it is sweeter;
And never was poem yet writ, but the meaning
    outmastered the metre.

Never a daisy that grows, but a mystery guideth
    the growing;
Never a river that flows, but a majesty sceptres the
    flowing;
Never a Shakespeare that soared, but a stronger
    than he did enfold him,
Nor ever a prophet foretells, but a mightier seer
    hath foretold him.

Back of the canvas that throbs the painter is hinted
    and hidden;
Into the statue that breathes the soul of the sculp-
    tor is bidden;
Under the joy that is felt lie the infinite issues of
    feeling;
Crowning the glory revealed is the glory that
    crowns the revealing.

Great are the symbols of being, but that which is
    symboled is greater;
Vast the create and beheld, but vaster the inward
    creator;

Back of the sound broods the silence, back of the
    gift stands the giving;
Back of the hand that receives thrill the sensitive
    nerves of receiving.

Space is as nothing to spirit, the deed is outdone by
    the doing;
The heart of the wooer is warm, but warmer the
    heart of the wooing;
And up from the pits where these shiver, and up
    from the heights where those shine,
Twin voices and shadows swim starward, and the
    essence of life is divine.

RICHARD REALF.

PROEM.

THERE is no rhyme that is half so sweet
As the song of the wind in the rippling wheat;
There is no metre that's half so fine
As the lilt of the brook under rock and vine;
And the loveliest lyric I ever heard
Was the wildwood strain of a forest bird.—
If the wind and the brook and the bird would teach
My heart their beautiful parts of speech,
And the natural art that they say these with,
My soul would sing of beauty and myth
In a rhyme and a metre that none before
Have sung in their love, or dreamed in their lore,
And the world would be richer one poet the more.

MADISON CAWEIN.

THE POET OF NATURE.

FROM "FESTUS."

He had no times of study, and no place ;
All places and all times to him were one.
His soul was like the wind-harp, which he loved,
And sounded only when the spirit blew,
Sometime in feasts and follies, for he went
Lifelike through all things ; and his thoughts then
    rose
Like sparkles in the bright wine, brighter still ;
Sometimes in dreams, and then the shining words
Would wake him in the dark before his face.
All things talked thoughts to him.   The sea went
    mad
To show his meaning ; and the awful sun
Thundered his thoughts into him ; and at night
The stars would whisper theirs, the moon sigh hers.

PHILIP JAMES BAILEY.

ABOVE THE CLOUDS.

'Mid white Sierras, that slope to the sea,
Lie turbulent lands.   Go dwell in the skies,
And the thundering tongues of Yosemitè
Shall persuade you to silence, and you shall be wise.

I but sing for the love of song and the few
Who loved me first and shall love me last ;
And the storm shall pass as the storms have passed,
For never were clouds but the sun came through.

JOAQUIN MILLER.

THE POET'S IMPULSE.

FROM "CHILDE HAROLD'S PILGRIMAGE," CANTO III.

Sky, mountains, river, winds, lake, lightnings! ye
With night, and clouds, and thunder, and a soul
To make these felt and feeling, well may be
Things that have made me watchful; the far roll
Of your departing voices is the knoll
Of what in me is sleepless,—if I rest.
But where of ye, O tempests! is the goal?
Are ye like those within the human breast?
Or do ye find, at length, like eagles, some high nest?

Could I embody and unbosom now
That which is most within me,—could I wreak
My thoughts upon expression, and thus throw
Soul, heart, mind, passions, feelings, strong or
    weak,
All that I would have sought, and all I seek,
Bear, know, feel, and yet breathe—into *one* word,
And that one word were Lightning, I would speak;
But as it is, I live and die unheard,
With a most voiceless thought, sheathing it as a
    sword.

LORD BYRON.

IMPRESSION.

In these restrained and careful times
Our knowledge petrifies our rhymes;
Ah! for that reckless fire men had
When it was witty to be mad,

When wild conceits were piled in scores,
And lit by flaring metaphors,
When all was crazed and out of tune,—
Yet throbbed with music of the moon.

If we could dare to write as ill
As some whose voices haunt us still,
Even we, perchance, might call our own
Their deep enchanting undertone.

We are too diffident and nice,
Too learnèd and too over-wise,
Too much afraid of faults to be
The flutes of bold sincerity.

For, as this sweet life passes by,
We blink and nod with critic eye ;
We 've no words rude enough to give
Its charm so frank and fugitive.

The green and scarlet of the Park,
The undulating streets at dark,
The brown smoke blown across the blue,
This colored city we walk through ;—

The pallid faces full of pain,
The field-smell of the passing wain,
The laughter, longing, perfume, strife,
The daily spectacle of life ;—

Ah ! how shall this be given to rhyme,
By rhymesters of a knowing time ?
Ah ! for the age when verse was glad,
Being godlike, to be bad and mad.

EDMUND GOSSE.

THE ANCIENT AND MODERN MUSES.

THE monument outlasting bronze
  Was promised well by bards of old ;
The lucid outline of their lay
Its sweet precision keeps for aye,
  Fixed in the ductile language-gold.

But we who work with smaller skill,
  And less refined material mould,—
This close conglomerate English speech,
Bequest of many tribes, that each
  Brought here and wrought at from of old,

Residuum rough, eked out by rhyme,
  Barbarian ornament uncouth,—
Our hope is less to last through Art
Than deeper searching of the heart,
  Than broader range of uttered truth.

One keen-cut group, one deed or aim
  Athenian Sophocles could show,
And rest content ; but Shakespeare's stage
Must hold the glass to every age,—
  A thousand forms and passions glow

Upon the world-wide canvas. So
  With larger scope our art we ply ;
And if the crown be harder won,
Diviner rays around it run,
  With strains of fuller harmony.

FRANCIS TURNER PALGRAVE.

ON HIS "SONNETS OF THE WINGLESS HOURS."

I WROUGHT them like a targe of hammered gold
On which all Troy is battling round and round ;
Or Circe's cup, embossed with snakes that wound
Through buds and myrtles, fold on scaly fold ;
Or like gold coins, which Lydian tombs may hold
Stamped with winged racers, in the old red ground ;
Or twined gold armlets from the funeral mound
Of some great viking, terrible of old.
I know not in what metal I have wrought ;
Nor whether what I fashioned will be thrust
Beneath the clouds that hide forgotten thought ;
But if it is of gold it will not rust ;
And when the time is ripe it will be brought
Into the sun, and glitter through its dust.

EUGENE LEE-HAMILTON.

THE POET OF TO-DAY.

MORE than the soul of ancient song is given
   To thee, O poet of to-day !—thy dower
Comes, from a higher than Olympian heaven,
   In holier beauty and in larger power.

To thee Humanity, her woes revealing,
   Would all her griefs and ancient wrongs rehearse ;
Would make thy song the voice of her appealing,
   And sob her mighty sorrows through thy verse.

While in her season of great darkness sharing,
  Hail thou the coming of each promise-star
Which climbs the midnight of her long despairing,
  And watch for morning o'er the hills afar.

Wherever Truth her holy warfare wages,
  Or freedom pines, there let thy voice be heard;
Sound like a prophet-warning down the ages
  The human utterance of God's living word.

But bring not thou the battle's stormy chorus,
  The tramp of armies, and the roar of fight,
Not war's hot smoke to taint the sweet morn o'er us
  Nor blaze of pillage, reddening up the night.

O, let thy lays prolong that angel-singing,
  Girdling with music the Redeemer's star,
And breathe God's peace, to earth "glad tidings"
    bringing
  From the near heavens, of old so dim and far!

SARAH JANE LIPPINCOTT (*Grace Greenwood*).

UNKNOWN POETS.

FROM "THE EXCURSION," BOOK I.

O, MANY are the poets that are sown
By nature; men endowed with highest gifts,
The vision and the faculty divine;
Yet wanting the accomplishment of verse
(Which, in the docile season of their youth,
It was denied them to acquire, through lack
Of culture and the inspiring aid of books,
Or haply by a temper too severe,
Or a nice backwardness afraid of shame),

Nor having e'er, as life advanced, been led
By circumstance to take unto the height
The measure of themselves, these favored beings,
All but a scattered few, live out their time,
Husbanding that which they possess within,
And go to the grave, unthought of. Strongest minds
Are often those of whom the noisy world
Hears least.

WILLIAM WORDSWORTH.

THE BALLAD OF PROSE AND RHYME.

WHEN the ways are heavy with mire and rut,
  In November fogs, in December snows,
When the North Wind howls, and the doors are
    shut,—
    There is place and enough for the pains of prose ;
    But whenever a scent from the whitethorn blows,
And the jasmine-stars at the casement climb,
    And a Rosalind-face at the lattice shows,
Then hey ! for the ripple of laughing rhyme !

When the brain gets dry as an empty nut,
  When the reason stands on its squarest toes,
When the mind (like a beard) has a " formal cut,"—
    There is place and enough for the pains of prose ;
    But whenever the May-blood stirs and glows,
And the young year draws to the " golden prime,"
    And Sir Romeo sticks in his ear a rose,—
Then hey ! for the ripple of laughing rhyme !

In a theme where the thoughts have a pedant-strut,
  In a changing quarrel of " Ayes " and " Noes,"

In a starched procession of " If " and " But,"—
    There is place and enough for the pains of prose ;
    But whenever a soft glance softer grows
And the light hours dance to the trysting-time,
    And the secret is told " that no one knows,"—
Then hey ! for the ripple of laughing rhyme !

ENVOY.

In the work-a-day world,—for its needs and woes,
There is place and enough for the pains of prose ;
But whenever the May-bells clash and chime,
Then hey ! for the ripple of laughing rhyme !

AUSTIN DOBSON.

ON FIRST LOOKING INTO CHAPMAN'S HOMER.

Much have I travelled in the realms of gold,
And many goodly states and kingdoms seen ;
Round many western islands have I been
Which bards in fealty to Apollo hold.
Oft of one wide expanse had I been told
That deep-browed Homer ruled as his demesne ;
Yet did I never breathe its pure serene
Till I heard Chapman speak out loud and bold :
Then felt I like some watcher of the skies
When a new planet swims into his ken ;
Or like stout Cortez, when with eagle eyes
He stared at the Pacific—and all his men
Looked at each other with a wild surmise—
Silent, upon a peak in Darien.

JOHN KEATS.

THE ODYSSEY.

PREFACING THE BUTCHER-LANG TRANSLATION.

As one that for a weary space has lain
  Lulled by the song of Circe and her wine
  In gardens near the pale of Proserpine,
Where that Ææan Isle forgets the Main,
And only the low lutes of love complain,
  And only shadows of wan lovers pine ;
  As such an one were glad to know the brine
Salt on his lips, and the large air again,—
So, gladly from the songs of modern speech
  Men turn, and see the stars, and feel the free
    Shrill wind beyond the close of heavy flowers ;
  And through the music of the languid hours,
They hear like ocean on a western beach
  The surge and thunder of the Odyssey.

ANDREW LANG.

SONNET.

FROM " ASTROPHEL AND STELLA."

Loving in truth, and fain in verse my love to show,
That she, dear she, might take some pleasure of my
    pain,—
Pleasure might cause her read, reading might make
    her know,
Knowledge might pity win, and pity grace obtain,—
I sought fit words to paint the blackest face of woe ;

Studying inventions fine, her wits to entertain,
Oft turning others' leaves, to see if thence would flow
Some fresh and fruitful showers upon my sun-burned
    brain.
But words came halting forth, wanting Invention's
    stay ;
Invention, Nature's child, fled step-dame Study's
    blows ;
And others' feet still seemed but strangers in my way.
Thus, great with child to speak, and helpless in my
    throes,
Biting my truant pen, beating myself for spite;
Fool, said my Muse to me, look in thy heart, and
    write.

SIR PHILIP SIDNEY.

THE SINGER OF ONE SONG.

HE sang one song and died—no more but that :
A single song and carelessly complete.
He would not bind and thresh his chance-grown
    wheat,
Nor bring his wild fruit to the common vat,
To store the acid rinsings, thin and flat,
Squeezed from the press or trodden under feet.
A few slow beads, blood-red and honey-sweet,
Oozed from the grape, which burst and spilled its
    fat.
But Time, who soonest drops the heaviest things
That weight his pack, will carry diamonds long.
So through the poets' orchestra, which weaves
One music from a thousand stops and strings,

Pierces the note of that immortal song :
" High over all the lonely bugle grieves." *
HENRY AUGUSTIN BEERS.

THE SONNET.

W HAT is a sonnet?   'T is the pearly shell
That murmurs of the far-off murmuring sea ;
A precious jewel carved most curiously ;
It is a little picture painted well.
What is a sonnet?   'T is the tear that fell
From a great poet's hidden ecstasy ;
A two-edged sword, a star, a song,—ah me !
Sometimes a heavy-tolling funeral bell.
This was the flame that shook with Dante's breath,
The solemn organ whereon Milton played,
And the clear glass where Shakespeare's shadow falls :
A sea this is,—beware who ventureth !
For like a fiord the narrow floor is laid
Mid-ocean deep to the sheer mountain walls.
RICHARD WATSON GILDER.

AN AUTOGRAPH.

O'ER the wet sands an insect crept
Ages ere man on earth was known—
And patient Time, while Nature slept,
The slender tracing turned to stone.

'T was the first autograph : and ours ?
Prithee, how much of prose or song,
In league with the creative powers,
Shall 'scape Oblivion's broom so long ?
JAMES RUSSELL LOWELL.

* See Vol. VIII. p. 327.

ART.

I.

Art's use; what is it but to touch the springs
Of nature?   But to hold a torch up for
Humanity in Life's large corridor,
To guide the feet of peasants and of kings!
What is it but to carry union through
Thoughts alien to thoughts kindred, and to merge
The lines of color that should not diverge,
And give the sun a window to shine through!
What is it but to make the world have heed
For what its dull eyes else would hardly scan!
To draw in a stark light a shameless deed,
And show the fashion of a kingly man!
To cherish honor, and to smite all shame,
To lend hearts voices, and give thoughts a name!

II.

But wherein shall art work?   Shall beauty lead
It captive, and set kisses on its mouth?
Shall it be strained unto the breast of youth,
And in a garden live where grows no weed?
Shall it, in dalliance with the flaunting world,
Play but soft airs, sing but sweet-tempered songs?
Veer lightly from the stress of all great wrongs,
And lisp of peace 'mid battle-flags unfurled?
Shall it but pluck the sleeve of wantonness,
And gently chide the folly of our time?
But wave its golden wand at sin's duress,

And say, " Ah me! ah me!" to fallow crime?
Nay; Art serves Truth, and Truth, with Titan
   blows,
Strikes fearless at all evil that it knows.

SIR GILBERT PARKER.

BROKEN MUSIC.

" A note
All out of tune in this world's instrument."

—AMY LEVY.

I KNOW not in what fashion she was made,
   Nor what her voice was, when she used to speak,
Nor if the silken lashes threw a shade
      On wan or rosy cheek.

I picture her with sorrowful vague eyes
   Illumed with such strange gleams of inner light
As linger in the drift of London skies
      Ere twilight turns to night.

I know not; I conjecture.   'T was a girl
   That with her own most gentle desperate hand
From out God's mystic setting plucked life's pearl—
      'T is hard to understand.

So precious life is!   Even to the old
   The hours are as a miser's coins, and she—
Within her hands lay youth's unminted gold
      And all felicity.

The winged impetuous spirit, the white flame
   That was her soul once, whither has it flown?

Above her brow gray lichens blot her name
    Upon the carven stone.

This is her Book of Verses—wren-like notes,
  Shy franknesses, blind gropings, haunting fears;
At times across the chords abruptly floats
    A mist of passionate tears.

A fragile lyre too tensely keyed and strung,
  A broken music, weirdly incomplete:
Here a proud mind, self-baffled and self-stung,
    Lies coiled in dark defeat.

THOMAS BAILEY ALDRICH.

THE MODERN POET.

A SONG OF DERIVATIONS.

I COME from nothing; but from where
Come the undying thoughts I bear?
  Down, through long links of death and birth,
  From the past poets of the earth.
My immortality is there.

I am like the blossom of an hour.
But long, long vanished sun and shower
  Awoke my breath i' the young world's air.
  I track the past back everywhere
Through seed and flower and seed and flower.

Or I am like a stream that flows
Full of the cold springs that arose
  In morning lands, in distant hills;
  And down the plain my channel fills
With melting of forgotten snows.

Voices I have not heard possessed
My own fresh songs ; my thoughts are blessed
    With relics of the far unknown ;
    And mixed with memories not my own
The sweet streams throng into my breast.

Before this life began to be,
The happy songs that wake in me
    Woke long ago, and far apart
    Heavily on this little heart
Presses this immortality.

ALICE MEYNELL.

THE JESTER'S PLEA.

[Published in a volume by several authors for the benefit of the starving weavers of Lancashire during the American civil war.]

THE World!   Was jester ever in
    A viler than the present ?
Yet if it ugly be—as sin,
    It almost is—as pleasant !
It is a merry world (*pro tem.*) ;
    And some are gay, and therefore
It pleases them—but some condemn
    The fun they do not care for.

It is an ugly world.   Offend
    Good people—how they wrangle !
The manners that they never mend !
    The characters they mangle !
They eat, and drink, and scheme, and plot
    And go to church on Sunday ;

And many are afraid of God—
    And more of *Mrs. Grundy.*

The time for Pen and Sword was when
    " My ladye fayre " for pity
Could tend her wounded knight, and then
    Grow tender at his ditty !
Some ladies now make pretty songs,
    And some make pretty nurses ;
Some men are good for righting wrongs
    And some for writing verses.

I wish We better understood
    The tax that poets levy !
I know the Muse is very *good* —
    I think she 's rather heavy.
She now compounds for winning ways
    By morals of the sternest :
Methinks the lays of nowadays
    Are painfully in earnest.

When Wisdom halts, I humbly try
    To make the most of Folly ;
If Pallas be unwilling, I
    Prefer to flirt with Polly :
To quit the goddess for the maid
    Seems low in lofty musers ;
But Pallas is a haughty jade—
    And beggars can't be choosers.

I do not wish to see the slaves
    Of party, stirring passion ;
Or psalms quite superseding staves,
    Or piety " the fashion."

I bless the hearts where pity glows,
   Who, here together banded,
Are holding out a hand to those
   That wait so empty-handed !

A righteous work !—My Masters, may
   A Jester by confession,
Scarce noticed join, half sad, half gay,
   The close of your procession ?
The motley here seems out of place
   With graver robes to mingle ;
But if one tear bedews his face,
   Forgive the bells their jingle.

                FREDERICK LOCKER-LAMPSON.

VERSES WHY BURNT.

How many verses have I thrown
Into the fire because the one
Peculiar word, the wanted most,
Was irrecoverably lost !

                WALTER SAVAGE LANDOR.

SWEET NATURE'S VOICE.

FROM " SUSAN : A POEM OF DEGREES."

HER Master gave the signal, with a look :
Then, timidly as if afraid, she took
In her rough hands the Laureate's dainty book,
And straight began.   But when she did begin,
Her own mute sense of poesy within

Broke forth to hail the poet, and to greet
His graceful fancies and the accents sweet
In which they are expressed. Oh, lately lost,
Long loved, long honored, and whose Captain's post
No living bard is competent to fill—
How strange, to the deep heart that now is still,
And to the vanished hand, and to the ear
Whose soft melodious measures are so dear
To us who cannot rival them—how strange,
If thou, the lord of such a various range,
Hadst heard this new voice telling Arden's tale !
For this was no prim maiden, scant and pale,
Full of weak sentiment, and thin delight
In pretty rhymes, who mars the resonant might
Of noble verse with arts rhetorical
And simulated frenzy : not at all !
This was a peasant woman ; large and strong,
Redhanded, ignorant, unused to song—
Accustomed rather to the rudest prose.
And yet, there lived within her rustic clothes
A heart as true as Arden's ; and a brain,
Keener than his, that counts it false and vain
To seem aught else than simply what she is.
How singular, her faculty of bliss !
Bliss in her servile work ; bliss deep and full
In things beyond the vision of the dull,
Whate'er their rank : things beautiful as these
Sonorous lines and solemn harmonies
Suiting the tale they tell of ; bliss in love—
Ah, chiefly that ! which lifts her soul above
Its common life, and gives to labors coarse
Such fervor of imaginative force
As makes a passion of her basest toil.

Surely this servant-dress was but a foil
To her more lofty being! As she read,
Her accent was as pure, and all she said
As full of interest and of varied grace
As were the changeful moods, that o'er her face
Passed, like swift clouds across a windy sky,
At each sad stage of Enoch's history.
Such ease, such pathos, such abandonment
To what she uttered, moulded as she went
Her soft sweet voice, and with such self-control
Did she, interpreting the poet's soul,
Bridle her own, that when the tale was done
I looked at her, amazed: she seemed like one
Who from some sphere of music had come down,
And donned the white cap and the cotton gown
As if to show how much of skill and art
May dwell unthought of, in the humblest heart.
Yet there was no great mystery to tell:
She felt it deeply, so she read it well.

ARTHUR JOSEPH MUNBY.

GENIUS.

FAR out at sea—the sun was high,
    While veered the wind, and flapped the sail—
We saw a snow-white butterfly
    Dancing before the fitful gale,
                    Far out at sea!

The little wanderer, who had lost
    His way, of danger nothing knew;
Settled awhile upon the mast,
    Then fluttered o'er the waters blue,
                    Far out at sea.

Above, there gleamed the boundless sky ;
 Beneath, the boundless ocean sheen ;
Between them danced the butterfly,
 The spirit-life of this vast scene,
                    Far out at sea.

The tiny soul then soared away,
 Seeking the clouds on fragile wings,
Lured by the brighter, purer ray
 Which hope's ecstatic morning brings,
                    Far out at sea.

Away he sped with shimmering glee !
 Scarce seen—now lost—yet onward borne !
Night comes !—with wind and rain—and he
 No more will dance before the Morn,
                    Far out at sea.

He dies unlike his mates, I ween ;
 Perhaps not sooner, or worse crossed ;
And he hath felt, thought, known, and seen
 A larger life and hope—though lost
                    Far out at sea !
             RICHARD HENRY HENGIST HORNE.

———

ONE DAY I WROTE HER NAME.

FROM " AMORETTI." SONNET LXXV.

ONE day I wrote her name upon the strand,
 But came the waves, and washèd it away :
Agayne, I wrote it with a second hand ;
 But came the tyde, and made my paynes his prey.

Vayne man, say'd she, that doest in vayne assay
  A mortall thing so to immortalize ;
For I my selve shall like to this decay,
  And eke my name bee wipèd out likewise.
Not so, quod I ; let baser things devize
  To dy in dust, but thou shall live by fame :
My verse your vertues rare shall éternize,
  And in the heavens wryte your glorious name,
    Where, when as death shall all the world subdew,
    Our love shall live, and later life renew.

EDMUND SPENSER.

THE POET'S DEATH.

FROM "THE LAY OF THE LAST MINSTREL," CANTO V.

CALL it not vain :—they do not err,
  Who say, that when the poet dies,
Mute nature mourns her worshipper,
  And celebrates his obsequies ;
Who say tall cliff, and cavern lone,
For the departed bard make moan ;
That mountains weep in crystal rill ;
That flowers in tears of balm distill ;
Through his loved groves that breezes sigh
And oaks, in deeper groan, reply ;
And rivers teach their rushing wave
To murmur dirges round his grave.

Not that, in sooth, o'er mortal urn
Those things inanimate can mourn ;
But that the stream, the wood, the gale,
Is vocal with the plaintive wail

Of those, who, else forgotten long,
Lived in the poet's faithful song,
And, with the poet's parting breath,
Whose memory feels a second death.
The maid's pale shade, who wails her lot,
That love, true love, should be forgot,
From rose and hawthorn shakes the tear
Upon the gentle minstrel's bier :
The phantom knight, his glory fled,
Mourns o'er the field he heaped with dead
Mounts the wild blast that sweeps amain,
And shrieks along the battle-plain :
The chief, whose antique crownlet long
Still sparkled in the feudal song,
Now, from the mountain's misty throne,
Sees, in the thanedom once his own,
His ashes undistinguished lie,
His place, his power, his memory die :
His groans the lonely caverns fill,
His tears of rage impel the rill ;
All mourn the minstrel's harp unstrung,
Their name unknown, their praise unsung.

SIR WALTER SCOTT.

THY SONGS AND MINE.

Sing thou my songs for me when I am dead !
   Soul of my soul, some day thou wilt awake
   To see the morning on the hilltops break,
And the far summits flame with rosy red—
But I shall wake not, though above my head

Armies should thunder; nor for Love's sweet
sake,
Though he the tenderest pilgrimage should
make
Where I am lying in my grassy bed.
I shall be silent, with my song half sung;
I shall be dumb, with half the story told;
I shall be mute, leaving the half unsaid.
Take thou the harp ere it be yet unstrung—
Wake thou the lyre ere yet its chords be
cold—
Sing thou my songs, and thine, when I am
dead!

JULIA C. R. DORR.

THE SHARING OF THE EARTH.

" TAKE the world," cried the God from his heaven
To men—" I proclaim you its heirs;
To divide it amongst you 't is given:
You have only to settle the shares."

Each takes for himself as it pleases,
Old and young have alike their desire:
The harvest the husbandman seizes;
Through the wood and the chase sweeps the
squire.

The merchant his warehouse is locking;
The abbot is choosing his wine;
Cries the monarch, the thoroughfare blocking,
" Every toll for the passage is mine!"

All too late, when the sharing was over,
Comes the poet,—he came from afar;

Nothing left can the laggard discover,
  Not an inch but its owners there are.

" Woe is me ! is there nothing remaining
  For the son who best loves thee alone ! "
Thus to Jove went his voice in complaining,
  As he fell at the Thunderer's throne.

" In the land of thy dreams if abiding,"
  Quoth the god, " Can'st thou murmur at *me ?*
Where wert *thou* when the earth was dividing ? "
  " *I was,*" said the poet, " *by thee !*

" Mine eye by thy glory was captured,
  Mine ear by thy music of bliss :
Pardon him whom *thy* world so enraptured
  As to lose him his portion in this ! "

" Alas," said the god, " earth is given !
  Field, forest, and market, and all !
What say you to quarters in heaven ?
  We 'll admit you whenever you call ! "

From the German of J. C. FRIEDRICH VON SCHILLER.
Translation of LORD BULWER-LYTTON.

THE IMMORTALITY OF GENIUS.

ORPHEUS, 't is said, the Thracian lyre-strings sweep-
    ing,
  Stayed the swift stream and soothed the savage
      brute ;
Cithæron's rocks, to Thebes spontaneous leaping,
  Rose into walls before Amphion's lute.

With dripping steeds did Galatea follow,
    'Neath Ætna's crags, lone Polyphemus's song:
Is 't strange the loved of Bacchus and Apollo
    Leads captive with his lay the maiden throng?

Though no Tænarian blocks uphold my dwelling,
    Nor ivory panels shine 'tween gilded beams;
No orchards mine Phæacia's woods excelling,
    No chiselled grots where Marcian water streams,—

Yet Song is mine; my strain the heart engages;
    Faint from the dance sinks the lithe Muse with
        me:
O happy maid whose name adorns my pages!
    Each lay a lasting monument to thee!

The pyramids that cleave heaven's jewelled portal;
    Elean Jove's star-spangled dome; the tomb
Where rich Mausolus sleeps,—are not immortal,
    Nor shall escape inevitable doom.

Devouring fire and rains will mar their splendor;
    The weight of years will drag the marble down:
Genius alone a name can deathless render,
    And round the forehead wreathe the unfading
        crown.

> From the Latin of SEXTUS PROPERTIUS.
> Translation of Dr. JAMES CRANSTOUN.

WRITTEN ON A FLY-LEAF OF THEOCRITUS.

THOSE were good times, in olden days,
    Of which the poet has his dreams,

When gods beset the woodland ways,
  And lay in wait by all the streams.

One could be sure of something then
  Severely simple, simply grand,
Or keenly, subtly sweet, as when
  Venus and Love went hand in hand.

Now I would give (such is my need)
  All the world's store of rhythm and rhyme
To see Pan fluting on a reed
  And with his goat-hoof keeping time!

MAURICE THOMPSON.

BOOKS.

FROM " THE KALÉDER OF SHEPERDES," 1528.

He that many bokes redys,
Cunnyinge shall he be.
Wysedome is soone caught;
In many leues it is sought:
But slouth, that no boke bought,
For reason taketh no thought;
His thryfte cometh behynde.

ANONYMOUS.

THE SCHOLAR.

FROM " EDWIN THE FAIR."

This life, and all that it contains, to him
Is but a tissue of illuminous dreams

Filled with book-wisdom, pictured thought and love
That on its own creations spends itself.
All things he understands, and nothing does.
Profusely eloquent in copious praise
Of action, he will talk to you as one
Whose wisdom lay in dealings and transactions;
Yet so much action as might tie his shoe
Cannot his will command; himself alone
By his own wisdom not a jot the gainer.
Of silence, and the hundred thousand things
'T is better not to mention, he will speak,
And still most wisely.

SIR HENRY TAYLOR.

THE BOOK-STALL.

It stands in a winding street,
  A quiet and restful nook,
Apart from the endless beat
  Of the noisy heart of Trade;
  There 's never a spot more cool
  Of a hot midsummer day
  By the brink of a forest pool,
  Or the bank of a crystal brook
  In the maples' breezy shade,
  Than the book-stall old and gray.

Here are precious gems of thought
  That were quarried long ago,
Some in vellum bound, and wrought
  With letters and lines of gold;
  Here are curious rows of " calf,"

And perchance an Elzevir ;
Here are countless " mos " of chaff,
And a parchment folio,
Like leaves that are cracked with cold,
All puckered and brown and sear.

In every age and clime
Live the monarchs of the brain :
And the lords of prose and rhyme,
Years after the long last sleep
Has come to the kings of earth
And their names have passed away,
Rule on through death and birth ;
And the thrones of their domain
Are found where the shades are deep
In the book-stall old and gray.

CLINTON SCOLLARD.

BOOKS.

FOR why, who writes such histories as these
Doth often bring the reader's heart such ease,
As when they sit and see what he doth note,
Well fare his heart, say they, this book that wrote !

JOHN HIGGINS.

V.

THE ARTS.

INFLUENCE OF MUSIC.

FROM " KING HENRY EIGHTH," ACT III. SC. 1.

ORPHEUS, with his lute, made trees,
And the mountain-tops that freeze,
  Bow themselves when he did sing ;
To his music plants and flowers
Ever sprung, as sun and showers
  There had made a lasting Spring

Every thing that heard him play,
Even the billows of the sea,
  Hung their heads, and then lay by.
In sweet music is such art,
  Killing care, and grief of heart—
  Fall asleep, or, hearing, die !

SHAKESPEARE.

MUSIC.

FROM " THE MERCHANT OF VENICE," ACT V. SC. 1.

LORENZO.—How sweet the moonlight sleeps upon
  this bank !
Here will we sit, and let the sounds of music

Creep in our ears: soft stillness, and the night,
Become the touches of sweet harmony.
Sit, Jessica: look, how the floor of heaven
Is thick inlaid with patines of bright gold:
There 's not the smallest orb which thou behold'st,
But in his motion like an angel sings,
Still quiring to the young-eyed cherubins;
Such harmony is in immortal souls:
But whilst this muddy vesture of decay
Doth grossly close it in, we cannot hear it.

.   .   .   .   .

JESSICA.—I am never merry when I hear sweet
  music.
LORENZO.—The reason is your spirits are attentive.

.   .   .   .   .

Therefore the poet
Did feign that Orpheus drew trees, stones, and
    floods;
Since naught so stockish, hard, and full of rage,
But music for the time doth change his nature.
The man that hath no music in himself,
Nor is not moved with concord of sweet sounds,
Is fit for treasons, stratagems, and spoils;
The motions of his spirit are dull as night,
And his affections dark as Erebus:
Let no such man be trusted.

SHAKESPEARE.

TO ——.

Music, when soft voices die,
Vibrates in the memory,—
Odors, when sweet violets sicken,
Live within the sense they quicken.

Rose-leaves, when the rose is dead,
Are heaped for the belovèd's bed ;
And so thy thoughts, when thou art gone,
Love itself shall slumber on.

PERCY BYSSHE SHELLEY.

THE CELLO.

WHEN late I heard the trembling cello play,
In every face I read sad memories
That from dark, secret chambers where they lay
Rose, and looked forth from melancholy eyes.
So every mournful thought found there a tone
To match despondence : sorrow knew its mate ;
Ill fortune sighed, and mute despair made moan ;
And one deep chord gave answer, " Late,—too late."
Then ceased the quivering strain, and swift returned
Into its depths the secret of each heart ;
Each face took on its mask, where lately burned
A spirit charmed to sight by music's art ;
But unto one who caught that inner flame
No face of all can ever seem the same.

RICHARD WATSON GILDER.

A SONG FOR SAINT CECILIA'S DAY, 1687.

FROM harmony, from heavenly harmony,
This universal frame began ;
When Nature underneath a heap
Of jarring atoms lay,
And could not heave her head

The tuneful voice was heard from high,
 Arise, ye more than dead!
Then cold and hot, and moist and dry,
 In order to their stations leap,
 And Music's power obey.
From harmony, from heavenly harmony,
 This universal frame began:
 From harmony to harmony,
Through all the compass of the notes it ran,
 The diapason closing full in man.

What passion cannot Music raise and quell?
 When Jubal struck the chorded shell,
 His listening brethren stood around,
 And, wondering, on their faces fell,
 To worship that celestial sound.
Less than a God they thought there could not dwell
 Within the hollow of that shell,
 That spoke so sweetly and so well.
What passion cannot Music raise and quell?

 The trumpet's loud clangor
  Excites us to arms,
 With shrill notes of anger,
  And mortal alarms.
The double double double beat
  Of the thundering drum
  Cries, Hark! the foes come;
Charge, charge, 't is too late to retreat!

 The soft complaining flute
 In dying notes discovers
 The woes of hopeless lovers,
Whose dirge is whispered by the warbling lute.

Sharp violins proclaim
Their jealous pangs, and desperation,
Fury, frantic indignation,
Depth of pains, and height of passion
For the fair, disdainful dame.

But O, what art can teach,
What human voice can reach,
The sacred organ's praise ?
Notes inspiring holy love,
Notes that wing their heavenly ways
To mend the choirs above.

Orpheus could lead the savage race ;
And trees uprooted left their place,
Sequacious of the lyre ;
But bright Cecilia raised the wonder higher ;
When to her organ vocal breath was given,
An angel heard, and straight appeared
Mistaking earth for heaven.

GRAND CHORUS.

As from the power of sacred lays
The spheres began to move,
And sung the great Creator's praise
To all the blessed above ;
So, when the last and dreadful hour
This crumbling pageant shall devour,
The trumpet shall be heard on high,
The dead shall live, the living die,
And music shall untune the sky.

JOHN DRYDEN.

THE SPELL.

"Son joyeux, importun, d'un clavecin sonore."
—PÉTRUS BOREL

THE keyboard, over which two slim hands float,
  Shines vaguely in the twilight pink and gray,
Whilst with a sound like wings, note after note
  Takes flight to form a pensive little lay
That strays, discreet and charming, faint, remote,
  About the room where perfumes of Her stray.

What is this sudden quiet cradling me
  To that dim ditty's dreamy rise and fall?
What do you want with me, pale melody?
  What is it that you want, ghost musical,
That fades toward the window waveringly,
  A little open on the garden small?

From the French of PAUL VERLAINE.
Translation of GERTRUDE HALL.

THE PASSIONS.

AN ODE FOR MUSIC.

WHEN Music, heavenly maid, was young,
While yet in early Greece she sung,
The Passions oft, to hear her shell,
Thronged around her magic cell,—
Exulting, trembling, raging, fainting,—
Possessed beyond the muse's painting;
By turns they felt the glowing mind
Disturbed, delighted, raised, refined;

Till once, 't is said, when all were fired,
Filled with fury, rapt, inspired,
From the supporting myrtles round
They snatched her instruments of sound ;
And, as they oft had heard apart
Sweet lessons of her forceful art,
Each (for madness ruled the hour)
Would prove his own expressive power.

First Fear his hand, its skill to try,
   Amid the chords bewildered laid,
And back recoiled, he knew not why,
   E'en at the sound himself had made.

Next Anger rushed ; his eyes, on fire,
   In lightnings owned his secret stings :
In one rude clash he struck the lyre,
   And swept with hurried hand the strings.

With woful measures wan Despair,
   Low, sullen sounds, his grief beguiled,—
A solemn, strange, and mingled air ;
   'T was sad by fits, by starts 't was wild.

But thou, O Hope, with eyes so fair,—
   What was thy delightful measure?
Still it whispered promised pleasure,
   And bade the lovely scenes at distance hail!
Still would her touch the strain prolong ;
   And from the rocks, the woods, the vale,
She called on Echo still, through all the song ;
   And where her sweetest theme she chose,
   A soft responsive voice was heard at every close ;
And Hope, enchanted, smiled, and waved her golden
     hair.

And longer had she sung—but, with a frown,
    Revenge impatient rose ;
He threw his blood-stained sword in thunder down ;
    And, with a withering look,
  The war-denouncing trumpet took,
And blew a blast so loud and dread,
Were ne'er prophetic sounds so full of woe !
    And ever and anon he beat
    The doubling drum with furious heat ;
And though, sometimes, each dreary pause between,
    Dejected Pity, at his side,
    Her soul-subduing voice applied,
Yet still he kept his wild, unaltered mien,
While each strained ball of sight seemed bursting
    from his head.

  Thy numbers, Jealousy, to naught were fixed,—
    Sad proof of thy distressful state ;
  Of differing themes the veering song was mixed ;
    And now it courted Love,—now, raving, called
    on Hate.

With eyes upraised, as one inspired,
Pale Melancholy sate retired ;
And from her wild sequestered seat,
In notes by distance made more sweet,
  Poured through the mellow horn her pensive
    soul :
    And, dashing soft from rocks around,
    Bubbling runnels joined the sound ;
  Through glades and glooms the mingled measure
    stole ;
  Or o'er some haunted stream, with fond delay,
    Round an holy calm diffusing,

Love of peace, and lonely musing,
In hollow murmurs died away.

But O, how altered was its sprightlier tone
When Cheerfulness, a nymph of healthiest hue,
Her bow across her shoulder flung,
Her buskins gemmed with morning dew,
Blew an inspiring air, that dale and thicket rung,—
The hunter's call, to faun and dryad known!
The oak-crowned sisters, and their chaste-eyed
queen,
Satyrs and sylvan boys, were seen
Peeping from forth their alleys green :
Brown Exercise rejoiced to hear ;
And Sport leapt up, and seized his beechen spear.

Last came Joy's ecstatic trial :
He, with viny crown advancing,
First to the lively pipe his hand addrest ;
But soon he saw the brisk-awakening viol,
Whose sweet entrancing voice he loved the best ;
They would have thought, who heard the strain,
They saw, in Tempe's vale, her native maids
Amidst the festal-sounding shades,
To some unwearied minstrel dancing,
While, as his flying fingers kissed the strings,
Love framed with Mirth a gay fantastic round :
Loose were her tresses seen, her zone unbound ;
And he, amidst his frolic play,
As if he would the charming air repay,
Shook thousand odors from his dewy wings.

O Music ! sphere-descended maid,
Friend of pleasure, wisdom's aid !

Why, goddess, why, to us denied,
Lay'st thou thy ancient lyre aside?
As, in that loved Athenian bower,
You learned an all-commanding power,
Thy mimic soul, O nymph endeared,
Can well recall what then it heard.
Where is thy native simple heart,
Devote to virtue, fancy, art?
Arise, as in that elder time,
Warm, energetic, chaste, sublime!
Thy wonders, in that godlike age,
Fill thy recording sister's page;
'T is said—and I believe the tale—
Thy humblest reed could more prevail,
Had more of strength, diviner rage,
Than all which charms this laggard age,—
E'en all at once together found,—
Cecilia's mingled world of sound.
O, bid our vain endeavors cease;
Revive the just designs of Greece!
Return in all thy simple state,—
Confirm the tales her sons relate!

WILLIAM COLLINS.

INVOCATION.

FROM "THE DAVIDEIS."

Awake, awake, my Lyre!
And tell thy silent master's humble tale
In sounds that may prevail;
Sounds that gentle thoughts inspire:
Though so exalted she,
And I so lowly be,

Tell her, such different notes make all thy harmony.

Hark! how the strings awake:
And, though the moving hand approach not near,
Themselves with awful fear
A kind of numerous trembling make.
Now all thy forces try;
Now all thy charms apply;
Revenge upon her ear the conquests of her eye.
Weak Lyre! thy virtue sure
Is useless here, since thou art only found
To cure, but not to wound,
And she to wound, but not to cure.
Too weak, too, wilt thou prove
My passion to remove;
Physic to other ills, thou 'rt nourishment to love.

Sleep, sleep again, my Lyre!
For thou canst never tell my humble tale
In sounds that will prevail,
Nor gentle thoughts in her inspire;
All thy vain mirth lay by,
Bid thy strings silent lie,
Sleep, sleep again, my Lyre, and let thy master die.

ABRAHAM COWLEY.

ALEXANDER'S FEAST; OR, THE POWER OF MUSIC.

AN ODE.

'T was at the royal feast, for Persia won
By Philip's warlike son:

Aloft in awful state
The godlike hero sate
  On his imperial throne :
His valiant peers were placed around,
Their brows with roses and with myrtles bound
  (So should desert in arms be crowned);
The lovely Thais, by his side,
Sate like a blooming Eastern bride
In flower of youth and beauty's pride.
  Happy, happy, happy pair !
    None but the brave,
    None but the brave,
None but the brave deserves the fair.

CHORUS.

* Happy, happy, happy pair !*
*   None but the brave,*
*   None but the brave,*
* None but the brave deserves the fair.*

Timotheus, placed on high
  Amid the tuneful choir,
  With flying fingers touched the lyre ;
The trembling notes ascend the sky,
  And heavenly joys inspire.
The song began from Jove,
Who left his blissful seats above
(Such is the power of mighty love).
A dragon's fiery form belied the god ;
Sublime on radiant spires he rode,
  When he to fair Olympia pressed,
  And while he sought her snowy breast ;
Then round her slender waist he curled,

And stamped an image of himself, a sovereign of
    the world.
The listening crowd admire the lofty sound,
A present deity ! they shout around ;
A present deity ! the vaulted roofs rebound.
       With ravished ears
       The monarch hears,
       Assumes the god,
       Affects to nod,
    And seems to shake the spheres.

CHORUS.

*   With ravished ears*
*   The monarch hears,*
*   Assumes the god,*
*   Affects to nod,*
And seems to shake the spheres.

The praise of Bacchus then the sweet musician sung,
    Of Bacchus—ever fair and ever young:
      The jolly god in triumph comes ;
      Sound the trumpets ; beat the drums :
        Flushed with a purple grace
        He shows his honest face :
Now give the hautboys breath. He comes ! he
      comes !
    Bacchus, ever fair and young,
      Drinking joys did first ordain ;
    Bacchus' blessings are a treasure,
    Drinking is the soldier's pleasure ;
       Rich the treasure,
       Sweet the pleasure,
    Sweet is pleasure after pain.

CHORUS.

Bacchus' blessings are a treasure,
Drinking is the soldier's pleasure ;
Rich the treasure,
Sweet the pleasure,
Sweet is pleasure after pain.

Soothed with the sound the king grew vain ;
Fought all his battles o'er again ;
And thrice he routed all his foes, and thrice he slew
the slain.
The master saw the madness rise ;
His glowing cheeks, his ardent eyes ;
And, while he heaven and earth defied,
Changed his hand and checked his pride.
He chose a mournful muse,
Soft pity to infuse :
He sung Darius, great and good,
By too severe a fate,
Fallen, fallen, fallen, fallen,
Fallen from his high estate,
And weltering in his blood ;
Deserted, at his utmost need,
By those his former bounty fed ;
On the bare earth exposed he lies,
With not a friend to close his eyes.
With downcast looks the joyless victor sate,
Revolving in his altered soul
The various turns of chance below ;
And, now and then, a sigh he stole ;
And tears began to flow.

CHORUS.

Revolving in his altered soul

> *The various turns of chance below ;*
> *And, now and then, a sigh he stole ;*
> *And tears began to flow*

The mighty master smiled, to see
That love was in the next degree ;
'T was but a kindred sound to move,
For pity melts the mind to love.
  Softly sweet, in Lydian measures,
  Soon he soothed his soul to pleasures.
War, he sung, is toil and trouble ;
Honor, but an empty bubble ;
  Never ending, still beginning,
  Fighting still, and still destroying :
  If the world be worth thy winning,
  Think, O, think it worth enjoying !
  Lovely Thais sits beside thee,
  Take the good the gods provide thee.
The many rend the skies with loud applause ;
So Love was crowned, but Music won the cause.
  The prince, unable to conceal his pain,
    Gazed on the fair
    Who caused his care,
  And sighed and looked, sighed and looked,
  Sighed and looked, and sighed again :
At length, with love and wine at once oppressed,
The vanquished victor sunk upon her breast.

CHORUS.

> *The prince, unable to conceal his pain,*
> * Gazed on the fair*
> * Who caused his care,*
> *And sighed and looked, sighed and looked,*
> *Sighed and looked, and sighed again :*

At length with love and wine at once oppressed,
The vanquished victor sunk upon her breast.

Now strike the golden lyre again :
A louder yet, and yet a louder strain.
Break his bands of sleep asunder,
And rouse him, like a rattling peal of thunder.
    Hark, hark, the horrid sound
      Has raised up his head ;
      As awaked from the dead,
    And amazed, he stares around.
Revenge ! revenge ! Timotheus cries,
    See the furies arise !
  See the snakes that they rear,
  How they hiss in their hair,
And the sparkles that flash from their eyes !
  Behold a ghastly band,
  Each a torch in his hand !
Those are Grecian ghosts, that in battle were slain,
    And unburied remain,
    Inglorious on the plain :
    Give the vengeance due
    To the valiant crew.
Behold how they toss their torches on high,
  How they point to the Persian abodes,
And glittering temples of their hostile gods !
The princes applaud with a furious joy ;
And the king seized a flambeau with zeal to destroy ;
    Thais led the way,
    To light him to his prey,
And, like another Helen, fired another Troy !

CHORUS.

And the king seized a flambeau with zeal to destroy :

Thais led the way,
To light him to his prey,
And, like another Helen, fired another Troy!

Thus, long ago,
Ere heaving bellows learned to blow,
While organs yet were mute ;
Timotheus, to his breathing flute,
And sounding lyre,
Could swell the soul to rage, or kindle soft desire.
At last divine Cecilia came,
Inventress of the vocal frame ;
The sweet enthusiast, from her sacred store,
Enlarged the former narrow bounds,
And added length to solemn sounds,
With nature's mother-wit, and arts unknown before.
Let old Timotheus yield the prize,
Or both divide the crown ;
He raised a mortal to the skies,
She drew an angel down.

GRAND CHORUS.

At last divine Cecilia came,
Inventress of the vocal frame ;
The sweet enthusiast, from her sacred store,
Enlarged the former narrow bounds,
And added length to solemn sounds,
With nature's mother-wit, and arts unknown before.
Let old Timotheus yield the prize,
Or both divide the crown ;
He raised a mortal to the skies,
She drew an angel down.

JOHN DRYDEN.

BEETHOVEN'S THIRD SYMPHONY.

Passion and pain, the outcry of despair,
   The pang of the unattainable desire,
   And youth's delight in pleasures that expire,
And sweet high dreamings of the good and fair
Clashing in swift soul-storm, through which no
      prayer
   Uplifted stays the destined death-stroke dire.
   Then through a mighty sorrowing, as through fire,
The soul burnt pure yearns forth into the air
Of the dear earth and, with the scent of flowers
   And song of birds assuaged, takes heart again,
   Made cheerier with this drinking of God's wine,
And turns with healing to the world of men,
And high above a sweet strong angel towers,
   And Love makes life triumphant and divine.
RICHARD HOVEY.

PAN IN WALL STREET.

Just where the Treasury's marble front
   Looks over Wall Street's mingled nations;
Where Jews and Gentiles most are wont
   To throng for trade and last quotations;
Where, hour by hour, the rates of gold
   Outrival, in the ears of people,
The quarter-chimes, serenely tolled
   From Trinity's undaunted steeple,—

Even there I heard a strange, wild strain
   Sound high above the modern clamor,

Above the cries of greed and gain,
    The curbstone war, the auction's hammer;
And swift, on Music's misty ways,
    It led, from all this strife for millions,
To ancient, sweet-do-nothing days
    Among the kirtle-robed Sicilians.

And as it stilled the multitude,
    And yet more joyous rose, and shriller,
I saw the minstrel, where he stood
    At ease against a Doric pillar:
One hand a droning organ played,
    The other held a Pan's-pipe (fashioned
Like those of old) to lips that made
    The reeds give out that strain impassioned.

'T was Pan himself had wandered here
    A-strolling through this sordid city,
And piping to the civic ear
    The prelude of some pastoral ditty!
The demigod had crossed the seas,—
    From haunts of shepherd, nymph, and satyr,
And Syracusan times,—to these
    Far shores and twenty centuries later.

A ragged cap was on his head;
    But—hidden thus—there was no doubting
That, all with crispy locks o'erspread,
    His gnarlèd horns were somewhere sprouting;
His club-feet, cased in rusty shoes,
    Were crossed, as on some frieze you see them,
And trousers, patched of divers hues,
    Concealed his crooked shanks beneath them.

He filled the quivering reeds with sound,
   And o'er his mouth their changes shifted,
And with his goat's-eyes looked around
   Where'er the passing current drifted ;
And soon, as on Trinacrian hills
   The nymphs and herdsmen ran to hear him,
Even now the tradesmen from their tills,
   With clerks and porters, crowded near him.

The bulls and bears together drew
   From Jauncey Court and New Street Alley,
As erst, if pastorals be true,
   Came beasts from every wooded valley ;
The random passers stayed to list,—
   A boxer Ægon, rough and merry,
A Broadway Daphnis, on his tryst
   With Nais at the Brooklyn Ferry.

A one-eyed Cyclops halted long
   In tattered cloak of army pattern,
And Galatea joined the throng,—
   A blowsy, apple-vending slattern ;
While old Silenus staggered out
   From some new-fangled lunch-house handy,
And bade the piper, with a shout,
   To strike up Yankee Doodle Dandy !

A newsboy and a peanut-girl
   Like little Fauns began to caper :
His hair was all in tangled curl,
   Her tawny legs were bare and taper ;
And still the gathering larger grew,
   And gave its pence and crowded nigher,
While aye the shepherd-minstrel blew
   His pipe, and struck the gamut higher.

O heart of Nature, beating still
 With throbs her vernal passion taught her,—
Even here, as on the vine-clad hill,
 Or by the Arethusan water!
New forms may fold the speech, new lands
 Arise within these ocean-portals,
But Music waves eternal wands,—
 Enchantress of the souls of mortals!

So thought I,—but among us trod
 A man in blue, with legal baton,
And scoffed the vagrant demigod,
 And pushed him from the step I sat on.
Doubting I mused upon the cry,
 "Great Pan is dead!"—and all the people
Went on their ways:—and clear and high
 The quarter sounded from the steeple.

EDMUND CLARENCE STEDMAN.

ON AN INTAGLIO HEAD OF MINERVA.

BENEATH the warrior's helm, behold
 The flowing tresses of the woman!
Minerva, Pallas, what you will—
 A winsome creature, Greek or Roman.

Minerva? No! 't is some sly minx
 In cousin's helmet masquerading;
If not—then Wisdom was a dame
 For sonnets and for serenading!

I thought the goddess cold, austere,
 Not made for love's despairs and blisses;

Did Pallas wear her hair like that?
  Was Wisdom's mouth so shaped for kisses?

The Nightingale should be her bird,
  And not the Owl, big-eyed and solemn.
How very fresh she looks, and yet
  She's older far than Trajan's column!

The magic hand that carved this face,
  And set this vine-work round it running,
Perhaps ere mighty Phidias wrought
  Had lost its subtle skill and cunning.

Who was he? Was he glad or sad,
  Who knew to carve in such a fashion?
Perchance he graved the dainty head
  For some brown girl that scorned his passion.

Perchance, in some still garden-place,
  Where neither fount nor tree to-day is,
He flung the jewel at the feet
  Of Phryne, or perhaps 't was Lais.

But he is dust: we may not know
  His happy or unhappy story;
Nameless, and dead these centuries,
  His work outlives him—there 's his glory!

Both man and jewel lay in earth
  Beneath a lava-buried city;
The countless summers came and went,
  With neither haste, nor hate, nor pity.

Years blotted out the man, but left
  The jewel fresh as any blossom,

Till some Visconti dug it up—
  To rise and fall on Mabel's bosom!

O nameless brother! see how Time
  Your gracious handiwork has guarded:
See how your loving, patient art
  Has come, at last, to be rewarded!

Who would not suffer slights of men,
  And pangs of hopeless passion also,
To have his carven agate-stone
  On such a bosom rise and fall so!

THOMAS BAILEY ALDRICH.

THE ARTIST.

He wrought with patience long and weary years
Upon his masterpiece, entitled " Fate,"
And dreamed sweet dreams, the while his crust he
    ate,
And gave his work his soul, his strength, and tears.
His task complete at last, he had no fears
The world would not pronounce his genius great,
But poor, unknown—pray, what could *he* create?
The mad world laughed, and gave not praise, but
    jeers.
Impelled to ask wherein his work was wrong,
He sought, despairing, one whose art was dead,
But on whose brow were wreathed the bays of
    Fame:
The master gazed upon the picture long;
" It lacks one thing to make it great," he said,
And signed the canvas with his own great name!

ARTHUR GRISSOM.

A PAINTED FAN.

Roses and butterflies snared on a fan,
  All that is left of summer gone by ;
Of swift, bright wings that flashed in the sun,
  And loveliest blossoms that bloomed to die !

By what subtle spell did you lure them here,
  Fixing a beauty that will not change,—
Roses whose petals never will fall,
  Bright, swift wings that never will range ?

Had you owned but the skill to snare as well
  The swift-winged hours that came and went,
To prison the words that in music died,
  And fix with a spell the heart's content,

Then had you been of magicians the chief ;
  And loved and lovers should bless your art,
If you could but have painted the soul of the
      thing,—
  Not the rose alone, but the rose's heart !

Flown are those days with their winged delights,
  As the odor is gone from the summer rose ;
Yet still, whenever I wave my fan,
  The soft, south wind of memory blows.

                    LOUISE CHANDLER MOULTON.

ON A FAN

THAT BELONGED TO THE MARQUISE DE POMPADOUR.

(BALLADE.)

Chicken-skin, delicate, white,
  Painted by Carlo Vanloo,

Loves in a riot of light,
  Roses and vaporous blue;
  Hark to the dainty *frou-frou!*
Picture above, if you can,
  Eyes that could melt as the dew,—
This was the Pompadour's fan!

See how they rise at the sight,
  Thronging the *Œil de Bœuf* through,
Courtiers as butterflies bright,
  Beauties that Fragonard drew,
  Talon-rouge, falaba, queue,
Cardinal, duke,—to a man,
  Eager to sigh or to sue,—
This was the Pompadour's fan!

Ah, but things more than polite
  Hung on this toy, *voyez-vous!*
Matters of state and of might,
  Things that great ministers do;
Things that, maybe, overthrew
  Those in whose brains they began;—
Here was the sign and the cue,—
  This was the Pompadour's fan!

ENVOY.

Where are the secrets it knew?
  Weavings of plot and of plan?
—But where is the Pompadour, too?
  This was the Pompadour's *fan!*

AUSTIN DOBSON.

VI.

LABOR AND REST.

HACK AND HEW.

Hack and Hew were the sons of God
   In the earlier earth than now:
One at his right hand, one at his left,
   To obey as he taught them how.

And Hack was blind, and Hew was dumb,
   But both had the wild, wild heart;
And God's calm will was their burning will,
   And the gist of their toil was art.

They made the moon and the belted stars,
   They set the sun to ride;
They loosed the girdle and veil of the sea,
   The wind and the purple tide.

Both flower and beast beneath their hands
   To beauty and speed outgrew,—
The furious, fumbling hand of Hack,
   And the glorying hand of Hew.

Then, fire and clay, they fashioned a man,
   And painted him rosy brown;
And God himself blew hard in his eyes:
   " Let them burn till they smoulder down! "

And "There!" said Hack, and "There!" thought
    Hew,
  "We'll rest, for our toil is done."
But "Nay," the Master Workman said,
  "For your toil is just begun.

"And ye who served me of old as God
  Shall serve me anew as man,
Till I compass the dream that is in my heart,
  And perfect the vaster plan."

And still the craftsman over his craft,
  In the vague white light of dawn,
With God's calm will for his burning will,
  While the mounting day comes on,

Yearning, wind-swift, indolent, wild,
  Toils with those shadowy two,—
The faltering, restless hand of Hack,
  And the tireless hand of Hew.

                       BLISS CARMAN.

THE AXE.

FROM "MALCOLM'S KATIE."

HIGH grew the snow beneath the low-hung sky,
And all was silent in the wilderness;
In trance of stillness Nature heard her God
Rebuilding her spent fires, and veiled her face
While the Great Worker brooded o'er His work.

  "Bite deep and wide, O Axe, the tree!
  What doth thy bold voice promise me?"

"I promise thee all joyous things
That furnish forth the lives of kings!

"For every silver ringing blow,
Cities and palaces shall grow!"

"Bite deep and wide, O Axe, the tree!
Tell wider prophecies to me."

"When rust hath gnawed me deep and red,
A nation strong shall lift his head.

"His crown the very Heavens shall smite,
Æons shall build him in his might!"

"Bite deep and wide, O Axe, the tree;
Bright Seer, help on thy prophecy!"

Max smote the snow-weighed tree, and lightly
    laughed.
"See, friend," he cried to one that looked and
    smiled,
"My axe and I—we do immortal tasks—
We build up nations—this my axe and I!"

ISABELLA VALANCEY CRAWFORD.

LABOR.

PAUSE not to dream of the future before us;
Pause not to weep the wild cares that come o'er us;
Hark! how Creation's deep, musical chorus,
    Unintermitting, goes up into Heaven!
Never the ocean-wave falters in flowing;
Never the little seed stops in its growing;
More and more richly the rose-heart keeps glowing,
    Till from its nourishing stem it is riven.

" Labor is worship ! "—the robin is singing ;
" Labor is worship ! "—the wild-bee is ringing ;
Listen ! that eloquent whisper upspringing
    Speaks to thy soul from out Nature's great heart.
From the dark cloud flows the life-giving shower ;
From the rough sod blows the soft-breathing
        flower ;
From the small insect, the rich coral bower ;
    Only man, in the plan, shrinks from his part.

Labor is life ! 'T is the still water faileth ;
Idleness ever despaireth, bewaileth ;
Keep the watch wound, for the dark rust assaileth ;
    Flowers droop and die in the stillness of noon.
Labor is glory !—the flying cloud lightens ;
Only the waving wing changes and brightens ;
Idle hearts only the dark future frightens :
    Play the sweet keys, wouldst thou keep them in
        tune !

Labor is rest from the sorrows that greet us,
Rest from all petty vexations that meet us,
Rest from sin-promptings that ever entreat us,
    Rest from world-sirens that lure us to ill,
Work—and pure slumbers shall wait on thy pillow ;
Work—thou shalt ride over Care's coming billow ;
Lie not down wearied 'neath Woe's weeping-willow ;
    Work with a stout heart and resolute will !

Labor is health ! Lo ! the husbandman reaping,
How through his veins goes the life-current leaping !
How his strong arm, in its stalwart pride sweeping,
    True as a sunbeam the swift sickle guides !
Labor is wealth—in the sea the pearl groweth ;

Rich the queen's robe from the frail cocoon floweth ;
From the fine acorn the strong forest bloweth :
  Temple and statue the marble block hides.

Droop not, though shame, sin, and anguish are round
      thee !
Bravely fling off the cold chain that hath bound
      thee !
Look to yon pure Heaven smiling beyond thee ;
  Rest not content in thy darkness—a clod !
Work—for some good, be it ever so slowly ;
Cherish some flower, be it ever so lowly ;
Labor !—all labor is noble and holy !
  Let thy great deeds be thy prayer to thy God !

FRANCES SARGENT OSGOOD.

THE SONG OF THE LOWER CLASSES.

We plough and sow—we 're so very, very low
  That we delve in the dirty clay,
Till we bless the plain with the golden grain,
  And the vale with the fragrant hay.
Our place we know—we 're so very low,
  'T is down at the landlord's feet :
We 're not too low the bread to grow,
  But too low the bread to eat.

Down, down we go—we 're so very, very low—
  To the hell of the deep-sunk mines,
But we gather the proudest gems that glow
  When the crown of a despot shines.
And whenever he lacks, upon our backs
  Fresh loads he deigns to lay :

We 're far too low to vote the tax,
But not too low to pay.

We 're low—we 're low—mere rabble, we know;
But at our plastic power,
The mold at the lordling's feet will grow
Into palace and church and tower;
Then prostrate fall in the rich man's hall,
And cringe at the rich man's door :
We 're not too low to build the wall,
But too low to tread the floor.

We 're low,—we 're low—we 're very, very low,—
Yet from our fingers glide
The silken flow and the robes that glow
Round the limbs of the sons of pride.
And what we get, and what we give,
We know, and we know our share :
We 're not too low the cloth to weave,
But too low the cloth to wear!

We 're low—we 're low—we 're very, very low ;
And yet when the trumpets ring,
The thrust of a poor man's arm will go
Through the heart of the proudest king.
We 're low—we 're low—our place we know,
We 're only the rank and file :
We 're not too low to kill the foe,
But too low to touch the spoil.

ERNEST CHARLES JONES.

"THE MAN WITH THE HOE."

WRITTEN AFTER SEEING MILLET'S WORLD-FAMOUS PAINTING.

> " God made man in His own image,
>   In the image of God made He him."—GENESIS.

BOWED by the weight of centuries he leans
Upon his hoe and gazes on the ground,
The emptiness of ages in his face,
And on his back the burden of the world.
Who made him dead to rapture and despair,
A thing that grieves not and that never hopes,
Stolid and stunned, a brother to the ox?
Who loosened and let down this brutal jaw?
Whose was the hand that slanted back this brow?
Whose breath blew out the light within this brain?

Is this the Thing the Lord God made and gave
To have dominion over sea and land;
To trace the stars and search the heavens for power;
To feel the passion of Eternity?
Is this the Dream He dreamed who shaped the suns
And marked their ways upon the ancient deep?
Down all the stretch of Hell to its last gulf
There is no shape more terrible than this—
More tongued with censure of the world's blind
        greed—
More filled with signs and portents for the soul—
More fraught with menace to the universe.

What gulfs between him and the seraphim!
Slave of the wheel of labor, what to him

Are Plato and the swing of Pleiades?
What the long reaches of the peaks of song,
The rift of dawn, the reddening of the rose?
Through this dread shape the suffering ages look;
Time's tragedy is in that aching stoop;
Through this dread shape humanity betrayed,
Plundered, profaned and disinherited,
Cries protest to the Judges of the World,
A protest that is also prophecy.

O masters, lords and rulers in all lands,
Is this the handiwork you give to God,
This monstrous thing distorted and soul-quenched?
How will you ever straighten up this shape;
Touch it again with immortality;
Give back the upward looking and the light;
Rebuild in it the music and the dream;
Make right the immemorial infamies,
Perfidious wrongs, immedicable woes?

O masters, lords and rulers in all lands,
How will the Future reckon with this Man?
How answer his brute question in that hour
When whirlwinds of rebellion shake the world?
How will it be with kingdoms and with kings—
With those who shaped him to the thing he is—
When this dumb Terror shall reply to God
After the silence of the centuries? *

EDWIN MARKHAM.

* From " The Man With the Hoe and Other Poems." Copyright, 1899, by Edwin Markham. Published by Doubleday & McClure Co.

"THE MAN WITH THE HOE."

A REPLY.

"Let us a little permit Nature to take her own way: she better understands her own affairs than we."—MONTAIGNE.

NATURE reads not our labels, "great" and "small";
Accepts she one and all

Who, striving, win and hold the vacant place;
All are of royal race.

Him, there, rough-cast, with rigid arm and limb,
The Mother moulded him,

Of his rude realm ruler and demigod,
Lord of the rock and clod.

With Nature is no "better" and no "worse,"
On this bared head no curse.

Humbled it is and bowed; so is he crowned
Whose kingdom is the ground.

Diverse the burdens on the one stern road
Where bears each back its load;

Varied the toil, but neither high nor low.
With pen or sword or hoe,

He that has put out strength, lo, he is strong;
Of him with spade or song

Nature but questions,—"This one, shall he stay?"
She answers "Yea," or "Nay,"

" Well, ill, he digs, he sings ; " and he bides on,
Or shudders, and is gone.

Strength shall he have, the toiler, strength and
    grace,
So fitted to his place

As he leaned, there, an oak where sea winds blow,
Our brother with the hoe.

No blot, no monster, no unsightly thing,
The soil's long-lineaged king ;

His changeless realm, he knows it and commands ;
Erect enough he stands,

Tall as his toil.   Nor does he bow unblest:
Labor he has, and rest.

Need was, need is, and need will ever be
For him and such as he ;

Cast for the gap, with gnarlèd arm and limb,
The Mother moulded him,—

Long wrought, and moulded him with mother's
    care,
Before she set him there.

And aye she gives him, mindful of her own,
Peace of the plant, the stone ;

Yea, since above his work he may not rise,
She makes the field his skies.

See ! she that bore him, and metes out the lot,
He serves her.   Vex him not

To scorn the rock whence he was hewn, the pit
And what was digged from it;

Lest he no more in native virtue stand,
The earth-sword in his hand,

But follow sorry phantoms to and fro,
And let a kingdom go.

JOHN VANCE CHENEY.

CORN–LAW HYMN.

LORD! call thy pallid angel,
    The tamer of the strong!
And bid him whip with want and woe
    The champions of the wrong!
O, say not thou to ruin's flood,
    " Up, sluggard! why so slow ? "
        But alone, let them groan,
        The lowest of the low;
And basely beg the bread they curse,
    Where millions curse them now!

No; wake not thou the giant
    Who drinks hot blood for wine;
And shouts unto the east and west,
    In thunder-tones like thine;
Till the slow to move rush all at once,
    An avalanche of men,
        While he raves over waves
        That need no whirlwind then;
Though slow to move, moved all at once,
    A sea, a sea of men!

EBENEZER ELLIOTT.

FOR A' THAT AND A' THAT.

Is there for honest poverty
  Wha hangs his head, and a' that?
The coward slave, we pass him by;
  We dare be poor for a' that.
For a' that, and a' that,
  Our toils obscure, and a' that;
The rank is but the guinea's stamp,—
  The man 's the gowd for a' that.

What though on hamely fare we dine,
  Wear hoddin gray, and a' that?
Gie fools their silks, and knaves their wine,—
  A man 's a man for a' that.
For a' that, and a' that,
  Their tinsel show, and a' that;
The honest man, though e'er sae poor,
  Is king o' men for a' that.

Ye see yon birkie ca'd a lord,
  Wha struts, and stares, and a' that,—
Though hundreds worship at his word,
  He 's but a coof for a' that;
For a' that, and a' that,
  His riband, star, and a' that;
The man of independent mind,
  He looks and laughs at a' that.

C prince can mak a belted knight,
  A marquis, duke, and a' that;
But an honest man 's aboon his might,—
  Guid faith, he maunna fa' that!

For a' that, and a' that;
  Their dignities, and a' that,
The pith o' sense, and pride o' worth,
  Are higher ranks than a' that.

Then let us pray that come it may,—
  As come it will for a' that,—
That sense and worth, o'er a' the earth,
  May bear the gree, and a' that.
For a' that, and a' that,
  It 's coming yet, for a' that,—
When man to man, the warld o'er,
  Shall brothers be for a' that !

ROBERT BURNS.

THE GOOD TIME COMING.

There 's a good time coming, boys.
  A good time coming:
We may not live to see the day,
But earth shall glisten in the ray
  Of the good time coming.
Cannon-balls may aid the truth,
  But thought 's a weapon stronger;
We 'll win our battle by its aid;—
  Wait a little longer.

There 's a good time coming, boys,
  A good time coming:
The pen shall supersede the sword,
And Right, not Might, shall be the lord
  In the good time coming.

Worth, not Birth, shall rule mankind,
　And be acknowledged stronger ;
The proper impulse has been given ;—
　Wait a little longer.

There 's a good time coming, boys,
　A good time coming :
War in all men's eyes shall be
A monster of iniquity
　In the good time coming.
Nations shall not quarrel then,
　To prove which is the stronger ;
Nor slaughter men for glory's sake ;—
　Wait a little longer.

There 's a good time coming, boys,
　A good time coming :
Hateful rivalries of creed
Shall not make their martyrs bleed
　In the good time coming.
Religion shall be shorn of pride,
　And flourish all the stronger ;
And Charity shall trim her lamp ;—
　Wait a little longer.

There 's a good time coming, boys,
　A good time coming :
And a poor man's family
Shall not be his misery
　In the good time coming.
Every child shall be a help
　To make his right arm stronger ;
The happier he, the more he has ;—
　Wait a little longer.

There 's a good time coming, boys,
  A good time coming:
Little children shall not toil
Under, or above, the soil
  In the good time coming;
But shall play in healthful fields,
  Till limbs and mind grow stronger;
And every one shall read and write;—
  Wait a little longer.

There 's a good time coming, boys,
  A good time coming:
The people shall be temperate,
And shall love instead of hate,
  In the good time coming.
They shall use, and not abuse,
  And make all virtue stronger;
The reformation has begun;—
  Wait a little longer.

There 's a good time coming, boys,
  A good time coming:
Let us aid it all we can,
Every woman, every man,
  The good time coming:
Smallest helps, if rightly given,
  Make the impulse stronger;
'T will be strong enough one day;—
  Wait a little longer.

CHARLES MACKAY.

THE LOTUS-EATERS.

I.

"Courage!" he said, and pointed toward the land;
"This morning wave shall roll us shoreward soon."
In the afternoon they came unto a land
In which it seemèd always afternoon.
All round the coast the languid air did swoon,
Breathing like one that hath a weary dream.
Full-faced above the valley stood the moon:
And, like a downward smoke, the slender stream
Along the cliff to fall, and pause, and fall did seem.

II.

A land of streams! some, like a downward smoke,
Slow-dropping veils of thinnest lawn, did go;
And some through wavering lights and shadows
　　broke,
Rolling a slumbrous sheet of foam below.
They saw the gleaming river seaward flow
From the inner land: far off, three mountain-tops,
Three silent pinnacles of aged snow,
Stood sunset-flushed: and, dewed with showery
　　drops,
Up-clomb the shadowy pine above the woven copse.

III.

The charmèd sunset lingered low adown
In the red west: through mountain-clefts the dale
Was seen far inland, and the yellow down
Bordered with palm, and many a winding vale
And meadow, set with slender galingale;
A land where all things always seemed the same!
And round about the keel, with faces pale,

Dark faces pale against that rosy flame,
The mild-eyed, melancholy Lotus-eaters came.

IV.

Branches they bore of that enchanted stem,
Laden with flower and fruit, whereof they gave
To each, but whoso did receive of them,
And taste, to him the gushing of the wave
Far, far away did seem to mourn and rave
On alien shores; and if his fellow spake,
His voice was thin, as voices from the grave;
And deep asleep he seemed, yet all awake,
And music in his ears his beating heart did make.

V.

They sat them down upon the yellow sand,
Between the sun and moon, upon the shore;
And sweet it was to dream of Father-land,
Of child, and wife, and slave; but evermore
Most weary seemed the sea, weary the oar,
Weary the wandering fields of barren foam.
Then some one said, " We will return no more; "
And all at once they sang, " Our island home
Is far beyond the wave ; we will no longer roam."

CHORIC SONG.

I.

There is sweet music here that softer falls
Than petals from blown roses on the grass,
Or night-dews on still waters between walls
Of shadowy granite, in a gleaming pass;
Music that gentlier on the spirit lies

Than tired eyelids upon tired eyes ;
Music that brings sweet sleep down from the bliss-
    ful skies.
Here are cool mosses deep,
And through the moss the ivies creep,
And in the stream the long-leaved flowers weep,
And from the craggy ledge the poppy hangs in
    sleep.

II.

Why are we weighed upon with heaviness,
And utterly consumed with sharp distress,
While all things else have rest from weariness ?
All things have rest : why should we toil alone ?
We only toil, who are the first of things,
And make perpetual moan,
Still from one sorrow to another thrown :
Nor ever fold our wings,
And cease our wanderings,
Nor steep our brows in slumber's holy balm ;
Nor hearken what the inner spirit sings,
" There is no joy but calm ! "
Why should we only toil, the roof and crown of
    things ?

III.

Lo ! in the middle of the wood,
The folded leaf is wooed from out the bud
With winds upon the branch, and there
Grows green and broad, and takes no care,
Sun-steeped at noon, and in the moon
Nightly dew-fed ; and turning yellow,
Falls, and floats adown the air.
Lo ! sweetened with the summer-light,

The full-juiced apple, waxing over-mellow,
Drops in a silent autumn night.
All its allotted length of days,
The flower ripens in its place,
Ripens and fades, and falls, and hath no toil,
Fast-rooted in the fruitful soil.

IV.

Hateful is the dark-blue sky,
Vaulted o'er the dark-blue sea.
Death is the end of life; ah! why
Should life all labor be?
Let us alone.   Time driveth onward fast,
And in a little while our lips are dumb.
Let us alone.   What is it that will last?
All things are taken from us, and become
Portions and parcels of the dreadful Past.
Let us alone.   What pleasure can we have
To war with evil?   Is there any peace
In ever climbing up the climbing wave?
All things have rest, and ripen toward the grave,
In silence ripen, fall, and cease:
Give us long rest or death, dark death of dreamful
ease!

V.

How sweet it were, hearing the downward stream,
With half-shut eyes ever to seem
Falling asleep in a half dream!
To dream and dream, like yonder amber light,
Which will not leave the myrrh-bush on the
height;
To hear each other's whispered speech;

Eating the Lotus, day by day,
To watch the crisping ripples on the beach,
And tender curving lines of creamy spray :
To lend our hearts and spirits wholly
To the influence of mild-minded melancholy ;
To muse and brood and live again in memory,
With those old faces of our infancy
Heaped over with a mound of grass,
Two handfuls of white dust, shut in an urn of
    brass !

VI.

Dear is the memory of our wedded lives,
And dear the last embraces of our wives,
And their warm tears ; but all hath suffered change ;
For surely now our household hearths are cold :
Our sons inherit us : our looks are strange :
And we should come like ghosts to trouble joy.
Or else the island princes, over-bold,
Have eat our substance, and the minstrel sings
Before them of the ten years' war in Troy,
And our great deeds as half-forgotten things.
Is there confusion in the little isle ?
Let what is broken so remain.
The gods are hard to reconcile :
'T is hard to settle order once again.
There *is* confusion worse than death,
Trouble on trouble, pain on pain,
Long labor unto aged breath,
Sore task to hearts worn out with many wars,
And eyes grown dim with gazing on the pilot-
    stars.

VII.

But, propt on beds of amaranth and moly,
How sweet (while warm airs lull us, blowing
        lowly),
With half-dropt eyelids still,
Beneath a heaven dark and holy,
To watch the long bright river drawing slowly
His waters from the purple hill—
To hear the dewy echoes calling
From cave to cave through the thick-twined vine
To hear the emerald-colored water falling
Through many a wov'n acanthus-wreath divine !
Only to hear and see the far-off sparkling brine,
Only to hear were sweet, stretched out beneath the
        pine.

VIII.

The Lotus blooms below the barren peak :
The Lotus blows by every winding creek :
All day the wind breathes low with mellower tone :
Through every hollow cave and alley lone
Round and round the spicy downs the yellow Lotus-
        dust is blown.
We have had enough of action, and of motion we,
Rolled to starboard, rolled to larboard, when the
        surge was seething free,
Where the wallowing monster spouted his foam-
        fountains in the sea.
Let us swear an oath, and keep it with an equal
        mind,
In the hollow Lotus-land to live and lie reclined
On the hills like gods together, careless of man-
        kind.

For they lie beside their nectar, and the bolts are
    hurled
Far below them in the valleys, and the clouds are
    lightly curled
Round their golden houses, girdled with the gleam-
    ing world;
Where they smile in secret, looking over wasted
    lands,
Blight and famine, plague and earthquake, roar-
    ing deeps and fiery sands,
Clanging fights, and flaming towns, and sinking
    ships, and praying hands.
But they smile, they find a music centred in a
    doleful song
Steaming up, a lamentation and an ancient tale of
    wrong,
Like a tale of little meaning, though the words are
    strong;
Chanted from an ill-used race of men that cleave
    the soil,
Sow the seed, and reap the harvest with enduring
    toil,
Storing yearly little dues of wheat, and wine, and
    oil;
Till they perish and they suffer—some, 't is whis-
    pered—down in hell
Suffer endless anguish, others in Elysian valleys
    dwell,
Resting weary limbs at last on beds of asphodel.
Surely, surely, slumber is more sweet than toil, the
    shore
Than labor in the deep mid-ocean, wind and wave
    and oar;

O rest ye, brother mariners, we will not wander
    more.

ALFRED, LORD TENNYSON.

DELAY.

I DO affirm that thou hast saved the race
As much as thou hast ever made it lose :
Men of quick action may thy name abuse,
But the world's life and theirs attest thy grace.
An hour of thee doth sometimes turn the face
Of men and kingdoms, bidding them refuse
What, chosen last, it had been death to choose :
Through thee alone, they missed the fatal place.
How often dies the guileful thought or end
When guileless eyes detain us on our way !
What sin and shame that hindrance may forefend,
Which we so hate and storm against to-day !
What mighty evils over all impend,
Averted graciously by kind Delay !

CHARLOTTE FISKE BATES.

THE HAPPY HEART.

FROM "PATIENT GRISSELL," ACT I. SC. 1.

ART thou poor, yet hast thou golden slumbers ?
    O sweet content !
Art thou rich, yet is thy mind perplexed ?
    O punishment !
Dost thou laugh to see how fools are vexed
To add to golden numbers, golden numbers ?
O sweet content ! O sweet, O sweet content !

Work apace, apace, apace, apace ;
Honest labor bears a lovely face ;
Then hey nonny nonny, hey nonny nonny !

Canst drink the waters of the crispèd spring ?
          O sweet content !
Swimm'st thou in wealth, yet sink'st in thine own
               tears ?
          O punishment !
Then he that patiently want's burden bears
No burden bears, but is a king, a king !
O sweet content ! O sweet, O sweet content !
     Work apace, apace, apace, apace ;
     Honest labor bears a lovely face ;
Then hey nonny nonny, hey nonny nonny !

THOMAS DEKKER.

THE COBBLER AND THE FINANCIER.

A COBBLER sang from morn till night :
'T was sweet and marvellous to hear ;
His trills and quavers told the ear
Of more contentment and delight,
Enjoyed by that laborious wight,
Than e'er enjoyed the sages seven,
Or any mortals short of heaven.
His neighbor, on the other hand,
With gold in plenty at command,
But little sang, and slumbered less,—
A financier of great success.
If e'er he dozed at break of day,
The cobbler's song drove sleep away ;
And much he wished that Heaven had made

Sleep a commodity of trade,
In market sold, like food and drink,
So much an hour, so much a wink.
At last, our songster did he call
To meet him in his princely hall.
Said he, " Now, honest Gregory,
What may your yearly earnings be ? "
" My yearly earnings ! faith, good sir,
I never go, at once, so far,"
   The cheerful cobbler said,
   And queerly scratched his head,—
" I never reckon in that way,
But cobble on from day to day,
   Content with daily bread."
   " Indeed ! Well, Gregory, pray,
What may your earnings be per day ? "
" Why, sometimes more and sometimes less.
The worst of all, I must confess,
(And but for which our gains would be
A pretty sight indeed to see,)
Is that the days are made so many
In which we cannot earn a penny.
The sorest ill the poor man feels :
They tread upon each other's heels,
Those idle days of holy saints !
   And though the year is shingled o'er,
   The parson keeps a-finding more ! "
With smile provoked by these complaints,
Replied the lordly financier,
   " I 'll give you better cause to sing.
These hundred pounds I hand you here
   Will make you happy as a king.
Go, spend them with a frugal heed :

They 'll long supply your every need."
The cobbler thought the silver more
Than he had ever dreamed, before,
The mines for ages could produce,
Or world with all its people use.
He took it home, and there did hide,
And with it laid his joy aside.
No more of song, no more of sleep,
   But cares, suspicions, in their stead,
   And false alarms, by fancy fed.
His eyes and ears their vigils keep,
And not a cat can tread the floor
But seems a thief slipped through the door.
       At last, poor man !
Up to the financier he ran,—
Then in his morning nap profound :
   " Oh, give me back my songs," cried he,
   " And sleep, that used so sweet to be,
And take the money, every pound ! "

From the French of JEAN DE LA FONTAINE.
Translation of ELIZUR WRIGHT.

LABOR DONE.

FROM "SONG OF THE BELL."

Let us with care observe
  What from our strength, yet weakness, springs ;
For he respect can ne'er deserve
  Who hands alone to labor brings.
'T is only this which honors man ;
  His mind with heavenly fire was warmed,

That he with deepest thought might scan
  The work which his own hand has formed.

.   .   .   .   .   .

Cheerful in the forest gloom,
  The wanderer turns his weary steps
To his loved, though lowly home.
    Bleating flocks draw near the fold ;
          And the herds,
Wide-horned, and smooth, slow-pacing come
    Lowing from the hill,
      The accustomed stall to fill.
          Heavy rolls
          Along the wagon,
          Richly loaded.
          On the sheaves,
          With gayest leaves
          They form the wreath ;
And the youthful reapers dance
          Upon the heath.
Street and market all are quiet,
And round each domestic light
Gathers now a circle fond,
While shuts the creaking city-gate.
          Darkness hovers
          O'er the earth.
Safety still each sleeper covers
          As with light,
That the deeds of crime discovers ;
  For wakes the law's protecting might.

Holy Order ! rich with all
The gifts of Heaven, that best we call,—
Freedom, peace, and equal laws,—

Of common good the happy cause !
She the savage man has taught
What the arts of life have wrought ;
Changed the rude hut to comfort, splendor,
And filled fierce hearts with feelings tender
And yet a dearer bond she wove,—
Our home, our country, taught to love.

A thousand active hands, combined
   For mutual aid, with zealous heart,
In well apportioned labor find
   Their power increasing with their art.
Master and workmen all agree,
   Under sweet Freedom's holy care,
And each content in his degree,
   Warns every scorner to beware.
Labor is the poor man's pride,—
   Success by toil alone is won.
Kings glory in possessions wide,—
   We glory in our work well done.

From the German of J. C. FRIEDRICH VON SCHILLER.
Translation of SAMUEL ATKINS ELIOT.

HASTE NOT! REST NOT!

" Ohne Hast, ohne Rast."

Without haste ! without rest !
Bind the motto to thy breast ;
Bear it with thee as a spell :
Storm and sunshine guard it well !
Heed not flowers that round thee bloom,
Bear it onward to the tomb.

Haste not! Let no thoughtless deed
Mar for aye the spirit's speed ;
Ponder well, and know the right ;
Onward, then, with all thy might.
Haste not! Years can ne'er atone
For one reckless action done.

Rest not! Life is sweeping by ;
Go and dare before you die :
Something mighty and sublime
Leave behind to conquer time!
Glorious 't is to live for aye,
When these forms have passed away.

Haste not! Rest not! Calmly wait ;
Meekly bear the storms of fate!
Duty be thy polar guide,—
Do the right, whate'er betide!
Haste not! Rest not! Conflicts past,
God shall crown thy work at last.

From the German of JOHANN WOLFGANG VON GOETHE.

WORK.

LET me but do my work from day to day,
　In field or forest, at the desk or loom,
　In roaring market-place, or tranquil room ;
Let me but find it in my heart to say,
When vagrant wishes beckon me astray—
　"This is my work ; my blessing, not my doom ;
　Of all who live, I am the one by whom
This work can best be done, in the right way."

Then shall I see it not too great, nor small,
    To suit my spirit and to prove my powers ;
    Then shall I cheerful greet the laboring hours,
And cheerful turn, when the long shadows fall
At eventide, to play and love and rest,
Because I know for me my work is best.

HENRY VAN DYKE.

A WISH.

THIS only grant me, that my means may lie
Too low for envy, for contempt too high.
    Some honor I would have,
Not from great deeds, but good alone ;
The unknown are better than ill known :
    Rumor can ope the grave.
Acquaintance I would have, but when 't depends
Not on the number, but the choice, of friends.

Books should, not business, entertain the light,
And sleep, as undisturbed as death, the night.
    My house a cottage more
Than palace ; and should fitting be
For all my use, no luxury.
    My garden painted o'er
With Nature's hand, not Art's ; and pleasures yield,
Horace might envy in his Sabine field.

Thus would I double my life's fading space ;
For he that runs it well twice runs his race.
    And in this true delight,
These unbought sports, this happy state,
I would not fear, nor wish, my fate ;

But boldly say each night,
To-morrow let my sun his beams display,
Or in clouds hide them ; I have lived to-day.

ABRAHAM COWLEY

CONTENTMENT.

I WEIGH not fortune's frown or smile ;
  I joy not much in earthly joys ;
I seek not state, I reck not style ;
  I am not fond of fancy's toys :
I rest so pleased with what I have,
I wish no more, no more I crave.

I quake not at the thunder's crack ;
  I tremble not at news of war ;
I swound not at the news of wrack ;
  I shrink not at a blazing star ;
I fear not loss, I hope not gain,
I envy none, I none disdain.

I see ambition never pleased ;
  I see some Tantals starved in store ;
I see gold's dropsy seldom eased ;
  I see even Midas gape for more ;
I neither want nor yet abound,—
Enough 's a feast, content is crowned.

I feign not friendship where I hate ;
  I fawn not on the great (in show) ;
I prize, I praise a mean estate,—
  Neither too lofty nor too low :
This, this is all my choice, my cheer,—
A mind content, a conscience clear.

JOSHUA SYLVESTER.

CONTENT.

FROM "FAREWELL TO FOLLIE," 1617.

Sweet are the thoughts that savor of content;
   The quiet mind is richer than a crown;
Sweet are the nights in careless slumber spent,—
   The poor estate scorns Fortune's angry frown:
Such sweet content, such minds, such sleep, such
     bliss,
Beggars enjoy, when princes oft do miss.

The homely house that harbors quiet rest,
   The cottage that affords no pride or care,
The mean, that 'grees with country music best,
   The sweet consort of mirth's and music's fare.
Obscurèd life sets down a type of bliss;
A mind content both crown and kingdom is.

ROBERT GREENE.

SONG.

He that is down need fear no fall;
   He that is low, no pride;
He that is humble ever shall
   Have God to be his guide.

I am content with what I have,
   Little be it or much;
And, Lord, contentment still I crave,
   Because thou savest such.

Fulness to such a burden is
   That go on pilgrimage;

Here little, and hereafter bliss,
  Is best from age to age.

JOHN BUNYAN.

IN PRISON.

BEAT on, proud billows; Boreas, blow;
  Swell, curlèd waves, high as Jove's roof;
Your incivility doth show
  That innocence is tempest proof;
Though surly Nereus frown, my thoughts are calm;
Then strike, Affliction, for thy wounds are balm.

That which the world miscalls a jail
  A private closet is to me;
Whilst a good conscience is my bail,
  And innocence my liberty:
Locks, bars, and solitude together met,
Make me no prisoner, but an anchoret.

I, whilst I wisht to be retired,
  Into this private room was turned;
As if their wisdoms had conspired
  The salamander should be burned;
Or like those sophists, that would drown a fish,
I am constrained to suffer what I wish.

The cynic loves his poverty;
  The pelican her wilderness;
And 't is the Indian's pride to be
  Naked on frozen Caucasus:
Contentment cannot smart; stoics we see
Make torments easier to their apathy.

These manacles upon my arm
  I as my mistress' favors wear;
And for to keep my ankles warm
  I have some iron shackles there:
These walls are but my garrison; this cell,
Which men call jail, doth prove my citadel.

I 'm in the cabinet lockt up,
  Like some high-prizèd margarite,
Or, like the Great Mogul or Pope,
  Am cloistered up from public sight:
Retiredness is a piece of majesty,
And thus, proud Sultan, I 'm as great as thee.

SIR ROGER L'ESTRANGE.

CLEON AND I.

CLEON hath a million acres, ne'er a one have I;
Cleon dwelleth in a palace, in a cottage I;
Cleon hath a dozen fortunes, not a penny I;
Yet the poorer of the twain is Cleon, and not I.

Cleon, true, possesseth acres, but the landscape I;
Half the charms to me it yieldeth money cannot buy.
Cleon harbors sloth and dulness, freshening vigor I;
He in velvet, I in fustian, richer man am I.

Cleon is a slave to grandeur, free as thought am I;
Cleon fees a score of doctors, need of none have I;
Wealth-surrounded, care-environed, Cleon fears to
    die;
Death may come, he 'll find me ready,—happier man
    am I.

Cleon sees no charms in nature, in a daisy I ;
Cleon hears no anthems ringing in the sea and sky ;
Nature sings to me forever, earnest listener I ;
State for state, with all attendants, who would
    change ? Not I.

CHARLES MACKAY.

THE WANTS OF MAN.

" MAN wants but little here below,
    Nor wants that little long."
'T is not with *me* exactly so ;
    But 't is so in the song.
My wants are many and, if told,
    Would muster many a score ;
And were each wish a mint of gold,
    I still should long for more.

What first I want is daily bread—
    And canvas-backs—and wine—
And all the realms of nature spread
    Before me, when I dine.
Four courses scarcely can provide
    My appetite to quell ;
With four choice cooks from France beside,
    To dress my dinner well.

What next I want, at princely cost,
    Is elegant attire :
Black sable furs for winter's frost,
    And silks for summer's fire,
And Cashmere shawls, and Brussels lace
    My bosom's front to deck,—

And diamond rings my hands to grace,
    And rubies for my neck.

I want (who does not want ?) a wife,—
    Affectionate and fair ;
To solace all the woes of life,
    And all its joys to share.
Of temper sweet, of yielding will,
    Of firm, yet placid mind,—
With all my faults to love me still
    With sentiment refined.

And as Time's car incessant runs,
    And Fortune fills my store,
I want of daughters and of sons
    From eight to half a score.
I want (alas ! can mortal dare
    Such bliss on earth to crave ?)
That all the girls be chaste and fair,
    The boys all wise and brave.

I want a warm and faithful friend,
    To cheer the adverse hour ;
Who ne'er to flatter will descend,
    Nor bend the knee to power,—
A friend to chide me when I 'm wrong,
    My inmost soul to see ;
And that my friendship prove as strong
    For him as his for me.

I want the seals of power and place,
    The ensigns of command ;
Charged by the People's unbought grace
    To rule my native land.

Nor crown nor sceptre would I ask
But from my country's will,
By day, by night, to ply the task
Her cup of bliss to fill.

I want the voice of honest praise
To follow me behind,
And to be thought in future days
The friend of human kind,
That after ages, as they rise,
Exulting may proclaim
In choral union to the skies
Their blessings on my name.

These are the Wants of mortal Man,—
I cannot want them long,
For life itself is but a span,
And earthly bliss—a song.
My last great Want—absorbing all—
Is, when beneath the sod,
And summoned to my final call,
The Mercy of my God.

JOHN QUINCY ADAMS.

CONTENTMENT.

"MAN WANTS BUT LITTLE HERE BELOW."

LITTLE I ask; my wants are few;
I only wish a hut of stone,
(A *very plain* brown stone will do,)
That I may call my own;
And close at hand is such a one,
In yonder street that fronts the sun.

Plain food is quite enough for me;
 Three courses are as good as ten;—
If nature can subsist on three,
  Thank Heaven for three. Amen!
I always thought cold victual nice;—
My *choice* would be vanilla-ice.

I care not much for gold or land;—
 Give me a mortgage here and there,—
Some good bank-stock,—some note of hand,
  Or trifling railroad share,—
I only ask that Fortune send
A *little* more than I shall spend.

Honors are silly toys, I know,
 And titles are but empty names;
I would, *perhaps*, be Plenipo,—
  But only near St. James;
I 'm very sure I should not care
To fill our Gubernator's chair.

Jewels are baubles; 't is a sin
 To care for such unfruitful things;—
One good-sized diamond in a pin,—
  Some, *not so large*, in rings,—
A ruby, and a pearl or so,
Will do for me;—I laugh at show.

My dame should dress in cheap attire;
 (Good heavy silks are never dear;)—
I own perhaps I *might* desire
  Some shawls of true Cashmere,—
Some marrowy crapes of China silk,
Like wrinkled skins on scalded milk.

I would not have the horse I drive
  So fast that folks must stop and stare;
An easy gait—two, forty-five—
    Suits me; I do not care;—
Perhaps, for just a *single spurt*,
Some seconds less would do no hurt.

Of pictures, I should like to own
  Titians and Raphaels three or four—
I love so much their style and tone—
    One Turner, and no more,
(A landscape—foreground golden dirt—
The sunshine painted with a squirt.)

Of books but few,—some fifty score
  For daily use, and bound for wear;
The rest upon an upper floor;—
    Some *little* luxury *there*
Of red morocco's gilded gleam,
And vellum rich as country cream.

Busts, cameos, gems,—such things as these,
  Which others often show for pride,
I value for their power to please,
    And selfish churls deride;
One Stradivarius, I confess,
Two meerschaums, I would fain possess.

Wealth's wasteful tricks I will not learn,
  Nor ape the glittering upstart fool;
Shall not carved tables serve my turn,
    But *all* must be of buhl?
Give grasping pomp its double share,—
I ask but *one* recumbent chair.

Thus humble let me live and die,
   Nor long for Midas' golden touch;
If Heaven more generous gifts deny,
   I shall not miss them *much*, —
Too grateful for the blessing lent
Of simple tastes and mind content!

OLIVER WENDELL HOLMES.

ULYSSES.

I⊤ little profits that, an idle king,
By this still hearth, among these barren crags,
Matched with an aged wife, I mete and dole
Unequal laws unto a savage race,
That hoard, and sleep, and feed, and know not me.
I cannot rest from travel: I will drink
Life to the lees: all times I have enjoyed
Greatly, have suffered greatly, both with those
That loved me, and alone; on shore, and when
Through scudding drifts the rainy Hyades
Vext the dim sea: I am become a name;
For always roaming with a hungry heart
Much have I seen and known; cities of men
And manners, climates, councils, governments,
Myself not least, but honored of them all;
And drunk delight of battle with my peers,
Far on the ringing plains of windy Troy.
I am a part of all that I have met;
Yet all experience is an arch wherethrough
Gleams that untravelled world, whose margin fades
Forever and forever when I move.
How dull it is to pause, to make an end,

To rust unburnished, not to shine in use !
As though to breathe were life.   Life piled on life
Were all too little, and of one to me
Little remains: but every hour is saved
From that eternal silence, something more,
A bringer of new things ; and vile it were
For some three suns to store and hoard myself,
And this gray spirit yearning in desire
To follow knowledge, like a sinking star,
Beyond the utmost bound of human thought.

   This is my son, mine own Telemachus,
To whom I leave the sceptre and the isle—
Well-loved of me, discerning to fulfil
This labor, by slow prudence to make mild
A rugged people, and through soft degrees
Subdue them to the useful and the good.
Most blameless is he, centred in the sphere
Of common duties, decent not to fail
In offices of tenderness, and pay
Meet adoration to my household gods,
When I am gone.   He works his work, I mine.

   There lies the port : the vessel puffs her sail :
There gloom the dark broad seas.   My mariners,
Souls that have toiled, and wrought, and thought
     with me—
That ever with a frolic welcome took
The thunder and the sunshine, and opposed
Free hearts, free foreheads—you and I are old.
Old age hath yet his honor and his toil ;
Death closes all : but something, ere the end,
Some work of noble note, may yet be done,
Not unbecoming men that strove with gods.
The lights begin to twinkle from the rocks :

The long day wanes : the slow moon climbs : the
    deep
Moans round with many voices. Come, my friends,
'T is not too late to seek a newer world.
Push off, and sitting well in order smite
The sounding furrows ; for my purpose holds
To sail beyond the sunset, and the baths
Of all the western stars, until I die.
It may be that the gulfs will wash us down :
It may be we shall touch the Happy Isles,
And see the great Achilles, whom we knew.
Though much is taken, much abides ; and though
We are not now that strength which in old days
Moved earth and heaven; that which we are, we
    are ;
One equal temper of heroic hearts,
Made weak by time and fate, but strong in will
To strive, to seek, to find, and not to yield.

ALFRED, LORD TENNYSON.

TO ALL IN HAVEN.

ALL ye who have gained the haven of safe days,
    And rest at ease, your wanderings being done,
    Except the last, inevitable one,
Be well content, I say, and hear men's praise :
Yet in the quiet of your sheltered bays, —
    Bland waters shining in an equal sun, —
    Forget not that the awful storm-tides run
In far, unsheltered, and tempestuous ways :

Remember near what rocks, and through ·what
    shoals.

Worn, desperate mariners strain with all their
    might :
They may not come to your sweet restful goals,
    Your waters placid in the level light :—
Their graves wait in that sea no moon controls,
    That is in dreadful fellowship with Night.

PHILIP BOURKE MARSTON.

A WOMAN'S WISH.

Would I were lying in a field of clover,
    Of clover cool and soft, and soft and sweet,
With dusky clouds on deep skies hanging over,
    And scented silence at my head and feet.

Just for one hour to slip the leash of Worry,
    In eager haste, from Thought's impatient neck,
And watch it coursing, in its heedless hurry
    Disdaining Wisdom's call or Duty's beck !

Ah ! it were sweet, where clover clumps are
    meeting
And daisies hiding, so to hide and rest ;
No sound except my own heart's steady beating,
    Rocking itself to sleep within my breast ;—

Just to lie there, filled with the deeper breathing
    That comes of listening to a wild bird's song !
Our souls require at times this full unsheathing, —
    All swords will rust if scabbard-kept too long :

And I am tired,—so tired of rigid duty,
    So tired of all my tired hands find to do !

I yearn, I faint, for some of life's free beauty,
   Its loose beads with no straight string running
      through.

Aye, laugh, if laugh you will, at my crude speech
   But women sometimes die of such a greed,—
Die for the small joys held beyond their reach,
   And the assurance they have all they need!
                MARY ASHLEY TOWNSEND.

THE WORLD AND THE QUIETIST.

   " WHY, when the world's great mind
   Hath finally inclined,
Why," you say, Critias, " be debating still?
   Why, with these mournful rhymes
   Learned in more languid climes,
   Blame our activity
   Who, with such passionate will,
   Are what we mean to be?"

   Critias, long since, I know
   (For Fate decreed it so),
Long since the world hath set its heart to live ;
   Long since, with credulous zeal
   It turns life's mighty wheel,
   Still doth for laborers send
   Who still their labor give,
   And still expects an end.

   Yet, as the wheel flies round,
   With no ungrateful sound
Do adverse voices fall on the world's ear.

Deafened by his own stir
The rugged laborer
Caught not till then a sense
So glowing and so near
Of his omnipotence.

So, when the feast grew loud
In Susa's palace proud,
A white-robed slave stole to the Great King's side.
He spake—the Great King heard ;
Felt the slow-rolling word
Swell his attentive soul ;
Breathed deeply as it died,
And drained his mighty bowl.

MATTHEW ARNOLD.

REST.

To spend the long warm days
Silent beside the silent-stealing streams,
To see, not gaze,—
To hear, not listen, thoughts exchanged for dreams :

See clouds that slowly pass
Trailing their shadows o'er the far faint down,
And ripening grass,
While yet the meadows wear their starry crown :

To hear the breezes sigh
Cool in the silver leaves like falling rain,
Pause and go by,
Tired wanderers o'er the solitary plain :

See far from all affright
Shy river creatures play hour after hour,
    And night by night
Low in the West the white moon's folding flower.

    Thus lost to human things,
To blend at last with Nature and to hear
    What songs she sings
Low to herself when there is no one near.

MARGARET L. WOODS.

INVOCATION TO SLEEP.

FROM " VALENTINIAN."

COME, Sleep, and with thy sweet deceiving
    Lock me in delight awhile ;
    Let some pleasing dreams beguile
    All my fancies, that from thence
    I may feel an influence,
All my powers of care bereaving !

Though but a shadow, but a sliding,
    Let me know some little joy !
    We that suffer long annoy
    Are contented with a thought,
    Through an idle fancy wrought :
O, let my joys have some abiding !

JOHN FLETCHER.

SLEEP.

Come, gentle sleep! attend thy votary's prayer,
And, though death's image, to my couch repair;
How sweet, though lifeless, yet with life to lie,
And, without dying, O how sweet to die!

DR. JOHN WOLCOTT (*Peter Pindar*).

SLEEP.

FROM "ASTROPHEL AND STELLA."

Come, Sleep, O Sleep, the certain knot of peace,
The baiting-place of wit, the balm of woe,
The poor man's wealth, the prisoner's release,
The indifferent judge between the high and low,
With shield of proof shield me from out the prease *
Of those fierce darts Despair at me doth throw;
O, make me in those civil wars to cease:
I will good tribute pay, if thou do so.
Take thou of me smooth pillows, sweetest bed,
A chamber deaf to noise, and blind to light,
A rosy garland, and a weary head:
And if these things, as being thine in right,
Move not thy heavy grace, thou shalt in me
Livelier than elsewhere Stella's image see.

SIR PHILIP SIDNEY.

SLEEP.

FROM "SECOND PART OF HENRY IV.," ACT III. SC. 1.

KING HENRY.—How many thousand of my poorest
    subjects
Are at this hour asleep!—O sleep! O gentle sleep!

* Press, throng.

Nature's soft nurse, how have I frighted thee,
That thou no more wilt weigh my eyelids down,
And steep my senses in forgetfulness?
Why rather, sleep, liest thou in smoky cribs,
Upon uneasy pallets stretching thee,
And hushed with buzzing night-flies to thy slumber,
Than in the perfumed chambers of the great,
Under the canopies of costly state,
And lulled with sounds of sweetest melody?
O thou dull god! why liest thou with the vile,
In loathsome beds, and leav'st the kingly couch
A watch-case, or a common 'larum-bell?
Wilt thou upon the high and giddy mast
Seal up the ship-boy's eyes, and rock his brains
In cradle of the rude imperious surge,
And in the visitation of the winds,
Who take the ruffian billows by the top,
Curling their monstrous heads, and hanging them
With deafening clamors in the slippery clouds,
That, with the hurly, death itself awakes?
Canst thou, O partial sleep! give thy repose
To the wet sea-boy in an hour so rude;
And in the calmest and most stillest night,
With all appliances and means to boot,
Deny it to a king?   Then, happy low, lie down;
Uneasy lies the head that wears a crown.

SHAKESPEARE

SLEEPLESSNESS.

A FLOCK of sheep that leisurely pass by
One after one; the sound of rain, and bees
Murmuring; the fall of rivers, winds and seas,

Smooth fields, white sheets of water, and pure
    sky ;—
I 've thought of all by turns, and still I lie
Sleepless ; and soon the small birds' melodies
Must hear, first uttered from my orchard trees,
And the first cuckoo's melancholy cry.
Even thus last night, and two nights more, I lay,
And could not win thee, Sleep, by any stealth :
So do not let me wear to-night away ;
Without thee what is all the morning's wealth ?
Come, blessèd barrier between day and day,
Dear mother of fresh thoughts and joyous health !

WILLIAM WORDSWORTH.

WATCHING.

IN BURMAH.

SLEEP, love, sleep !
The dusty day is done.
Lo ! from afar the freshening breezes sweep
Wide over groves of balm;
Down from the towering palm,
In at the open casement cooling run,
And round thy lowly bed,
Thy bed of pain,
Bathing thy patient head,
Like grateful showers of rain,
They come ;
While the white curtains, waving to and fro,
Fan the sick air ;
And pityingly the shadows come and go,
With gentle human care,
Compassionate and dumb.

The dusty day is done,
The night begun ;
While prayerful watch I keep,
Sleep, love, sleep !
Is there no magic in the touch
Of fingers thou dost love so much ?
Fain would they scatter poppies o'er thee now ;
Or, with its mute caress,
The tremulous lip some soft nepenthe press
Upon thy weary lid and aching brow ;
While prayerful watch I keep,
Sleep, love, sleep !

On the pagoda spire
The bells are swinging,
Their little golden circlet in a flutter
With tales the wooing winds have dared to utter,
Till all are ringing,
As if a choir
Of golden-nested birds in heaven were singing,
And with a lulling sound
The music floats around,
And drops like balm into the drowsy ear ;
Commingling with the hum
Of the Sepoy's distant drum,
And lazy beetle ever droning near.
Sounds these of deepest silence born,
Like night made visible by morn ;
So silent that I sometimes start
To hear the throbbings of my heart,
And watch, with shivering sense of pain,
To see thy pale lids lift again.

The lizard, with his mouse-like eyes,

Peeps from the mortise in surprise
At such strange quiet after day's harsh din ;
Then boldly ventures out,
And looks about,
And with his hollow feet
Treads his small evening beat,
Darting upon his prey
In such a tricky, winsome sort of way,
His delicate marauding seems no sin.
And still the curtains swing,
But noiselessly ;
The bells a melancholy murmur ring,
As tears were in the sky :
More heavily the shadows fall,
Like the black foldings of a pall,
Where juts the rough beam from the wall ;
The candles flare
With fresher gusts of air ;
The beetle's drone
Turns to a dirge-like, solitary moan ;
Night deepens, and I sit, in cheerless doubt alone.

EMILY CHUBBUCK JUDSON.

THE VOYAGE OF SLEEP.

To sleep I give myself away,
Unclasp the fetters of the mind,
Forget the sorrows of the day,
The burdens of the heart unbind.

With empty sail this tired bark
Drifts out upon the sea of rest,
While all the shore behind grows dark
And silence reigns from east to west.

At last awakes the hidden breeze
That bears me to the land of dreams,
Where music sighs among the trees
And murmurs in the winding streams.

O weary day, O weary day,
That dawns in fear and ends in strife,
That brings no cooling draught to allay
The burning fever thirst of life ;

O sacred night, when angel hands
Are pressed upon the throbbing brow,
And when the soul on shining sands
Descends with angels from the prow,

And sees soft skies and meadows sweet,
And blossoming lanes that wind and wind
To bowers where friends long parted meet
And sit again with arms entwined,

And catch the perfumed breeze that blows
From pink-plumed orchards sloping fair
And every fresh-expanding rose
That throws sweet kisses to the air.

O sacred night, O silvery shore,
O blossoming lanes that wind and wind,
Ye are my refuge more and more
From ghosts that haunt the waking mind.

To sleep I give myself away,
Forget the visions of unrest
That came through all the clamorous day,
And drift into the silent west.

ARTHUR WENTWORTH EATON.

THE TWO OCEANS.

Two seas, amid the night,
  In the moonshine roll and sparkle—
Now spread in the silver light,
  Now sadden, and wail, and darkle.

The one has a billowy motion,
  And from land to land it gleams;
The other is sleep's wide ocean,
  And its glimmering waves are dreams.

The one, with murmur and roar,
  Bears fleets around coast and islet;
The other, without a shore,
  Ne'er knew the track of a pilot.
                    JOHN STERLING.

ODE TO SLEEP.

BEYOND the sunset and the amber sea
  To the lone depths of ether, cold and bare,
Thy influence, soul of all tranquillity,
  Hallows the earth and awes the reverent air;
Yon laughing rivulet quells its silvery tune;
  The pines, like priestly watchers tall and grim,
  Stand mute against the pensive twilight dim,
Breathless to hail the advent of the moon;
From the white beach the ocean falls away
  Coyly, and with a thrill; the sea-birds dart
  Ghostlike from out the distance, and depart
With a gray fleetness, moaning the dead day;

The wings of Silence, overfolding space,
  Droop with dusk grandeur from the heavenly
    steep,
And through the stillness gleams thy starry face,—
    Serenest Angel, Sleep!

Come! woo me here, amid these flowery charms;
  Breathe on my eyelids; press thy odorous lips
Close to mine own; enwreathe me in thine arms,
  And cloud my spirit with thy sweet eclipse;
No dreams! no dreams! keep back the motley
    throng,—
  For such are girded round with ghastly might,
And sing low burdens of despondent song,
  Decked in the mockery of a lost delight;
I ask oblivion's balsam! the mute peace
  Toned to still breathings, and the gentlest sighs;
  Not music woven of rarest harmonies
Could yield me such elysium of release:
The tones of earth are weariness,—not only
  'Mid the loud mart, and in the walks of trade,
But where the mountain Genius broodeth lonely,
  In the cool pulsing of the sylvan shade;
Then bear me far into thy noiseless land;
  Surround me with thy silence, deep on deep,
    Until serene I stand
Close by a duskier country, and more grand
  Mysterious solitude, than thine, O Sleep!

As he whose veins a feverous frenzy burns,
  Whose life-blood withers in the fiery drouth,
Feebly and with a languid longing turns
  To the spring breezes gathering from the south,
So, feebly and with languid longing, I

Turn to thy wished nepenthe, and implore
  The golden dimness, the purpureal gloom
Which haunt thy poppied realm, and make the
    shore
  Of thy dominion balmy with all bloom.
In the clear gulfs of thy serene profound,
Worn passions sink to quiet, sorrows pause,
  Suddenly fainting to still-breathèd rest :
Thou own'st a magical atmosphere, which awes
  The memories seething in the turbulent breast;
Which, muffling up the sharpness of all sound
Of mortal lamentation, solely bears
  The silvery minor toning of our woe,
  All mellowed to harmonious underflow,
Soft as the sad farewells of dying years,—
    Lulling as sunset showers that veil the west,
      And sweet as Love's last tears
When over-welling hearts do mutely weep :
    O griefs ! O wailings ! your tempestuous mad-
      ness,
    Merged in a regal quietude of sadness,
Wins a strange glory by the streams of sleep !

Then woo me here, amid these flowery charms ;
  Breathe on my eyelids, press thy odorous lips
Close to mine own ; enfold me in thine arms,
  And cloud my spirit with thy sweet eclipse ;
And while from waning depth to depth I fall,
Down lapsing to the utmost depths of all,
  Till wan forgetfulness obscurely stealing
    Creeps like an incantation on the soul,
And o'er the slow ebb of my conscious life
  Dies the thin flush of the last conscious feeling,

And like abortive thunder, the dull roll
Of sullen passions ebbs far, far away,—
O Angel! loose the chords which cling to strife,
Sever the gossamer bondage of my breath,
    And let me pass, gently as winds in May,
    From the dim realm which owns thy shadowy
    sway,
To thy diviner sleep, O sacred Death!

PAUL HAMILTON HAYNE.

THE FALLEN.
(In Memoriam, May 30.)
I.

Toll the slow bell,
Toll the low bell,
Toll, toll,
Make dole
For them that wrought so well.
Come, come,
With muffled drum
And wailing lorn
Of dolorous horn;
The solemn measure slow
Toll and beat and blow;
Put out all glories that adorn
The sweet, unheeding morn.
Come, come;
To the muffled drum
And the sad horns
Bring flowers for them that took the thorns.

Knell, knell;
Let the slow bell

Be struck and the troubled drum;
Come, come,
The solemn measure slow
Toll and beat and blow;
Rebuke this bright, unpitying light.
The solemn measure slow
Toll and beat and blow
For them our beauty and our might
Gone on the unreturning way,
For them that took the night
That we might have the day.

II.

Hark! voices, joyous voices break
From the green martyr-mounds : " Wake, wake!
The Lord our God, once more He saith,
This hand made all—it made not death.
Let the blithe bells ring
And the May air sing;
Strike the quick drum,
Smite sorrow dumb;
Blow the glad horn,
This glad May morn;
Lift the valiant measures high
Of the proud earth and sky
For them that tent
Beyond the firmament,
And on the field of light
Still gather to the fight.

" Blow the glad horn,
This glad May morn;
Stanch, undaunted measures blow,
Gathering courage as they go,—
Valiant measures high

Carolled of earth and sky ;
Set the bright, triumphal stave
For them that fought so well,
That faltered not nor fell ;
For them and all whereso yon colors wave,
Unto the four winds given
And the proud earth and heaven.
There believe and battle they
Whose face is toward the day,
The ever-living light,
Where is no night,
Where is no death nor shadow of the grave."

JOHN VANCE CHENEY.

INDEX: AUTHORS AND TITLES.

INDEX OF AUTHORS AND TITLES.

For occupation, nativity, etc., of Authors, and the American publishers of American poetical works, see General Index of Authors, Volume X.

AUTHORS AND TITLES. 459